CW01021872

To the Confucius Institute

with best wishes

*Singapore, Chinese Migration and the Making
of the British Empire, 1819–67*

WORLDS OF THE EAST INDIA COMPANY

ISSN 1752-5667

Series Editor
H. V. Bowen (Swansea University)

Editorial Board
Andrew Cook (British Library)
Rajat Datta (Jawaharlal Nehru University, New Delhi)
P. J. Marshall (King's College, London)
Nigel Rigby (National Maritime Museum)

This series offers high-quality studies of the East India Company, drawn from across a broad chronological, geographical and thematic range. The rich history of the Company has long been of interest to those who engage in the study of Britain's commercial, imperial, maritime and military past, but in recent years it has also attracted considerable attention from those who explore art, cultural and social themes within an historical context. The series will thus provide a forum for scholars from different disciplinary backgrounds, and for those who have interests in the history of Britain (London and the regions), India, China, Indonesia, as well as the seas and oceans.

The editors welcome submissions from both established scholars and those beginning their career; monographs are particularly encouraged but volumes of essays will also be considered. All submissions will receive rapid, informed attention. They should be sent in the first instance to:

Professor H. V. Bowen, Department of History, Swansea University, Swansea SA2 8PP. Email: h.v.bowen@swansea.ac.uk.

Previously published titles are listed at the back of this volume.

SINGAPORE, CHINESE MIGRATION AND THE MAKING OF THE BRITISH EMPIRE, 1819–67

Stan Neal

THE BOYDELL PRESS

© Stan Neal 2019

All Rights Reserved. Except as permitted under current legislation no part of this work may be photocopied, stored in a retrieval system, published, performed in public, adapted, broadcast, transmitted, recorded or reproduced in any form or by any means, without the prior permission of the copyright owner

The right of Stan Neal to be identified as the author of this work has been asserted in accordance with sections 77 and 78 of the Copyright, Designs and Patents Act 1988

First published 2019
The Boydell Press, Woodbridge

ISBN 978-1-78327-423-9

The Boydell Press is an imprint of Boydell & Brewer Ltd
PO Box 9, Woodbridge, Suffolk IP12 3DF, UK
and of Boydell & Brewer Inc.
668 Mt Hope Avenue, Rochester, NY 14620–2731, USA
website: www.boydellandbrewer.com

A CIP catalogue record for this title is available from the British Library

The publisher has no responsibility for the continued existence or accuracy of URLs for external or third-party internet websites referred to in this book, and does not guarantee that any content on such websites is, or will remain, accurate or appropriate

This publication is printed on acid-free paper

Printed and bound in Great Britain by
TJ International Ltd, Padstow, Cornwall

For Esther and Archie.

CONTENTS

ILLUSTRATIONS

Maps

Tables

ACKNOWLEDGEMENTS

There are numerous people whose help and support have been crucial to the completion of this book. Inevitably, the journey from initial proposal to completed project has required a great deal of different types of support, and I apologise in advance to anyone whose contribution has been omitted.

First, the support of Ulster University has been invaluable in the completion of this project. I have a particular appreciation for the John Springhall legacy fund, which financed my appointment as the John Springhall Post-Doctoral Lecturer in Modern British/Imperial History. Additionally, the support of Professor Ian Thatcher (Research Director – History) requires a special mention. Ulster University has provided generous funding for travel to archives and conferences at a time when many early career researchers working in higher education miss out on these opportunities due to financial constraints. I would also like to extend my thanks to the wider academic staff at Ulster University, who have been extremely helpful, insightful and supportive whenever needed.

Second, I must thank my former supervisors and colleagues at Northumbria University. The assistance and advice of Dr Joe Hardwick, Professor Tanja Bueltmann and Professor Tony Webster have been invaluable. They have always consistently provided me with detailed, useful feedback and have shown great patience as I developed, slowly, as a researcher. I would also like to extend my thanks to Professor David Gleeson and Professor Robert Bickers (University of Bristol) for their comments and feedback on the research that underpins this book. I must extend particular thanks to those who have read and offered specific guidance on early draft chapters. I am extremely grateful to Dr David Hope, Dr Peter O'Connor, Dr Jennifer Kain, Dr Sarah Hellawell and Dr Mark Wilson. I also wish to thank Northumbria University and the Economic History Society for financial support, which has allowed me to travel to various archives. Over several years, these trips have taken me to archives in Britain and Asia, where I encountered many enthusiastic and helpful archivists.

Beyond my immediate academic colleagues, I must also extend thanks to the wider academic community for facilitating my personal development. I have learned a great deal from debate and discussions at various conferences and events, such as EuroSEAS 2017 at Oxford University and Singapore 200 at Liverpool John Moores University, and have received excellent guidance and feedback on journal articles and book chapters from anonymous reviewers (*Modern Asian Studies*, *Journal of World History*, *History Australia*). In the development of this book specifically, the role played by Peter Sowden and Professor Huw Bowen deserves special praise, and I commend the work of Boydell & Brewer in promoting and supporting new research on the British Empire in Asia.

Finally, I would like to thank my parents, Cath and Terry, and my brothers, Alfie and Tommy, who have supported, and often distracted, me over decades of research and educational development. Cath deserves additional gratitude as her proofreading has helped to eliminate many of my most obvious grammatical errors. The errors and oversights that remain are mine alone. My wife, Esther, and son, Archie, require the most special acknowledgement. To put it simply, without their love this book would not exist.

LANGUAGE USAGE

In all cases this book uses the most common contemporary English-language usage. The language used in primary sources has not been modified. This is an important specification, as most of the authors discussed in this text were writing before the Wade-Giles or pinyin systems for the standard Romanisation of Chinese. A similar approach is applied when referencing the work of historians. For example, when describing Chinese associations in Singapore, *kongsi* is preferred over *gōngsī* as that is the most common usage in academic writing. Romanised Chinese terms are italicised throughout.

For consistency, the same approach is applied to proper nouns. Sri Lanka is referred to as Ceylon, and Xiamen is referred to as Amoy. Similarly, Karl Gützlaff is referred to by his commonly used anglicised title of Charles Gutzlaff, and Anglo-Chinese is preferred to Sino-British. Such nineteenth-century terminology is used to maintain consistency between extracts from primary sources and the voice of the book.

CHRONOLOGY: SINGAPORE, THE BRITISH EMPIRE AND ANGLO-CHINESE RELATIONS, 1819–67

1819

29 January: Stamford Raffles establishes an East India Company trading post at Singapore.

6 February: Singapore Treaty signed between Sultan Hussein of Johor, Temenggong Abdul Rahman and Stamford Raffles confirming the East India Company's right to establish a trading post. William Farquhar assumes the role of British Resident and Commandant in Singapore.

1823

27 May: John Crawfurd takes over from William Farquhar as the Resident of Singapore.

1824

17 March: Anglo-Dutch Treaty of London

2 August: The Treaty of Friendship and Alliance signed between the East India Company, Sultan Husain Shah and Temenggong Abdu'r Rahman. Singapore and surrounding islands were ceded to the East India Company in exchange for a lump sum and monthly allowance for the Sultan and Temenggong.

1826

27 November: Singapore becomes part of the Straits Settlements with Malacca and Penang. The Straits Settlements become the fourth presidency of India. Robert Fullerton is appointed first Governor of the Straits Settlements.

1829

2 May: Swan River Colony (later renamed Western Australia) founded.

1830

12 November: Robert Ibbetson appointed Governor of the Straits Settlements.

1832

7 December: Singapore becomes the centre of government of the Straits Settlements. Kenneth Murchison appointed Governor of the Straits Settlements.

1833

28 August: The Government of India Act is granted royal assent. Also known as the Charter Act or Saint Helena Act, this marked the end of the East India Company's monopoly of the China trade and ended the Company's commercial activities.

28 August: Slavery Abolition Act is granted royal assent. This Act abolished slavery in the British Empire, with exceptions for Ceylon and Saint Helena. Slave owners were compensated for the loss of their 'property' and slaves had to serve a period of 'apprenticeship' before they were free.

1836

18 November: Sir George Bonham appointed Governor of the Straits Settlements.

28 December: Colony of South Australia is founded.

1839

April–May: Commissioner Lin Zexu begins the destruction of British opium. After British merchants petition the British Government for compensation a Royal Navy force is dispatched to China and the First Opium War begins.

1841

20 January: After British military victories over China the Convention of Chuenpi cedes Hong Kong Island to the United Kingdom. Neither government ratified this agreement.

1842

29 August: The Treaty of Nanking (Nanjing) confirms the cession of Hong Kong to Britain, the opening of five treaty ports to foreign merchants, and mandates that reparations are owed by the Qing Government. This is the first of a number of agreements later branded 'unequal treaties'.

1843

January: Singapore ruled directly by the East India Company from January to August 1843.

August: William John Butterworth appointed Governor of the Straits Settlements.

1844

25 July: The Tan Tock Seng Hospital begins operation.

1851

11 January: Hong Xiuquan declares the Heavenly Kingdom after being influenced by Christianity. The conflict between the Heavenly Kingdom and the Qing dynasty, known as the Taiping Rebellion, lasted approximately fourteen years (1850–64), took an estimated 20 million lives through war and famine, and was suppressed by the Qing with the aid of Britain and France.

1 July: Victoria separates from New South Wales as a new colony.

1855

21 March: Edmund Augustus Blundell appointed Governor of the Straits Settlements.

6 August: Sir Orfeur Cavenagh appointed Governor of the Straits Settlements.

1856

23 October: In response to the Arrow incident, where Chinese officials arrested Chinese crew members of a British-registered ship, Britain attacks Canton, prompting the Second Opium War. France joins the conflict with Britain to force concessions from China.

1857

10 May 1857: Bengal Army troops in Meerut refuse to use the new Enfield rifle (the cartridge is greased with pork and beef fat causing religious offence), and they mutiny against superior officers. The Indian Rebellion lasts until the rebel defeat at Gwalior on 20 June 1858. The conflict leads to the dissolution of the East India Company and direct rule in the form of the British Raj.

1858

8 March: The Straits Settlements are placed under the control of the Government of India.

June: The Treaties of Tientsin (Tianjin) end the first phase of the Second Opium War. Concessions included opening more ports to foreign merchants, allowing foreign travel into China's interior, and residences in Beijing for Western envoys. Hostilities resume in June 1859.

1859

10 December: Queensland becomes a Crown Colony.

1860

24 October: After the British and French troops enter the Forbidden City and burn the Summer Palace, the Convention of Peking (Beijing) cedes the Kowloon peninsula (adjacent to Hong Kong) to Britain. The Treaties of Tientsin are ratified and the Xianfeng Emperor also signs agreements with France and Russia.

1867

1 April: The Straits Settlements come under direct British control as a Crown Colony.

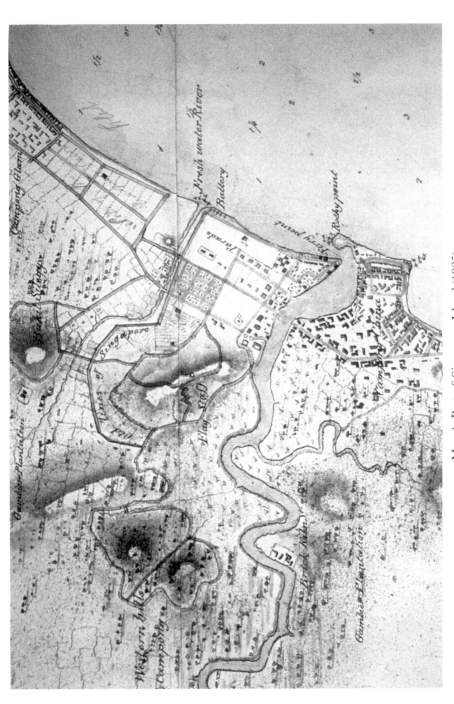

Map 1: Part of Singapore Island (1825)

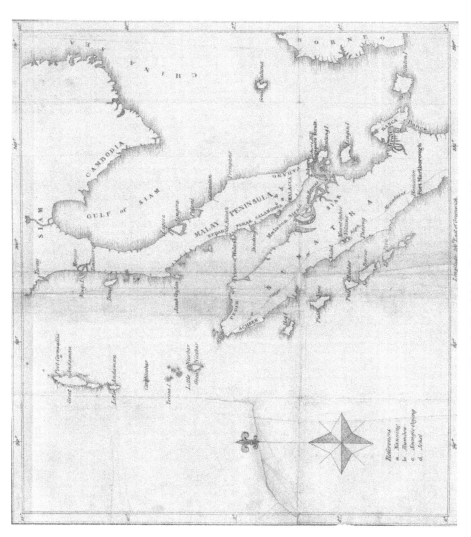

Map 2: The Malay Peninsula (1836)

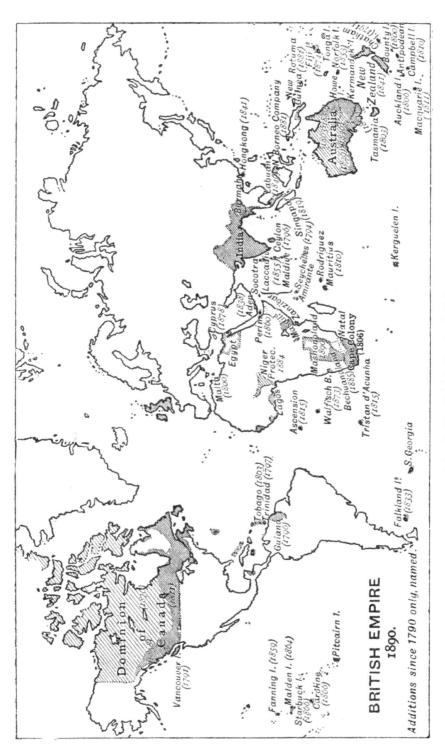

Map 3: The British Empire (1890)

INTRODUCTION

The year 2019 marks 200 years since the East India Company established a trading post on the island of Singapore. The conventional, historical narrative of the colonial experience emphasises how, by 1867, British colonisation had transformed this island of roughly 1,000 inhabitants into a centre for international trade and home to over 80,000 people, over two-thirds of whom were Chinese or descended from Chinese migrants.[1] Clearly, as we reflect on this bicentenary, we can see that the British Empire transformed Singapore.[2] However, this book focuses on the role of early colonial Singapore in the transformation of the British Empire. The central argument is that the colonial experience in Singapore shaped British ideas about colony building. In fact, the rapid growth and commercial success of early colonial Singapore led to various attempts to reproduce this colonial model through the recruitment of Chinese migrant labour. These attempts to replicate colonial Singapore were based on contemporary assumptions and ideas about race, economics and colonisation and contingent on rapid imperial and global change in the nineteenth century.

The Straits Settlements of Penang (ceded to the British in 1786), Singapore (ceded in 1824) and Malacca (ceded in 1824) were the first British colonies to rely on Chinese migrants, as both a labour force and a class of wealthy merchants.[3] Originally under the auspices of the East India Company, the economic success and political significance of these colonies meant that the Straits Settlements were granted Crown Colony status in 1867. Within this

---

[1]   The 1819 figure is from '1819 Singapore Treaty', *Singapore Government: National Library Board*, http://eresources.nlb.gov.sg/infopedia/articles/SIP_2014-05-16_133354.html (accessed 30 September 2018). The 1867 figure is from Straits Settlements Blue Book (1867), CO 277/1 (National Archives).

[2]   Note that despite colonial representations of pre-colonial Singapore as an unused backwater, Singapore has a much longer history. See: 'Origins', in John Curtis Perry, *Singapore: Unlikely Power* (New York: Oxford University Press, 2017), 3–22; John Miksic and Cheryl-Ann Low Mei Gek, eds, *Early Singapore, 1300s–1819: Evidence in Maps, Text and Artefacts* (Singapore: Singapore History Museum, 2004); Karl Hack and Jean-Louis Margolin, eds, *Singapore from Temasek to the 21st Century: Reinventing the Global City* (Singapore: National University of Singapore, 2010).

[3]   Philip A. Kuhn, *Chinese among Others: Emigration in Modern Times* (Lanham, MD: Rowman & Littlefield, 2008), 99. See Map 2 for the prominence of these colonies on the Malay Peninsula.

context the growth of Singapore was particularly important.[4] The contact zone of Singapore, which grew rapidly in terms of economic output and population from 1819 onwards, confirmed the idea that Chinese migrants were compatible with British colonialism and thus served as an example to colonial and metropolitan observers. Because of its success, Singapore became a template for migration to different colonial contexts. Chinese migration in the nineteenth century fits within a wider framework of empire building. Whilst colonial administrators celebrated the Chinese as an essential component of colonial Singapore's economic miracle, they maligned indigenous peoples as an obstacle to colonial development. As a result, colonial observers saw Chinese migrants as an economically productive replacement for indigenous populations. Moreover, the success of Singapore offered a model for colonial development as free trade and free labour became increasingly desirable in the British Empire from the 1830s onwards. Systems of indentured and voluntary migration, which were developed to service the labour shortages of the British Empire, were influenced by the Singapore model.

The key theme that underpinned the colonial desire to experiment with Chinese migrant labour was the idea of a distinctly Chinese racial character, which was constructed in the Anglo-Chinese contact zone of Singapore. As demonstrated by this book, British observers formed and disseminated sterotypes about Chinese migrants in various colonial contact zones in the mid-nineteenth century – such as Assam, Hong Kong and New South Wales – and these experiences were often underpinned by assumptions from colonial Singapore. Despite their primary roles as missionaries, merchants, diplomats, colonial officials or military officers, colonial observers also transmitted information about Chinese migrants, and China more broadly, to Britain and around the British Empire. These actors played a crucial role in defining and describing a specific Chinese character and in building a body of Western knowledge about Chinese migrants in the context of broader ideas about race, economics and colonisation.[5] The existing scholarly literature on Chinese migration focuses on anti-immigration movements from the 1850s onwards, meaning that the nature of these stereotypes about Chinese migrants has been generalised as either positive or negative. Given the range of China experts with different experiences, access and interests, ideas about the Chinese were neither uniform nor simple. Yet, if there was a common

---

[4]   Map 1 shows the limited beginnings of early colonial Singapore.

[5]   Songchuan Chen, 'An Information War Waged by Merchants and Missionaries at Canton: The Society for the Diffusion of Useful Knowledge in China, 1834–1839', *Modern Asian Studies*, 46, 6 (2012), 1705–35; Maxine Berg, 'Britain, Industry and Perceptions of China: Matthew Boulton, "Useful Knowledge" and the Macartney Embassy to China', *Journal of Global History*, 1, 2 (2006), 269–88. A major historiographical theme of the early 2000s was discussion about imperial information 'networks', best exemplified by Alan Lester, *Imperial Networks: Creating Identities in Nineteenth Century South Africa and Britain* (London: Routledge, 2001).

theme in colonial and imperial attitudes towards Chinese immigrants, it was that they were 'useful'.[6] At one end of colonial stratification, Chinese labourers formed a cheap and effective labour force that met the economic needs of the British Empire, whilst at the other end, Chinese merchants were valued collaborators in enabling colonial control. These colonial observers and the ways in which they used information networks were essential in confirming certain tropes about Chinese migrants – tropes as varied as being duplicitous, organised, criminal, frugal and entrepreneurial – which would later be appropriated in exclusionary rhetoric against Chinese immigrants in Britain's white settler colonies.

Singapore's rapid expansion, driven by Chinese immigration, preceded changes within the British Empire and Anglo-Chinese relations that made Chinese migration to Singapore a desirable model for other colonies. The economies and labour pools of the British Empire were in transition from the 1830s onwards. Most clearly, the abolition of slavery and the movement away from convict transportation ostensibly signalled the ending of forced labour in the British Empire.[7] At the same time, previously un-remunerative colonies came under pressure from metropolitan critics to increase the production of resources for export.[8] This desire for increased profitability whilst absorbing the costs of non-coercive labour meant that cheap Chinese labourers were in demand. The nineteenth century was also a crucial period of change in Anglo-Chinese relations. The 1830s marked a crisis point as the Qing Empire attempted to enforce its prohibition of opium. British merchants illegally smuggled Indian opium into China and used the profits to export Chinese tea to Europe.[9] In critiquing limits on Western trade, these British opium traders and their supporters depicted the Qing state as despotic and backward. Ultimately, these views prevailed in Britain as the military power of the British Empire forced open China to Western trade and established a British

---

[6] In the same way that certain forms of knowledge were prioritised and described as 'useful', often in terms of economic utility, Chinese migrants were often procured to fulfil a specific economic role.

[7] The year 1833 saw the abolition of slavery in the British Empire, and 1840 brought the suspension of convict transportation to New South Wales. In Chapters 4 and 5, systems of Chinese indentured labour are compared by colonial observers to both of these systems.

[8] Zoë Laidlaw, 'Investigating Empire: Humanitarians, Reform and the Commission of Eastern Inquiry', *The Journal of Imperial and Commonwealth History*, 40, 5 (2012), 749–68. Note that Singapore itself was part of this agricultural revolution: Lynn Hollen Lees, *Planting Empire, Cultivating Subjects: British Malaya, 1786–1941* (Cambridge: Cambridge University Press, 2017).

[9] Historically the tea trade had relied on Spanish silver, which was expensive for the East India Company to acquire. Using highly addictive opium to exchange for tea made this trade much more profitable. For a comprehensive history of opium consumption in Asia, see Hans Derks, *The History of the Opium Problem: The Assault on the East, ca.1600–1950* (Boston: Brill, 2012). For an overview of the role of the Anglo-Indian opium trade in the opening of China, see Robert Bickers, *The Scramble for China: Foreign Devils in the Qing Empire, 1832–1914* (London: Allen Lane, 2011).

colony at Hong Kong in the Opium Wars (1839–42 and 1856–60). These broader contexts of colonial development, the changing nature of labour, the ideological movement in favour of free trade and Anglo-Chinese relations are essential to understanding the motivations for colonial experiments with Chinese labour.

This book focuses on several specific experiments with Chinese migrant labour that sought to replicate early colonial Singapore. In doing so it draws on several, connected historiographical streams: recent work on Singapore and colonial port cities as contact zones; Western ideas about a specifically Chinese character in the context of scientific racism; and Chinese migration and racial exclusion in the British Empire and beyond. The first important point to make is that the idea of Singapore as a model transcends the early colonial period. This can take many forms, ranging from suggestions that the United Kingdom could follow a 'Singapore model' after it leaves the European Union, to Beijing's envy of Singaporean methods for dealing with political dissent.[10] In the modern era, this is based on the 'Singapore Story', famously articulated by Singapore's first Prime Minister, Lee Kuan Yew, as 'Third World to First'.[11] These contemporary discussions of Singapore as an economic miracle are analogous to discussions about early colonial Singapore in the nineteenth-century British Empire.

Recent years have seen scholarly interest in re-evaluating the development of early colonial Singapore. This encompasses innovative work to try to recover subaltern perspectives of colonial experiences as well as work that focuses on the colonial administration itself.[12] For example, there has been renewed scholarly interest in the colonial experiences of early colonial leaders such as Stamford Raffles and John Crawfurd.[13] In a similar vein, this book will examine the impact of Singapore on various British administrators, merchants and travellers and, as a result, Singapore's impact on various British colonies. From the earliest histories of Singapore, such as *One Hundred Years of Singapore* and *One Hundred Years' History of the Chinese in Singapore*, the significance of the Chinese community is ubiquitous.[14] The Chinese merchant elite,

---

[10] 'Sling the Singapore Model out of the Brexit Debate', *Financial Times*, 31 July 2017, www.ft.com/content/08726b32-75f2-11e7-a3e8-60495fe6ca71 (accessed 30 September 2018); Stephan Ortmann and Mark R. Thompson, 'China and the "Singapore Model"', *Journal of Democracy*, 27, 1 (2016), 39–48.

[11] Lee Kuan Yew, *From Third World to First: The Singapore Story, 1965–2000* (Singapore: Singapore Press Holdings, 2000).

[12] Lees, *Planting Empire, Cultivating Subjects*.

[13] Victoria Glendinning, *Raffles and the Golden Opportunity, 1781–1826* (London: Profile, 2012); Gareth Knapman, *Race and British Colonialism in Southeast Asia, 1770–1870: John Crawfurd and the Politics of Equality* (New York: Routledge, 2017). Note also the departure from more uncritical histories such as Edwin Lee, *The British as Rulers: Governing Multiracial Singapore, 1867–1914* (Singapore: Singapore University Press, 1991).

[14] Roland Braddell et al., *One Hundred Years of Singapore, 1819–1919, Vol. I* (London: John Murray, 1921); Ong Siang Song, *One Hundred Years' History of the Chinese in Singapore* (London:

as collaborators with colonial authority, were crucial to both the economic success and social cohesion of the colony. Specifically, the Chinese merchant community mediated between colonial authorities and the Chinese labour force, which constituted the largest group numerically.[15] This population of Chinese labourers, who worked on pepper, gambier and opium plantations as well as in Singapore's tin mines, was crucial to the colony's economic success. Whilst Singapore is famous as a trade entrepôt that benefited from its strategic position at the convergence of international shipping routes, the development of colonial agriculture and tax 'farms' on exported products were essential to growth in the early colonial period.[16] The Anglo-Chinese mixture of the colony's merchant elite contributed to the development of a 'regional economic identity'.[17] The result of this economic success meant that Chinese migration to the Straits Settlements became a model for migration to new colonial contexts.

There is also a broader historical interest in global port cities like Singapore as contact zones in which ideas, goods and people meet and exchange. Zones of British control in Southeast Asia were crucial in allowing missionaries, merchants and officials to form ideas about different racial groups. Contact zones are places – often trading ports, cities or borders – in which the movement of people, commodities and ideas brings different cultures into 'contact' with each other.[18] Port cities act as connectors between different empires, power structures and groups of people.[19] Crucially, in the nineteenth century, Western ideas about Chinese migrants were not constructed in the West but were already being formed in multi-racial Asian contact zones, where Chinese migrants played various social and economic roles. This book argues that Singapore was a particularly important contact zone that facilitated the development and spread of ideas about race, colonisation and economics as intertwined and mutually constituted.

John Murray, 1923).

[15] Mark Frost, *Singapore: A Biography* (London: Thames & Hudson, 2009), 87; Mark Ravinder Frost, 'Emporium in Imperio: Nanyang Networks and the Straits Chinese in Singapore, 1819–1914', *Journal of Southeast Asian Studies*, 36, 1 (2005), 29–66; Carl A. Trocki, *Opium and Empire: Chinese Society in Colonial Singapore, 1800–1910* (London: Cornell University Press, 1990); C. Trocki, 'Opium and the Beginnings of Chinese Capitalism in Southeast Asia', *Journal of Southeast Asian Studies*, 33, 2 (2002), 297–314.

[16] The opium 'farm' was not necessarily a literal farm but a description for the outsourcing of tax collection by the colonial state. Chapter 1 discusses this in more detail.

[17] Anthony Webster, 'The Development of British Commercial and Political Networks in the Straits Settlements 1800 to 1868: The Rise of a Colonial and Regional Economic Identity?', *Modern Asian Studies*, 45, 4 (2011), 899–929.

[18] This idea of the colonial 'contact zone' first appeared in Mary Louise Pratt, *Imperial Eyes: Travel Writing and Transculturation* (London: Routledge, 1992).

[19] Ulbe Bosma and Anthony Webster, eds, *Commodities, Ports and Asian Maritime Trade since 1750* (Basingstoke: Palgrave Macmillan, 2015); Nara Dillon and Jean C. Oi, eds, *At the Crossroads of Empires: Middlemen, Social Networks, and State-Building in Republican Shanghai* (Stanford, CA: Stanford University Press, 2008).

Discussions of Chinese migrant labour in the nineteenth-century British Empire also took place in a changing intellectual environment. The nineteenth century was a key period in terms of the development and institutionalisation of scientific racism.[20] Ideas such as polygenesis and Social Darwinism changed how race and racial difference were understood and articulated, particularly in Britain and the United States.[21] Importantly, some figures who are examined in this book, such as John Crawfurd, actively contributed to this hardening of racial attitudes and drew on their colonial experiences to present race as an immutable physical category. As a result, this book uses the terminology of 'race' rather than 'ethnicity'.[22] However, it is important to clarify that in the colonial correspondence and publications examined in this book, the language of civilisation, rather than pure physical distinctions of race, remained the dominant means for articulating differences between Britain and China or the British and the Chinese.[23] The concept of civilisation was particularly useful for implying British superiority and justifying the British legal authority over China and the Chinese.[24] The similarities and differences highlighted between the Chinese and other racial groups are particularly pertinent in English-language writing in the 1830s. Contemporary observers clearly identified Chinese culture as a distinguishing feature which set the Chinese apart from other racial groups in Asia. Of course, the acknowledgement of cultural difference within China and between Chinese migrants from different regions problematises the concept of 'the Chinese'.[25] Whilst there was no uniform definition of Chinese culture, it is clear from the sources examined that over the mid-nineteenth century the Chinese began to be perceived as a specific racial group, often defined and

---

[20] Kay Anderson, *Race and the Crisis of Humanism* (New York: UCL Press, 2006); David Hollinsworth, *Race and Racism in Australia* (Katoomba: Social Science Press, 1998).

[21] Douglas A. Lorimer, *Science, Race Relations and Resistance: Britain, 1870–1914* (Manchester: Manchester University Press, 2013).

[22] Contemporary discussions of these issues would use the language of 'ethnicity' to acknowledge differences of culture. These cultural differences were still relevant in the nineteenth century, but they were connected to physical, racial characteristics. For more on these distinctions, see Stephen M. Caliendo and Charlton D. McIlwain, eds, *The Routledge Companion to Race and Ethnicity* (London: Routledge, 2011).

[23] For a discussion of ideas such as 'the ladder of civilization', see Peter Mandler, '"Race" and "Nation" in Mid-Victorian Thought', in Stefan Collini, Richard Whatmore and Brian Young, eds, *History, Religion, and Culture: British Intellectual History, 1750–1950* (Cambridge: Cambridge University Press, 2000), 233.

[24] Adam McKeown, *Melancholy Order: Asian Migration and the Globalization of Borders* (New York: Columbia University Press, 2008), 8; Jennifer Pitts, *A Turn to Empire: The Rise of Imperial Liberalism in Britain and France* (Princeton: Princeton University Press, 2005).

[25] What constituted the 'genuine' Chinese character was often contested and confused. As Henrietta Harrison points out, this is hardly surprising if we consider how large and diverse the population that came under the umbrella of 'Chinese' was in terms of language, religion, cultural practices and ethnic identity. See Henrietta Harrison, *China: Inventing the Nation* (London: Bloomsbury Academic, 2011).

differentiated by their culture, even after centuries of settlement in a particular overseas location.

Connected to the presentation of the Chinese as a specific race was the idea that there was a specific Chinese character.[26] This interest in an inherent Chinese character was a theme that ran through English-language literature on China from the late eighteenth century onwards.[27] The conceptual development of a national character in Western thought was not solely applied to China or the Chinese. In Britain the language of a shared character was becoming increasingly common in the late eighteenth and early nineteenth century.[28] Histories of Anglo-Chinese relations have traditionally focused on the positive or negative attributes attached to these concepts of character. The most commonly, uncritically repeated argument has been that British, or Western, perspectives on China deteriorated from a largely positive view of Chinese culture, civilisation and technology in the eighteenth century to a negative view of Chinese despotism, vice and heathenism in the nineteenth century.[29] However, this positive to negative narrative is overly simplistic.[30] It is more appropriate to describe how the imagined Chinese character, and by extension Chinese migrant labour, was seen as economically useful, particularly in the context of colonial rule, rather than positive or negative.[31] We must also acknowledge that these ideas are long-lasting. For example, the description of the Chinese as a 'trade and business diaspora' fits within

[26] Arthur Henderson Smith's *Chinese Characteristics*, published over several editions in the 1890s, provides the clearest articulation of the importance of character. For Smith the Chinese character was defined by a 'Contempt for Foreigners' and 'The Absence of Public Spirit': Arthur Henderson Smith, *Chinese Characteristics* (New York: Fleming H. Revell Company, 1894).

[27] J. A. G. Roberts, 'On the Character of the Chinese', in J. A. G. Roberts, *China through Western Eyes: The Nineteenth Century* (Bath: Alan Sutton, 1991), deals specifically with the issue of defining the Chinese character in English-language literature.

[28] Peter Mandler, *The English National Character: The History of an Idea from Edmund Burke to Tony Blair* (London: Yale University Press, 2006), 3.

[29] William Edward Soothill, *China and the West: A Short History of Their Contact from Ancient Times to the Fall of the Manchu Dynasty* (London: Oxford University Press, 1925); Colin Mackerras, *Sinophiles and Sinophobes: Western Views of China* (New York: Oxford University Press, 2000); Roberts, *China through Western Eyes*. Similarly, Peter Kitson's acceptance of this orthodoxy is demonstrative of how the positive to negative narrative is handled in much scholarship: 'My thesis accepts the conventional view that the representation of the Qing Empire in the late eighteenth and early nineteenth centuries suffered a staggering reversal of fortune from admiration to degradation' (Peter J. Kitson, *Forging Romantic China: Sino-British Cultural Exchange, 1760–1840* (Cambridge: Cambridge University Press, 2013), 13).

[30] A number of scholars have emphasised the contradictions of definitions of Chinese character and the diverse motives and narratives of different Western observers: Ting Man Tsao, 'Representing China to the British Public in the Age of Free Trade, c. 1833–1844' (Ph.D. thesis, State University of New York at Stony Brook, 2000); Hao Gao, 'Sino-British Encounters: Perceptions and Attitudes from Macartney's Mission to the Opium War, 1792–1840' (Ph.D. thesis, Edinburgh, 2014); Laurence Williams, 'Anglo-Chinese Caresses: Civility, Friendship and Trade in English Representations of China, 1760–1800', *Journal for Eighteenth Century Studies*, 38, 2 (June 2015), 277.

[31] Berg, 'Britain, Industry and Perceptions of China', 269–88.

this broader history of ascribing an essential entrepreneurial character to 'the Chinese'.[32]

The history of Chinese migration into the British Empire and the West more generally is inseparable from a much broader historical theme: otherness. The mass movement of Chinese migrants in the nineteenth century, which had a significant impact on ideas about race, colonial politics, immigration laws, cultural change and the development of economic resources, means that there is a vast body of relevant literature. This existing literature focuses specifically on settler colonies – such as Lake and Reynolds' *Drawing the Global Colour Line*, McKeown's *Melancholy Order* and Atkinson's *The Burden of White Supremacy* – and treated these migrations to 'white men's countries' as separate from Chinese migrations to Southeast Asia.[33] There are two critical issues with the historiography of Chinese and Asian migration into the British Empire and the West. First, there are transnational themes in the history of Chinese migration and the subsequent responses to Chinese immigration, whether inter-colonial, imperial, continental, hemispheric or even global. Where these histories have taken a transnational approach, the focus has been overwhelmingly on the host nations and negative responses to Chinese immigration. As a result, these histories have dwelt on exclusion and exploitation and neglected the stories of those who promoted Chinese emigration and immigration. Second, the assumed linear development of movement and resistance is crucial to shaping our current understanding of migration and exclusion. The traditional analysis of exclusionary politics being born from white working-class reactions to labour competition in the late nineteenth century is too simplistic. Exclusion movements invoked, rather than created, stereotypes.[34] The mass migration of the late nineteenth century has been presented as an independent phenomenon that was unconnected to Anglo-Chinese tensions and exchanges from the 1830s onwards.[35] This book demonstrates that stereotypes about Chinese workers, formed in early colonial Singapore by colonial officials and employers who praised Chinese immigration, reappeared in the anti-immigrant narratives prominent in white settler colonies from the 1850s onwards.

[32] Robin Cohen, *Global Diasporas: An Introduction* (London: Routledge, 2008), 83.

[33] Marilyn Lake and Henry Reynolds, *Drawing the Global Colour Line: White Men's Countries and the International Challenge of Racial Equality* (Cambridge: Cambridge University Press, 2008); McKeown, *Melancholy Order*; David C. Atkinson, *The Burden of White Supremacy: Containing Asian Migration in the British Empire and the United States* (Chapel Hill: University of North Carolina Press, 2017).

[34] Older studies of exclusion movements have particularly neglected the earlier nineteenth century. For example, note the dates in the title of A. T. Yarwood, *Asian Migration to Australia: The Background to Exclusion 1896–1923* (Melbourne: Melbourne University Press, 1964).

[35] The disconnect is being revised by scholars. See Benjamin Mountford, *Britain, China and Colonial Australia* (Oxford: Oxford University Press, 2016).

This book examines a range of colonial contexts – Singapore, Assam, Ceylon, New South Wales, Mauritius, the West Indies, Hong Kong – and different forms of migration – free, credit-ticket and indentured – simultaneously. The focus is not on a specific colony but on how ideas about Chinese migrants moved around the British Empire through the books, letters, newspapers and reports of colonial officials, merchants, missionaries and travellers. These sources and colonial case studies offer comprehensive insight into the development of Singapore, Chinese migration and the growth of the British Empire in the nineteenth century.[36] The available source material has heavily influenced the approach taken in this work. The clandestine nature of Chinese emigration in this period makes the use of comparable or uniform statistical migration records impossible. The Qing Empire prohibited emigration until 1860 and it was, in theory if not in practice, punishable by death. Chinese and Western facilitators of emigration often recruited migrants from locations other than Canton, outside of Chinese or British oversight. Additionally, in both credit-ticket (where the cost of passage was repaid by workers) and indentured (where contracts were signed prior to embarkation) migration schemes, the level of consent was debatable.[37] Even after 1855, when the Passenger Act connected migrant numbers to ship tonnage, documentation on passenger numbers was routinely forged.[38] It was not until the rise of exclusion and mass migrations of the late nineteenth century that colonial censuses expanded in scope and regularity to allow for the longitudinal tracing of migrant movements.

This book does not seek to recapture migrant voices that have been omitted from conventional narratives, but to interrogate the vast colonial records on specific colonial experiments with Chinese migrant labour. The focus here is on the changing perceptions of, and demands for, Chinese migrants as colonists within a wider framework of empire building. An examination of a variety of sources gives an insight into various colonial experiments with Chinese migrant labour. These sources are divisible into four broad groups: official, commercial, private and public.

The main official documents are British Parliamentary Papers, Colonial Office Records and correspondence from the Singapore National Archives, which deal with imperial and colonial policy. The commercial sources refer to the business letters of merchant firms that were active in Asia, such as Jardine Matheson (Canton/Hong Kong), Davidson & Co. (Singapore) and Tait & Co. (Amoy). The infamous China-coast opium trader Jardine Matheson acts

[36] Map 3 demonstrates the territorial growth of the British Empire in the nineteenth century.
[37] The issue of debt slavery complicates the idea of 'free' labour. See Gwyn Campbell and Alessandro Stanziani, eds, *Bonded Labour and Debt in the Indian Ocean World* (London: Pickering & Chatto, 2013).
[38] Robert Lee Irick, 'Chi'ing Policy towards the Coolie Trade, 1847–1878' (Ph.D. thesis, Harvard University, 1971), 10; Parliamentary Papers, *Chinese Passenger Ships. A bill intituled an act for the regulation of Chinese passenger ships*, 1854–55 (293).

as a particularly useful source because of the firm's access to China in this period and the scale of the company's archive. The private sources category covers the unpublished letters and diaries of relevant individuals – from the Jardine Matheson archives, the British Library, the National Archives of Scotland and elsewhere. The public documents comprise a large amount of the sources analysed and include newspapers, journals, periodicals, reports and books intended for a mass contemporary audience. Many of these are available digitally, but archives in London and Hong Kong also provide printed material that discusses China and Chinese migration. Historians of migration often treat these types of colonial sources with caution. As instruments of colonial power these sources contain orientalist tropes and negative stereotypes, they provide no insight into the migrant experience and they often omit unrecorded population movement. However, in the context of this book, these sources are of interest precisely because they demonstrate attempts by colonial and imperial authorities to understand, control and manage migration. A critical analysis of these sources provides an insight into how the example of Singapore and the connected colonial assumptions about race, colonisation and economics shaped perceptions of Chinese migrants across the British Empire.

Chapter 1 outlines the rapid growth of Singapore in the 1820s and 1830s and some of the key explanations for the colony's economic success, which informed subsequent strategies of colonial development. It examines how systems of Chinese migration to Southeast Asia worked, how the Chinese in Singapore were perceived by colonial observers and the ways in which Singapore emerged as a colonial model. The key theme is that because of Singapore's rapid growth colonial observers saw British colonial governance and Chinese economic migration as an effective combination in the context of an empire that increasingly prioritised free trade and free labour. We can see here how ideas about race, economics and colonisation were intertwined in colonial Singapore. Chapter 2 explores how the key lesson of the colonial experience in Singapore – that liberal British rule and the economic contribution of Chinese migrants were an effective combination – was disseminated to the metropole and between different colonies. It examines the role of Singapore in the debates over the East India Company Charter, the broader development of ideas about Chinese character beyond Singapore, and the way that declining Anglo-Chinese relations shaped these discussions. We can see here how ideas about race, colonisation and economics moved through information, personal, bureaucratic and commercial networks around the British Empire. These chapters lay the groundwork for the experiments with Chinese labour in different colonial contexts, which are explored in the following chapters.

The following chapters examine different Chinese migration schemes and colonial experiences of Chinese migration from the 1830s to the 1860s. It is notable that many of these migration schemes met with huge problems, which led to abandonment, or were retrospectively considered failures. However, these schemes had a wider narrative significance in shaping perceptions of Chinese labour in the British Empire. Chapter 3 introduces the first case study that saw the use of Chinese labour migration outside of the existing patterns of migration to Southeast Asia. First, migration to Assam (Northeast India) built upon existing movements of Chinese labour and invoked assumptions about Chinese migrants and indigenous peoples detailed in previous chapters. We then see the significance of Singapore in influencing attempts to introduce Chinese colonists in colonial Ceylon. At the same time the issue of labour in the British Empire was subject to intense debate in London. The phasing out of coercive forms of employment – slave labour, convict labour and the suspension of Indian indentured labour – left questions about how colonies like Mauritius and the West Indies would cope with labour shortages. Chapter 4 turns attention to attempts to apply the Singapore model in the white settler colonies of Australia. It examines Gordon Forbes Davidson's Chinese migration scheme in New South Wales. In establishing this scheme, Davidson drew heavily on his time in Southeast Asia and explicitly attempted to extend the existing migration networks he had observed in colonial Singapore. We can also trace the continuing influence of Singapore during the gold rush era, which saw mass migration from China to the Australian colonies.

Chapter 5 provides the final case study with an examination of Chinese emigration from Hong Kong and the China coast from the 1850s. After Britain defeated China in the First Opium War, the Treaty of Nanking (1842) opened Chinese ports to Western trade, granted Britain Hong Kong as a new colony, and kick-started a new era of Chinese migration. This chapter details how colonial observers measured the new colony of Hong Kong against Singapore, how it disrupted Singapore's dominance as a point of emigration and how Singapore remained an important connection between China and the rest of the British Empire. Specifically, we can see the significance of Singapore as a stopping place for Chinese passenger ships departing Hong Kong and the Chinese treaty ports for new destinations, such as the West Indies.

By studying these examples this book traces early representations of and experiments with Chinese labour in the British Empire during the early period of colonial Singapore, from 1819 to 1867. It shows the role of Singapore in facilitating Chinese emigration and contributing to the formation of an imagined Chinese character. The attempts to apply ideas about race, colonisation and economics developed in Singapore to different colonial contexts offer a unique insight into the development of the British Empire in the nineteenth century. We see how Singapore shaped the development of plantation colonies, the contours of mass migration and the phasing out of slave labour. More broadly, modern concepts and systems of border control, which are a ubiquitous function of modern nation states, developed in response to Chinese mass migration.[39] Both physically and conceptually, this period of rapid change laid the foundations for the huge Chinese migrations that would shape so much of the British Empire, and the world, at the end of the nineteenth century. Beyond the specific historical period, the interconnected themes that informed attempts to replicate colonial Singapore continue to be relevant in the present day. In modern Britain, debates about migration, racism and globalisation demonstrate the centrality of these themes to Britain's relationship with the wider world. In the present, we continue to evaluate migrants according to economic utility, foster exclusionary racism as a political device and grapple with the tensions between free trade and the free movement of people. All of these issues came to the fore when British colonial administrators attempted to replicate the Singapore model of colonisation in the nineteenth century.

[39] McKeown, *Melancholy Order*.

Chapter 1

THE SINGAPORE MODEL

From the start of the colonial project in Singapore, British administrators recognised the importance of the Chinese population. Stamford Raffles, who founded a trading post at Singapore in 1819, recognised the suitability of Chinese migrants from the outset:

> That a speculating and industrious people like the Chinese, they must continue to operate in spite of political restrictions and partial exactions. It deserves remark that of all the inhabitants of the archipelago, the Chinese as well from their assimilating more with the customs of Europeans than the native Mahomedans, as from their habits of obedience and submission to power, are uniformly found to be the most peaceable and improvable ... Borneo and the Eastern Islands may become to China what America is already to the nations of Europe. The superabundant and overflowing population of China affords an almost inexhaustible source of colonization, while the new and fertile soil of these Islands offers the means of immediate and plentiful subsistence to any numbers who may settle in them.[1]

The 'power' to which Raffles believes the Chinese submit is British colonial rule. Similarly, the second Resident of Singapore, John Crawfurd, deemed that this Anglo-Chinese combination of mutual interests was so strong that he was able to refuse additional military support when negotiating the 1824 treaty that confirmed the island as a permanent British colony with indigenous leaders. Instead, Crawfurd was confident that he could draw on the support of the Chinese migrant population as a military force if negotiations turned violent.[2] This chapter charts the racialised explanations for the role of the Chinese in Singapore's economic success, which informed subsequent strategies of colonial development. Because of Singapore's rapid growth, colonial observers saw British colonial governance and Chinese economic migration

---

[1] Minute by Sir Stamford Raffles on the Establishment of a Malayan College at Singapore, 1 April 1823, in M2: Singapore: Letters from Bengal to the Resident (National Archives of Singapore).

[2] Knapman, *Race and British Colonialism in Southeast Asia*, 136, discusses this episode in detail.

as an effective combination in the context of an empire that increasingly prioritised free trade and free labour.

Between the establishment of a trading post in 1819 and the creation of the Straits Settlements as a Crown Colony in 1867 both Singapore's population and its economic output increased significantly. Singapore became famous as an entrepôt of free trade, a lucrative trading port between India and China, but also relied on often overlooked plantation agriculture.[3] As a site of both trade and cultivation, Singapore was a contact zone, where colonial observers developed and tested ideas about the Chinese character. Generally, Southeast Asia was the site of pre-existing systems of Chinese migration in the form of the seasonal junk trade, which carried labourers from southern China on credit-ticket contracts.[4] As a result of these large annual migrations, Singapore provided contemporary observers with an example of a significant Chinese population living and working under British governance. For example, during his time in Singapore, John Crawfurd formed ideas about Chinese labour and the Chinese character which would inform his understanding of racial hier-archy, his advocacy of free trade and his political liberalism for the rest of his life. Most colonial observers singled out elite Chinese merchants, who acted in compliance and partnership with colonial authority, as ideal colonists. As a crucial point of contact, Singapore both validated the credentials of Western experts and provided an example of how Chinese migrants fulfilled various economic roles. Colonial administrators were not the only ones who formed stereotypes about Chinese migrants. The account of Chinese businessman Seah Eu Chin reveals the agency of some Chinese elites in mediating colonial understandings of Chinese society within Singapore. Residence in Singapore was also a major influence on the British merchant Gordon Forbes Davidson, who went on to establish a Chinese migration scheme to Australia in the late 1830s. It was in Singapore that Davidson saw first-hand the utility of Chinese labour in a British colony and was familiarised with pre-existing systems of Chinese emigration. Singapore was a template. It provided both an example of pre-existing systems of Chinese migration as well as a large Chinese population, which could be 'exported' to other colonies.

Credit-Ticket Migration to Singapore and the Straits Settlements from the 1820s

In the early nineteenth century, imperial planners identified China, with its vast 'surplus' population, as a solution to imperial labour shortages.[5] For example, in 1810 a House of Commons Select Committee considered 'the

---

[3]   Lees, *Planting Empire, Cultivating Subjects*, gives a good overview of Singapore's agricultural development, which was crucial in the early colonial period.

[4]   Trocki, *Opium and Empire*, 30.

[5]   Jardine Matheson's newspaper, the *Canton Register*, frequently discussed the excess size of the Chinese population: *Canton Register*, 3 October 1829, 17 March 1831, 11 July 1837.

practicability and expediency of supplying our West India colonies with free labourers from the East'. This committee examined the possibility of replacing the recently prohibited African slave trade (1807) with a system of Chinese immigration. In the committee's report the Chinese were praised for having 'uniformly conducted themselves with the greatest propriety and order' and being 'distinguished by their orderly and industrious habits', though such a scheme was dismissed as impracticable.[6] Similarly, in colonial settings where there were labour shortages, such as the Australian colonies, colonial employers saw Chinese migrants as a possible solution from the turn of the nineteenth century.[7] These demands were driven by vast, Empire-wide changes. Colonies became more important as centres of production for the supply of raw materials to the rapidly industrialising British economy. The British colonial experience in the Straits Settlements over the 1820s and 1830s demonstrated the economic utility of Chinese migration. Migration schemes that were deemed impracticable at the start of the nineteenth century were established and operational by the 1850s, and it was a consequence of migration to the Straits Settlements.

Contact zones such as Singapore were crucial for providing knowledge of the practicalities of Chinese immigration and as locations in which racial hierarchies were constructed.[8] Whilst Southeast Asia had been home to Chinese expatriate communities for centuries, the increasing population movement between 1740 and 1840, which was partly driven by the infusion of European capital into the region, has been described by scholars as the 'Chinese century'.[9] Singapore was of particular significance in the 1830s because of its rapid development in the 1820s. Crucially, experience of early colonial Singapore had a significant impact on colonial observers who were later involved in establishing schemes for Chinese migration and diffusing ideas about an archetypal Chinese character. The best example of the connection between the colonial experience and ideas about race is the way that colonial life in Singapore shaped John Crawfurd's perceptions of Chinese migrants. John Crawfurd was a significant figure, serving as British Resident of Singapore from 1823 to 1826. His role in negotiating the 1824 treaty with the Temenggong of Johor on the status of Singapore means that he is often cited,

---

[6] Parliamentary Papers, *Report from the committee appointed to consider the practicability and expediency of supplying our West India colonies with free labourers from the East*, 1810–11 (225), 1.

[7] See Chapter 4 for a discussion of Chinese migration to Australia. These discussions first appear in the correspondence of Governor King; King to Hobart, 14 August 1804, in *Historical Records of Australia: Series I, Volume V* (The Library Committee of the Commonwealth Parliament, 1915), 8.

[8] Ulrike Hillemann, *Asian Empire and British Knowledge: China and the Networks of British Imperial Expansion* (New York: Palgrave MacMillan, 2009), 1–16.

[9] Nordin Hussin, *Trade and Society in the Straits of Melaka: Dutch Melaka and English Penang, 1780–1830* (Singapore: NUS Press, 2007), xxiv.

alongside Raffles, as the 'father' of the colony.[10] After travelling to Calcutta to work for the East India Company's Bengal Medical Service in 1803, Crawfurd had a long career in Asia, as an administrator and diplomat, before returning to Britain to contribute to the East India Company Charter debates in the 1830s. After several failed attempts to enter parliament as a Whig MP, Crawfurd later became President of the Ethnological Society of London (1861–68) and Vice President of the Royal Geographical Society (1861–68).[11] Gareth Knapman has detailed how Crawfurd combined his liberal politics with bold new ideas about race.[12] As a leading advocate of polygenesis, the idea that different races of human beings had different origins, Crawfurd regularly drew on his colonial experiences in Southeast Asia. Crucially, as this chapter demonstrates, Crawfurd viewed the Chinese as superior to the indigenous population due to their industriousness and economic importance to the colony. As a consequence of the colonial experience in Singapore, colonial observers routinely characterised the Chinese as the 'highest ranking Asians on the scale of civilization'.[13] Ideas about race and economic utility were mutually constituted in colonial Singapore, which provided a fertile ideological rationale for later colonial experiments with Chinese labour.

In Singapore, British colonial authorities and merchant elites exploited pre-existing systems of Chinese migration across the Malay Peninsula and Southeast Asia. Whilst contemporary Western critics chastised the insularity of the Qing Empire, there had long been semi-clandestine Chinese migration networks.[14] Significant population movement from China to the Philippines, Java, Siam, Borneo and Malaya had been recorded from the 1600s onwards.[15] These migrations were not just driven by economic pull factors but also by the growth of Amoy (Xiamen) as a thriving port city on China's south coast.[16] This long history has led to the designation of Southeast Asia as the '*Nanyang*', described by Craig Lockyard as a 'Chinese Mediterranean'.[17] The port towns that would be designated the Straits Settlements by the British

---

[10] C. M. Turnbull, 'Crawfurd, John (1783–1868)', *Oxford Dictionary of National Biography*, Oxford University Press, 2004, www.oxforddnb.com/view/article/6651 (accessed 30 September 2018). The Temenggong was an ancient Malay title of nobility, and the treaty agreement legally secured British control of Singapore. See also Ernest C. T. Chew, 'Dr. John Crawfurd (1783–1868): The Scotsman Who Made Singapore British', *The Literature, Culture and Society of Singapore*, www.postcolonialweb.org/singapore/history/chew/chew10.html (accessed 30 September 2018).

[11] Knapman, *Race and British Colonialism in Southeast Asia*, 8.

[12] Ibid., 7.

[13] Hillemann, *Asian Empire and British Knowledge*, 149.

[14] Whilst emigration was technically illegal until 1860, local Qing officials were aware of emigration from southern ports along existing trade routes. The movement of people was tacitly accepted by authorities.

[15] Trocki, *Opium and Empire*, 30.

[16] Kuhn, *Chinese among Others*, 35.

[17] Craig A. Lockard, 'Chinese Migration and Settlement in Southeast Asia before 1850: Making Fields from the Sea', *History Compass*, 11, 9 (2013): 765–781 at 766.

were already connected, through commerce and population movement, to China. Nordin Hussin's study of Penang and Malacca shows the growth of the Chinese populations across Southeast Asia in the eighteenth century, prior to British colonial control. As an example, the Chinese immigrant community in Malacca grew from three per cent of the total population in 1675 to twenty-two per cent by 1750.[18] These pre-existing Chinese communities were visible to Europeans in Southeast Asia. John Crawfurd suggested that of the total population of the Siamese Empire (which he estimated to be 2.8 million) more than 440,000 were Chinese, and that they made up 'one half of the population of Bangkok'.[19] Chinese migrants were important economic and social power brokers across Southeast Asia, often in areas outside of European colonial control. Why then, in a region where Chinese migrants were ubiquitous, was Singapore so significant? The answer is timing. Singapore's rapid expansion, driven by Chinese immigration, preceded changes within the British Empire and Anglo-Chinese relations that made Chinese labour migration to Singapore a desirable model for other colonies to follow.

Singapore provided an example of a large Chinese population, living under British rule, which could be 'exported' to other parts of the Empire via onward migration.[20] Over the 1820s Singapore became a vital trade point connected to India, Canton and ports across Southeast Asia.[21] Singapore's commercial success, proximity to China and shortage of labour quickly attracted migrant populations from Europe, China and areas within Southeast Asia. Notably, British observers tended to essentialise the large and diverse Chinese community into two categories: manual labourers and wealthy merchants. These two groups drew colonial interest because they were economically significant, with the rest of the intermediate economic roles performed by Chinese migrants largely ignored. Moreover, the 'rags to riches' narrative of poor labourers who became wealthy merchants further served Singapore's legend as a successful colony.[22] By the 1830s the island attracted between 5,000 and 8,000 Chinese labourers annually, mainly for work in tin mines and on rubber plantations. Additionally, this population movement both attracted and created a class of wealthy Chinese merchants, who by 1867

[18] Hussin, *Trade and Society in the Straits of Melaka*, 164–6.
[19] John Crawfurd, *Journal of an Embassy from the Governor-General of India to the Courts of Siam and Cochin China, Vol. II* (London: Henry Colburn and Richard Bentley, 1830), 221–4.
[20] For a broad history of Chinese migration in Southeast Asia see Craig A. Lockard, *Southeast Asia in World History* (Oxford: Oxford University Press, 2009); Carl A. Trocki, 'Singapore as a Nineteenth Century Migration Node', in Donna Gabaccia and Dirk Hoerder, eds, *Connecting Seas and Connected Ocean Rims: Indian, Atlantic, and Pacific Oceans and China Seas Migrations from the 1830s to the 1930s* (Leiden: Brill, 2011), 198–225.
[21] Frost, *Singapore*, 85. Singapore also acted as a connecting point between global and intra-Asian trade: see Atsushi Kobayashi, 'The Role of Singapore in the Growth of Intra-Southeast Asian Trade, c.1820s–1852', *Southeast Asian Studies*, 2, 3 (2013), 443–74.
[22] Lockard, *Southeast Asia in World History*, 100.

made up two-thirds of the colony's merchant community.[23] Different classes of Chinese colonists – whether labourers, artisans or merchants – were both interconnected and played different roles in colonial society. The colonial focus on labourers and merchants missed the complexities of Chinese life in Singapore, but this crude oversimplification was central to the creation of stereotypes that informed subsequent colonial experiments with Chinese migration.

In Singapore, stereotypes about Chinese migrants were developed in a multi-racial context. Anthony Webster has discussed how the Chinese, along with the native Malay population, were regularly subject to racism and ridicule in the English-language press.[24] By contrast, Webster has also revealed how the prominence of the Chinese in the Straits Settlements created a distinct Southeast Asian identity – amongst the colonial elite – that contributed to the growing 'regional, political and commercial consciousness [that] emerged in the 1830s and 1840s'.[25] British narratives of hierarchy in Singapore led to a racial stratification in which the Chinese were placed above other Asian racial groups, due to their economic contribution, but below Europeans, due to their perceived cultural and social inferiority.[26]

Most Chinese migrants to Singapore, and the Malay Peninsula in general, were credit-ticket migrants: manual labourers who signed contracts to get their 'tickets' from China to Singapore paid. Numerous scholars have detailed how this system long predated British colonial control.[27] The credit-ticket system largely worked to the benefit of employers seeking cheap labour. Workers signed contracts for a set period with a broker in China before they were taken to their destination (in this case Singapore) where the Chinese brokers would sell the contract to a Chinese or European employer. The sale of the contract acted as payment to the broker for passage and the labourers repaid their new employers for the purchase of the contract from their wages.[28] Alternatively some credit-ticket passengers were brought to Southeast Asia on the account of specific vessels, where on arrival the passengers would be detained until an employer secured their services by paying their expenses

---

23 Frost, *Singapore*, 87–91.
24 Webster, 'The Development of British Commercial and Political Networks in the Straits Settlements', 911.
25 Ibid., 908.
26 Syed Alatas, *The Myth of the Lazy Native: A Study of the Image of the Malays, Filipinos and Javanese from the 16th to the 20th Century and Its Function in the Ideology of Colonial Capitalism* (London: Cass and Co., 1977).
27 David Northrup, *Indentured Labour in the Age of Imperialism, 1834–1922* (Cambridge: Cambridge University Press, 1995), 54; Persia Crawfurd Campbell, *Chinese Coolie Emigration within the British Empire* (London: P.S. King & Son, 1923), xii. There are references to migrants 'pawning' themselves in this fashion as early as 1805.
28 Arnold J. Meagher, *The Coolie Trade: The Traffic in Chinese Laborers to Latin America, 1847–1874* (Philadelphia: Xlibris, 2008), 189.

and a margin of profit to the ship.[29] This 'junk trade' was conducted entirely by Chinese brokers and operated in some form across most of Southeast Asia.[30] These trading vessels often carried labourers as supplementary cargo, meaning that the movement of people followed existing trade routes. Trocki's periods of Chinese migration mark the early nineteenth century as an important shifting point, with European capital investment stimulating the growth of the existing Chinese trade.[31] The rapid economic development of Singapore vastly increased the demand for credit-ticket labourers, which, prior to 1842, was reliant on pre-existing Chinese trading networks.[32]

Many Chinese men (it was almost universally a system for male labourers) entered credit-ticket contracts willingly, but there were abuses within the system – including coercion, contract manipulation, and false promises of pay and conditions.[33] Debt was often exploited by both employers and brokers in order to extend contracts beyond their original terms.[34] Workers from China would enter into contracts often to repay debts incurred through opium addiction, gambling or financial mismanagement.[35] In the early colonial period the credit-ticket system was entirely unregulated by the colonial state and little information about population movement was recorded. Estimates from 1876 suggest that two-thirds of arriving Chinese labourers were credit-ticket as opposed to 'free'.[36] The account of W. A. Clubley, the Secretary to the Governor of the Straits Settlements, demonstrates the awareness of British colonial authorities of the problems with the system:

> With regard to the subject of Chinese emigrants arriving here, it may be only necessary to say, that of course they are, as stated, people of poor condition, and generally without the means to defray their passage money from China. Thus, on their arrival here, as is the case in other parts, their labour is

[29] Chen-tung Chang, 'Chinese Coolie Trade in the Straits Settlements in the Late Nineteenth Century', *Bulletin of the Institute of Ethnology Academia Sinica*, 65 (1988), 2.

[30] Elliot C. Arensmeyer, 'The Chinese Coolie Labour Trade and the Philippines: An Inquiry', *Philippine Studies*, 28 (1980), 189.

[31] Trocki, *Opium and Empire*, 30.

[32] From 1842 onwards there are a number of examples of British and European merchants engaged in transporting labourers from the British colony of Hong Kong to Singapore. For example, Hamilton, Gray & Co. were granted 'three special licences for the importation of Chinese immigrants' by Governor Butterworth, 18 January 1844, in Z15 Singapore: Letters from Governor (National Archives of Singapore).

[33] Campbell, *Chinese Coolie Emigration within the British Empire*, xii; Trocki, 'Singapore as a Nineteenth Century Migration Node', 198–225.

[34] Eli Murakami, 'Two Bonded Labour Emigration Patterns in Mid-Nineteenth-Century Southern China: The Coolie Trade and Emigration to Southeast Asia', in Campbell and Stanziani, *Bonded Labour and Debt in the Indian Ocean World*, 153–65.

[35] Alatas, *The Myth of the Lazy Native*, 84.

[36] Chang, 'Chinese Coolie Trade in the Straits Settlements in the Late Nineteenth Century', 3. The term 'free' here refers to labourers who were not bound by contract or debt upon arrival, yet it is used cautiously as the degree to which a choice of employer or employment was available was often questionable.

temporarily mortgaged to individuals, in consideration of the payment of their passage money, their Masters subsisting them for the year in which they are so engaged. Generally speaking, this debt amounts to 15 or 20 dollars and their first year is employed in this voluntary service, in gaining a knowledge of the nature and value of their future labour. Too frequently, the Chinese so engaged abscond from their service before the year expires, but although the Masters have frequent cause to complain of them, never have I known a complaint on the part of the Chinese themselves.[37]

Notably, though there is an awareness here of the potential for abuse, there is a reticence to intervene and Clubley presents Chinese workers as compliant. As new systems of migration to distant European colonies developed in the nineteenth century, Singapore became a favoured destination of emigrants from southern China. For potential migrants Southeast Asia was a desirable destination due to the ease of return migration. Many of the brokers involved in the Southeast Asian credit-ticket system were return migrants themselves.[38] For those planning to sojourn for purely economic reasons, the high level of return migration, as compared with later destinations such as the West Indies, was particularly reassuring and made colonies like Singapore favoured migrant destinations.

Measuring Singapore's Population

For the early period it is difficult to estimate the exact size of the Chinese population working under credit-ticket contracts in Singapore. The sojourning nature of the credit-ticket system meant the population was largely transient. Historians have been reluctant to cite Singapore's census results prior to the 1870s due to the irregularity of their timing and methodology. Different censuses from early colonial Singapore included different geographical areas and placed inhabitants into different racial or demographic categories. They were also highly irregular, with no detailed data for the 1850s and only general data, with no ethnic categories, from 1860. In 1859 an editorial in the *Straits Times* remarked that 'it is now ten years since a return was made of the population of Singapore, yet we do not hear of any steps being adopted for a new census'.[39] In terms of migration, there are even fewer records. In the first 'blue book' of the new Straits Settlements Crown Colony in 1867 the 'immigrants/emigrants' section reads 'Cannot be ascertained. No records being kept'.[40]

---

[37] W. A. Clubley, 16 June 1825, in A18: Penang Consultations (National Archives of Singapore).

[38] Murakami, 'Two Bonded Labour Emigration Patterns in Mid-Nineteenth-Century Southern China', 162.

[39] *The Straits Times*, 23 April 1859.

[40] Straits Settlements Blue Book (1867), CO 277/1 (National Archives). Before 1867 the Straits Settlements were not required to submit 'blue books'. This changed when the Straits

Early colonial accounts give a population of 200 on the island in February 1819; by April 1820 the figure was around 10,000 and in 1829 the population was over 21,000.[41] Though imprecise, these figures demonstrate the rapid expansion of the colony's population. This continued through the decade and colonial newspapers give a vague insight as to how this happened. In February 1828 the *Singapore Chronicle* reported that 'the number of Junks which have recently arrived this year is three, all of them from Canton. One of them has brought 500 passengers, another also 500, and the third 200, altogether 1,200.'[42]

Table 1 provides an overview of the available census data for Singapore pre-1867. The categories 'Chinese males', 'Chinese females' and 'grand total' appear in all of these censuses and are listed here comparatively.

Table 1   Chinese population of Singapore, 1827–51

Year	Chinese males	Chinese females	Total population	Percentage of total
1827	5,847	363	14,885	41.7
1828	7,163	412	17,664	42.9
1830	6,021	534	16,634	39.4
1840	15,518	1,661	39,681	43.3
1845	28,765	3,367	52,347	61.4
1849	24,790	1,460	52,891	49.6
1851	23,760	2,255	53,000	49.1

Sources: Singapore Shipping and Commerce, 1823–44, in IOR/V/17/450, India Office Records (British Library); *Singapore Chronicle*, 14 February 1828, 12 February 1829; *Singapore Free Press*, 21 August 1845; James White, 'Emigration from China to the West Indies', 21 June–17 November 1851, in CO 885/1/19 (National Archives).

Across the early colonial period the Chinese were consistently the largest racial group in Singapore, making up 39.4 per cent of the population at the lowest ebb in 1830.[43] There is a degree of fluctuation here due to the transient nature of much of the labouring population, which ebbed and flowed with Singapore's levels of agricultural output, as well as inconsistencies in the collection of data and parameters of the census.[44] Note that after the cession

---

Settlements became a Crown Colony.

[41] Clement Liew, 'Ordo ab Chao at the Far End of India: Chinese Settlers and Their Colonial Masters', *Journal of Asian History*, 50, 1 (2016), 144.

[42] *Singapore Chronicle*, 28 February 1828.

[43] Note that this remained the case up to the present day. There was also large-scale Indian immigration into Southeast Asia over the nineteenth century. See Lockard, *Southeast Asia in World History*, 100.

[44] For example, note that the total population for 1851 is an estimate.

of Hong Kong to Britain in 1842 the Chinese population as a percentage of the overall population is significantly larger. This phenomenon is discussed in Chapter 5 of this book.

Despite the inconsistencies in census data, this census information provided an important background for colonial decision-making. The 1827 census provides a good example of the presentation of early census data and how the colonial authorities categorised Singapore's population by racial categories. Colonial newspapers such as the *Singapore Chronicle* and *Canton Register* published Table 2 in 1828.

Table 2. Singapore census, 1827

	Males	**Females**
Europeans	85	23
Native Christians	119	74
Malays	2,850	2,486
Armenians	17	8
Chinese	5,847	363
Coromandel Coast	1,072	23
Bengal	237	57
Arabs	17	0
Bugese	877	375
Javanese	247	108
Total	11,368	3,517

Source: *Singapore Chronicle*, 14 February 1828.

A close examination of the 1827 census gives an indication of how colonial administrators perceived and categorised the population of the colony. Notably the total population of 14,885 was significantly higher than the estimated 200 inhabitants in 1819, when Stamford Raffles first established a trading post on the island.[45] The Chinese already constituted forty-two per cent of the total population by 1827. Strikingly, the Chinese population was significantly larger than the Malay population by this point, and dwarfed the European merchant population. Most interestingly, the listing of the different groups presents the population in a hierarchical form. For example, 'Europeans' and 'Native Christians' appear at the top of the census, despite their relative statistical insignificance. This was common across the British Empire, with colonial blue books regularly using broad categories such as 'coloured' or 'blacks' to describe colonial populations.

---

[45] Saw Swee-Hock, 'Population Trends in Singapore, 1819–1967', *Journal of Southeast Asian History*, 10, 1 (1969), 36–7.

The gender imbalance within the Chinese population was also well above average. For example, the Chinese population of Singapore was only six per cent female, compared to the figure of thirty-one per cent female for the colony as a whole.[46] The same trend of majority male Chinese migration continued later in the century and can be attributed to three main factors: the illegality of emigration until 1860; the exclusively male mining and plantation work available; and the temporary, sojourning nature of contract migration. Generally speaking, amongst credit-ticket migrant labourers, male 'breadwinners' from southern China left dependent wives and families in China and remitted surplus earnings.[47] The small amount of female emigration reflects the fact that the majority of Chinese migrants were single men working in mines and on plantations for temporary periods who planned to return to China. The gender imbalance of Singapore's total population was a major concern for colonial observers, as seen in this editorial commentary on Singapore's population in the *Singapore Chronicle*:

> We understand a large proportion of the murders committed at Singapore have originated in jealousy or revenge of which women have been the source and sometimes the victims. There is, in fact, too great a disparity in the numbers of the sexes in the settlement, the males being much more numerous than the females … The disproportion is very great and must sometimes excite a rivalry for the smiles of the fair cause of dissention very inimical to the peace and good order of the community.[48]

As demonstrated by the 1827 census data, the gender imbalance was especially high in the Chinese population. Colonial authorities expressing concern over the importation of Chinese males, without females, is a recurring theme in the way that Chinese immigrants were stereotyped throughout this book.[49]

By the late 1820s Singapore had a sizeable Chinese population, but the data shows it continued to grow even further in the 1830s. The growth of productive export industries in Singapore led to a consistently increasing annual influx of Chinese workers. The *Canton Press* reported the total number of annual Chinese arrivals in 1837 at 2,069, noting that 'from ports in the

---

[46] *Singapore Chronicle*, 14 February 1828. It is also worth clarifying that women did work on rubber plantations, on ships, in factories and in domestic service. See Kelvin E. Y. Low, 'Chinese Migration and Entangled Histories: Broadening the Contours of Migratory History', *Journal of Historical Sociology*, 27, 1 (2014), 78, for more on this.

[47] George Peffer, *If They Don't Bring Their Women Here: Chinese Female Immigration before Exclusion* (Urbana: University of Illinois Press, 1999), 5.

[48] *Singapore Chronicle*, 15 February 1827.

[49] Though outnumbered, Chinese women did emigrate. The ongoing Ph.D. work of Sandy Chang (provisionally titled 'Across the Nanyang: Gender, Intimate Labor, and Chinese Migration in British Asia, 1890–1939', University of Texas) demonstrates the significance of female migration.

province Fuk-heen, or Hokien, there are numerous emigrants'.[50] Though 'Hokkien' is more appropriately described as a language dialect related to certain communities as opposed to a geographical space, it is mainly spoken in Fujian province and indicates the regional focus of migrant origins.[51] The bulk of migrants came from southern China. Fukien (Fujian) and Kwan-tung (Guandong) provinces were the principal centres of emigration.[52] These geographical differences would prove crucial in the construction of the Western narrative of southern Han Chinese escaping the despotic northern Chinese to live under Western dominion.[53] Emigration from these regions continued to grow to such an extent that by 1840 there were over 5,000 new arrivals each year, with nearly one-third of Chinese migrants undertaking highly physical labour on gambier plantations.[54]

The credit-ticket labourers and miners were a prominent occupational majority, but as Singapore grew, so did the importance of the wealthy Chinese merchant community and Chinese artisans in various skilled industries.[55] There were regional and class differences within the Chinese community in Singapore. Seah Eu Chin (also styled Siah U'Chin) offered a unique insight into these distinctions. Seah was born and educated in Guangdong province and first arrived in Singapore in 1823 as a clerk on a trading junk.[56] After acquiring the necessary capital whilst working on trading vessels, he was able to invest in property in the 1830s and he married into the elite of the Straits Chinese by marrying the daughter of the Chinese Kapitan of Perak.[57] Invest-ment in pepper and gambier plantations secured Seah's fortune. He became the colony's first Chinese 'man of letters' and maintained connections with prominent European merchants.[58] Seah was an example of a wealthy Chinese businessman who collaborated with British colonial authority. He joined the Singapore Chamber of Commerce in 1840, became the first Chinese Justice of the Peace in 1872 and employed credit-ticket Chinese labourers on his

50 *Canton Press*, 28 March 1838.
51 For the relationship between Chinese dialects and geographical regions see Lynn Pan, ed., *The Encyclopaedia of the Chinese Overseas* (Richmond: Curzon, 1998), 23–60.
52 Arnold Joseph Meagher, 'The Introduction of Chinese Laborers to Latin America: The "Coolie Trade", 1847–1874' (Ph.D. thesis, University of California, Davis, 1975), 66.
53 For more on this separation of the Qing Empire and Chinese population see the sub-section 'The Chinese Character' in Chapter 2.
54 Campbell, *Chinese Coolie Emigration within the British Empire*, 8; Trocki, *Opium and Empire*, 68. The gambier plant was used to make dye for clothes and materials.
55 Webster, 'The Development of British Commercial and Political Networks in the Straits Settlements', 912.
56 See the following overviews of Seah Eu Chin's significance: Pan, *The Encyclopaedia of the Chinese Overseas*, 202; Frost, 'Emporium in Imperio', 36; Carl A. Trocki, *Singapore: Wealth, Power and the Culture of Control* (London: Routledge, 2006), 32.
57 Pan, *The Encyclopaedia of the Chinese Overseas*, 202. A 'Kapitan' was a leader who acted as the head of the local Chinese community; in Singapore the British sought to recognise less overtly political forms of community leadership in the 1830s; Kuhn, *Chinese among Others*, 58.
58 Frost, 'Emporium in Imperio', 36.

plantations.[59] Though Seah became part of the Chinese elite in Singapore, the overview he gave of the Chinese population was more nuanced than the observations of his British contemporaries.

Seah Eu Chin's account of Singapore's Chinese in the 1840s identified six different classes (mainly based on dialect groupings) amongst the then 40,000 strong community: Chinese from Hokien; Malacca-born Chinese; Chinese from Tio Chiu; Chinese from Canton; the Khe Chinese; and Chinese from Hai-nam.[60] From these different groups, which Seah called 'tribes', came a vast range of professions for Chinese migrants:

> The different trades and professions of the Chinese in Singapore, are School-masters, Writers, Cashiers, Shop-keepers, Apothecaries, Coffin-makers, Grocers, Gold-smiths, Silver-smiths, Tin-smiths, Blacksmiths, Dyers, Tailors, Barbers, Shoemakers, Basket-makers, Fishermen, Sawyers, Boat-builders, Cabinet-makers, Architects, Masons, Manufacturers of lime and bricks, Sailors, Ferrymen, Sago manufacturers, Distillers of Spirits, Cultivators of plantations of Gambier, Sugar, Siri, Pepper, and Nutmegs, Play actors, Sellers of cake and fruit, Carriers of burdens, Fortune tellers, idle vagabonds who have no work and of whom there are not a few, beggars, and, nightly, there are those villains the thieves.[61]

Within the Chinese community these different 'tribes' were believed to be predisposed to specific professions. As an example, the Hokkien dialect group was overrepresented in trading and finance in both Malacca and Singapore.[62] Seah's references to 'idle vagabonds' and 'those villains the thieves', demonstrate a class hierarchy within the Chinese community. The wealthy elite identified certain strata of colonial society as undesirable. Over time, the increasing group of Straits Chinese came to dominate Singapore socially and economically as they were able to draw upon multiple connections and networks.[63] The Chinese community and narratives about the Chinese as a community within Singaporean society were complex and diverse. Importantly, Chinese migration to Singapore influenced British perceptions of the Chinese, and consequently China, more generally.

---

[59] Pan, *The Encyclopaedia of the Chinese Overseas*, 202; Justin Corfield, *Historical Dictionary of Singapore* (Toronto: Scarecrow Press, 2011), 74.

[60] Siah U'Chin, 'The Chinese in Singapore', *Journal of the Indian Archipelago*, Vol. II (1848), 284. Note that Seah dictated his account to a 'Dr Oxley' who wrote the article in English. Oxley was an East India Company surgeon who purchased land to open nutmeg plantations in the 1830s: Gretchen Liu, *Singapore: A Pictorial History, 1819–2000* (Singapore: Archipelago Press, 1999), 20.

[61] Siah, 'The Chinese in Singapore', 284.

[62] Kuhn, *Chinese among Others*, 58; Trocki, 'Singapore as a Nineteenth Century Migration Node', 198–225.

[63] Frost, 'Emporium in Imperio', 40.

Chinese Colonists: Uncivilised or Industrious?

Both the colonial state and Western residents perceived the different classes of Chinese migrants in various ways at various points. Whilst certain Chinese migrants were criticised, and others were celebrated, the community at large was recognised as essential to the colony's economic development. For example, in 1829 the Governor, Robert Fullerton, analysed comparative census information with the aim of 'ridding the settlement of vagabond Chinese'.[64] Colonial correspondence and newspapers discussed concerns about a large Chinese population without employment at length.[65] See, for example, this extract from the *Singapore Chronicle*:

> The chief increase has been among the Chinese, and it is worthy of remark that, although agriculture is generally believed to have declined greatly of late, yet there are no less than 883 Chinese in the interior more than 1827. Of these a considerable proportion are without any visible means of livelihood and there is too much reason to fear from the frequent robberies which occur that they live entirely by plunder, a belief not entertained by Europeans alone but by the principal and best informed men among the Chinese themselves.[66]

As a solution, Fullerton advised the Superintendent of Lands to allow Chinese migrants free land rent, to 'afford encouragement to the settlement of industrious labourers in the cultivation of the land'.[67] Chinese migrants in Singapore were seen as both essential and problematic. Stereotypes about Chinese workers were intimately connected to employment, and to notions of labour and class.

Manual labourers emigrating from China found work in tin mines or in pepper, opium or gambier production. Increasing numbers of Chinese manual labourers supplemented the growing influence of clans known as *Kongsi* – ethnic associations, which acted in lieu of domestic familial networks.[68] The *Kongsi* associations allowed for disenfranchised Chinese workers to act collectively and pool capital and resources.[69] They performed important social functions, such as raising funds for funerals and burials for immigrants.[70] The

---

64 Robert Fullerton, 'Population of Singapore: Expediency of ridding the settlement of vagabond Chinese', 20 May 1829, in IOR/F/4/1271, India Office Records (British Library), 1.

65 J. G. Bonham, 'Extract of Singapore Consultations', 23 February 1829, in IOR/F/4/1271/51002A, India Office Records (British Library).

66 *Singapore Chronicle*, 12 February 1829.

67 Fullerton, 'Population of Singapore'.

68 Webster, 'The Development of British Commercial and Political Networks in the Straits Settlements', 912; Trocki, *Opium and Empire*; Wang Tai Peng, *The Origins of Chinese Kongsi* (Selangor: Pelanduk Publications, 1994); Ching-Hwang Yen, *The Chinese in Southeast Asia and Beyond: Socioeconomic and Political Dimensions* (London: World Scientific Publishing, 2008).

69 Trocki, 'Opium and the Beginnings of Chinese Capitalism in Southeast Asia', 301.

70 Seah Eu Chin was connected to the Ngee Ann Kongsi. There are two excellent biographies of Seah, which discuss these issues, written by his decadents: Shawn Seah, *Seah Eu Chin: His Life and Times* (Singapore, National Heritage Board, 2017) and Brandon Seah, 'Seah Eu Chin',

social and economic structures of these Chinese communities were important for the creation of the industrious stereotype that was applied to the
Chinese in contrast to the colonial view of the 'lazy native'.[71] The supposed
industriousness of the labouring Chinese in colonial Singapore was driven
by economic necessity – namely debt. The nature of the credit-ticket system
allowed for manipulation of workers, as employers deducted payments for
passage, food, shelter, clothing and debts (incurred due to opium addiction,
gambling or financial mismanagement), to extend contracts until workers
had repaid debts. This led to employment well beyond the initial contract's
original terms.[72]

A major cause of migrant debt was opium addiction. Opium acted as
a form of control over the workforce, with supply established through the
Kongsi. Expenditure on opium in excess of income meant contract extensions
were necessary in order to repay the initial debts incurred as part of the
credit-ticket system.[73] Trocki's view of this relationship between addiction
and the labour supply is substantiated by the account of Seah Eu Chin who,
as an owner of gambier and pepper plantations, was well aware of addiction
amongst his employees.[74] He explained in an article for the *Journal of the Indian
Archipelago* why workers would regularly extend their contracts in Singapore:

> Those who originally intended to return to their native country after 3 years,
> and yet after the lapse of more than 10 years have not been able to fulfil their
> wish; but what is the reason of it? It is because they become addicted to the
> prevailing vice of Opium smoking.[75]

Where colonial observers attributed the long contracts of Chinese labourers
to an innate industriousness of the Chinese character, employers such as
Seah were aware of the financial necessity for extended employment. Opium
addiction was extremely profitable for multiple groups. Opium revenue
farming provided a lucrative income for the *Kongsi*.[76] The ethnic associations
connected the different Chinese classes: 'there existed a bourgeoisie and a
working class, which were linked together by systems of commodity production and consumption'.[77] As the different Chinese classes were symbiotic,
observers like Fullerton could not neatly separate the 'industrious' Chinese
from the 'vagabond' Chinese as he might have hoped. Not only did opium

http://seaheuchin.info/ (accessed 30 September 2018).
[71] For more on the notion of the 'lazy native' see Alatas, *The Myth of the Lazy Native*.
[72] Hillemann, *Asian Empire and British Knowledge*, 127.
[73] Trocki, *Opium and Empire*, 2.
[74] Claude Markovits, 'The Political Economy of Opium Smuggling in Early Nineteenth
Century India: Leakage or Resistance?', *Modern Asian Studies*, 43, 1 (2009), 89; Pan, *The Encyclopaedia of the Chinese Overseas*, 202.
[75] Siah, 'The Chinese in Singapore', 285. J. R. Logan published and edited the *Journal of the
Indian Archipelago* at Singapore's Mission Press.
[76] Trocki, 'Opium and the Beginnings of Chinese Capitalism in Southeast Asia', 301.
[77] Ibid., 300.

addiction provide the employers with a cheap labour force, it also provided a profit for British merchants and colonial revenues. The first Resident of Singapore, William Farquhar, had created opium, liquor and gambling 'farms' that raised revenue for the colony and subsidised Singapore's status as a duty-free port.[78] These were not physical farms, but taxes placed on these products and activities, which were outsourced to private 'farmers' for collection. Opium exports from Singapore increased from 1,285 chests in 1835 to 7,550 by 1841.[79] Whilst opium addiction presented a social problem, and one that was used to criticise Chinese 'vagabonds', it was also a profitable export for the colonial state.

Whilst opium provided the colonial government with revenue and respected European and Chinese merchants profited from the system, addiction and its negative effects were attributed to the lack of self-control of the consumers: 'the victim had come to stand for the crime'.[80] Again, in spite of his personal economic interest in the use of debt from addiction to entrap workers, Seah Eu Chin reflected on the negative social consequences of addiction:

> They become addicted to the prevailing vice of Opium smoking. After a continued residence here they learn the habit, which afterwards becomes fixed. Many of the Chinese labourers after having earned a little money, waste it upon opium or expend it in gambling … when these opium smokers are reduced to straits from want of money they resort to schemes of plunder and robbery.[81]

As Seah mentions, in addition to opium smoking, gambling was seen as a distinctly Chinese vice. John Crawfurd described the Chinese of Singapore as 'the most debauched of gamesters', and in criticising the possible relaxing of gambling restrictions the *Singapore Chronicle* warned that 'every Chinaman's shop would become a receptacle of villainous sharpers'.[82] Notably, the early colonial period was defined by colonial confusion over how to address these social problems. Famously, on his return to Singapore, the founder of the original trading post, Stamford Raffles, was unhappy that opium and gambling had

---

[78] Ellen C. Cangi, 'Civilising the People of Southeast Asia: Sir Stamford Raffles' Town Plan for Singapore, 1819–1823', *Planning Perspectives*, 8, 2 (1993), 174. Though Stamford Raffles is often credited as the founder of Singapore, Farquhar's policies actually defined Singapore's early development: Nadia Helen Wright, 'Image Is All: Lt-Colonel William Farquhar, Sir Stamford Raffles, and the Founding and Early Development of Colonial Singapore' (Ph.D. thesis, University of Melbourne, 2012).

[79] Hans Derks, *The History of the Opium Problem: The Assault on the East, c. 1600–1950* (Boston: Brill, 2012), 746.

[80] Ibid., 2; Webster, 'The Development of British Commercial and Political Networks in the Straits Settlements', 942; Trocki, *Opium and Empire*, 1.

[81] Siah, 'The Chinese in Singapore', 285.

[82] John Crawfurd, *History of the Indian Archipelago, Vol. I* (Edinburgh: Archibald, Constable & Co., 1820), 112; note that Crawfurd maintained the opium farm and classed opium alongside alcohol as a tradable commodity: see Knapman, *Race and British Colonialism in Southeast Asia*, 133. *Singapore Chronicle*, 27 February 1836.

been legalised. Farquhar's response to Raffles highlighted how the colonial administrators were beginning to attribute the behaviour of Chinese workers to unchanging character traits: 'any attempt to abolish a custom [gambling] so completely rooted in Chinese character and so intimately combined with all their ceremonies will not only give general dissatisfaction but prove abortive in its effort'.[83] A good example of how colonial administrators struggled to control the Chinese population with little or no knowledge of Chinese culture is that when the government proposed to abolish gambling in the 1830s the plan was to make it legal for fifteen days around Chinese New Year because it was believed to be part of Chinese religion.[84]

Despite their important economic role, the Chinese labouring classes were perceived to be fundamentally immoral and a troublesome social presence by colonial authorities. The gender imbalance of the Chinese population, highlighted in the census data, was also believed to exacerbate immorality. By the 1830s the preference of many British observers was for the immigration of families. The *Chronicle* hoped that 'the tide of emigration should return in our favour, with married emigrants'.[85] The idea that innate Chinese immorality could be subdued through abstinence and marriage held a particular irony as it was the expense of opium consumption and the system of familial remittance, where young single men sent excess earnings back to family in China, that made the Chinese plantation workers such a cost-effective workforce in the first place.

Colonial authorities also perceived the majority Chinese population as fundamentally untrustworthy. Most Asian communities in the colony outnumbered the European community, but it was an organised Chinese labour force that presented the clearest political threat. As Anthony Webster has suggested, the Chinese were perceived as an intimidating presence, especially during outbreaks of violence in the 1840s.[86] The associations formed by the Chinese were a source of concern. The social institution of the *Kongsi* often came into conflict with the free market ideology of European merchants and colonial authorities.[87] In particular, the *Kongsi* organisations aroused European suspicions because they regularly overlapped and were confused with secret societies. For example, the Ngee Ann Kongsi and the Ngee Heng Kongsi both performed charitable economic functions in Singapore, but the Ngee Heng was a secret society that had originally evolved from political opposition to

---

[83] Acting Secretary to the Lieutenant Governor to W. Farquhar (Singapore), 16 April 1823, in L15: Raffles: Letters from Singapore (National Archives of Singapore).

[84] Jim Baker, *Crossroads: A Popular History of Malaysia and Singapore* (Singapore: Marshall Cavendish, 2008), 96.

[85] *Singapore Chronicle*, 15 October 1836.

[86] Webster, 'The Development of British Commercial and Political Networks in the Straits Settlements', 911.

[87] Trocki, *Opium and Empire*, 4.

the Manchu-led Qing Empire in southern China.[88] Fears of Chinese secret societies sat within a broader colonial fear of the Chinese criminal organisation: the triad society.

In the early colonial period, the main source of English-language information on the triad society was an article by the missionary William Milne written in 1826. Milne conceded that many of his assertions were speculative as the society was secret and it was virtually impossible to distinguish between members and non-members.[89] This mystique added to the threat of the society, which was notable for organised criminal activity. According to Milne, the society's activities involved 'theft, robbery, overthrow of government, and aiming for political power'.[90] The triad society was supposedly present in colonial Singapore. Milne suggested that 'the idle, gambling, opium-smoking Chinese (particularly of the lower classes), frequently belong to this fraternity'.[91] The clandestine nature of such societies prevented the collation of membership information. However, by the 1880s the colonial authorities estimated that the largest secret societies – the Ghee Hin, Ghee Hok and Hai Sin – had a membership of over 33,000.[92] The accusation of secret society membership was a useful tool to collectively denote the Chinese as deceitful and threatening. The triad society became a catch-all slur for Chinese organisations and associations that the colonial state did not recognise as legitimate.[93]

The very earliest colonial records demonstrate the concern of the colonial state with the activities of various Chinese societies and organisations in the context of fears about political unrest and the desire to maintain an orderly workforce. There are numerous correspondences containing information from Chinese prisoners, informers and merchants about 'Chinese clubs'.[94] Colonial authorities saw these organisations as a trans-colonial threat across the Straits Settlements. For example, this extract from the period when Penang was capital of the Straits Settlements demonstrates the way that authorities linked membership of societies, or clubs, to the evaluation of Chinese colonists:[95]

---

88 Seah, 'Seah Eu Chin'.

89 William Milne, 'Account of a Secret Association in China, Entitled the Triad Society', *Transactions of the Royal Asiatic Society of Great Britain and Ireland*, 1, 2 (1826), 244–5.

90 Ibid., 241.

91 Ibid., 241.

92 James Francis Warren, *Rickshaw Coolie: A People's History of Singapore, 1880–1940* (Singapore: Singapore University Press, 2003), 17.

93 Note that the secret societies persisted as a threat through the colonial and postcolonial period. See Kamaludeen Mohamed Nasir, 'Protected Sites: Reconceptualising Secret Societies in Colonial and Postcolonial Singapore', *Journal of Historical Sociology*, 29, 2 (2016), 232–49.

94 'Information of Shimyip or Shimyen, a Chinese man of the Tribe Choah, Prisoner in the House of Correction', 1 May 1825, in M4: Singapore: Letters from Bengal to the Resident (National Archives of Singapore).

95 Note that Penang had a long history as a key trading port in its own right. See Tomotaka

This club has been established about 2 years. It consists of about 1,000 members, of the lowest class of Macau Chinese day labourers, carpenters, gardeners &ca.; they are all poor, not a merchant or respectable trader amongst them; they are looked upon as bad characters; good people do not join such clubs.[96]

Again, the colonial state was reliant on Chinese intermediaries for information about Chinese culture and social organisation. When William A. Pickering took up the post of Chinese Protector in 1877 he was one of only two European residents in Singapore, which had a Chinese population of 54,000, with a working knowledge of the Chinese language.[97] Throughout the early colonial period, administrators would rely on Chinese merchant community leaders to diffuse riots and disorder in the Chinese community.[98]

In a reflection of the multi-racial hierarchies of colonial Singapore, colonial observers also presented Chinese immigrants as a threat to the Malay population. Sandra Manickam has written about the use of 'race as a strategy of colonial rule' in Singapore and particularly the emphasis on comparisons between Malay and Chinese colonists as a justification of British governance.[99] Sir John Bowring, Governor of Hong Kong during the Second Opium War, saw the movement of Chinese migrants into Southeast Asia as an ultimately destructive force:

Immigration of the black-haired races is changing the whole character of society, the Indian Archipelago being the field where the battle of the nationalities is constantly fought, and where the expulsion of the less civilised by the more civilised may be studied.[100]

Notably, though Bowring recognised the economic utility of Chinese migrants in Southeast Asia, he saw the Chinese population as a replacement for indigenous peoples. The use of the term 'battle' in this context is especially

Kawamura, 'Maritime Asian Trade and Colonization of Penang, c.1786–1830', in Taukasa Mizushima, George Bryan Souza and Dennis O. Flynn, eds, *Hinterlands and Commodities: Place, Space, Time and Political Economic Development of Asia over the Long Eighteenth Century* (Leiden: Brill, 2015), 145–65.

[96] 'Examination of Che Sung, Che Toah, Beng and Keat, the head Chinese merchants in George Town, by the Hon'ble the Governor and Chief Judge', 10 June 1825, in A18: Penang Consultations (National Archives of Singapore).

[97] Michelle T. King, 'Replicating the Colonial Expert: The Problem of Translation in the Late Nineteenth-Century Straits Settlements', *Social History*, 34, 4 (2009), 434.

[98] J. Burn to the Resident Councillor at Prince of Wales Island (Singapore), 31 November 1859, in U39: Governor: Letters to Resident Councillors (National Archives of Singapore). See also Liew, 'Ordo ab Chao at the Far End of India', 162.

[99] Sandra Khor Manickam, 'Common Ground: Race and the Colonial Universe in British Malaya', *Journal of Southeast Asian Studies*, 40, 3 (2009), 595.

[100] John Bowring, *Autobiographical Recollections of Sir John Bowring* (London: Henry S. King, 1877), 213.

revealing. Evidently the civilisational disparity between Chinese and other Asian colonists made the ascendancy of Straits Chinese inevitable.

Similarly, it was the view of John Crawfurd that the British acted as stewards of the Malay population, which the powerful Chinese majority would exploit and destroy in the absence of colonial rule. Crawfurd's long experience of observing Chinese migration in Southeast Asia provided a grounding for these views. Crawfurd warned that the wily Chinese, if left to their own devices, would deceive 'the simple natives'.[101] Crawfurd illustrated his warning with an example from his time in Java, which was home to a large Chinese population under Dutch colonial rule:

> A Javanese boatman … was accosted by a Chinese from the bank requesting a passage … when the victim of this piece of roguery awoke, he found himself lying stark naked in a forest fifteen miles distant from the place where he had taken in the Chinese – robbed of his canoe, and all his property.[102]

Whilst the Chinese migrant population was essential to Singapore's prosperity, such cautionary tales perpetuated stereotypes about the Chinese as innately treacherous and untrustworthy. Moreover, these concerns legitimised the control of a small governing class of Europeans over a Chinese majority population, which would ultimately mistreat other groups if allowed the opportunity.

Despite colonial criticism and a fear of the Chinese population, the perceived Chinese propensity for hard work and entrepreneurship led Stamford Raffles to praise 'the splendid foundation they form for the business prosperity of Singapore'.[103] John Crawfurd, despite his criticisms of Chinese duplicity, recognised the economic benefits of Chinese migrant labour across Southeast Asia. He specifically praised the 'two most industrious, intelligent, and wealthy classes, the Europeans and the Chinese'.[104] After his experiences in India, Burma, Siam and Java, Crawfurd published accounts of his travels.[105] His experience of different social contexts across Southeast Asia fed into his praise of Chinese merchants in Singapore. For Crawfurd, the Chinese merchant elite were vitally important to economic development across Southeast Asia. For example, Crawfurd's account of Java regularly praised the Chinese contribution to the local economy.[106] He asserted that

---

101   Crawfurd, *History of the Indian Archipelago, Vol. I*, 466.

102   Ibid., 466.

103   Braddell et al., *One Hundred Years of Singapore*, 376.

104   Crawfurd, *Journal of an Embassy from the Governor-General of India to the Courts of Siam and Cochin China, Vol. II*, 390.

105   See Turnbull, 'Crawfurd, John (1783–1868)', for an overview of Crawfurd's travel writing.

106   See the work of Roger Knight for more on the development of Java in the nineteenth century. See Roger Knight, *Sugar, Steam and Steel: The Industrial Project in Colonial Java, 1830–1885* (Adelaide: University of Adelaide Press, 2014).

'the natives are indebted to the ingenuity of the Chinese, who are always the workmen', and that silk production in the region 'under the direction of the indefatigable and enterprising Chinese can hardly fail'.[107] In Siam, Crawfurd observed that the Chinese took up skilled occupations and formed an artisan class. He noted the 'superiority of the Chinese in industry, intelligence and enterprise'.[108] This Chinese 'superiority' was evident across Southeast Asia.

Crawfurd believed that the presence of Chinese labourers in Singapore was such a factor in the colony's economic success that he attempted to quantify their impact. According to Crawfurd's calculations in 1830, 'the Chinese amount to 8,595. About five-sixths of the whole number are unmarried men, in the prime of life: so that, in fact, the Chinese population, in point of effective labour, may be estimated as equivalent to an ordinary population of above 37,000.'[109] As a result of this increased output, Chinese migrants were paid more than other workers. As Crawfurd estimated, 'the average value of the labour, skill, and intelligence of a Chinese to be in the proportion of three to one to those of a native of the continent of India', it followed that 'the wages of other classes of inhabitants are much lower than the Chinese'.[110] Crucially, the perceived superiority of Chinese labourers over indigenous or other alternative sources mitigated the perceived deficiencies of their moral conduct.

The Chinese merchant community in Singapore was particularly eulogised by Western observers, from colonial administrators to Western merchants and transient visitors. In contrast to the perceived threat posed by the large Chinese labouring population, and their mysterious secret societies, Chinese merchants were crucial to British authority as a 'go-between' with the wider Chinese community.[111] For example, as a member of the Chinese elite, Seah Eu Chin fulfilled important social roles in Singapore. He helped to fund the Tan Tock Seng Hospital, mediated the Hokkien-Teochiu riots of 1854, served as a Grand Juror and became a Justice of the Peace in 1872.[112] Wealthy Chinese merchants and businessmen acted as community leaders through different social roles. The 'Kapitan' system of community leadership, which was used in European colonies across Southeast Asia, was not used in Singapore due to its overt centralisation of political power, and was

---

[107] Crawfurd, *History of the Indian Archipelago, Vol. I*, 181–93.
[108] Crawfurd, *Journal of an Embassy from the Governor-General of India to the Courts of Siam and Cochin China, Vol. I*, 77.
[109] Ibid., 30.
[110] Ibid., 384–5.
[111] Trocki, *Opium and Empire*, 222.
[112] Pan, *The Encyclopaedia of the Chinese Overseas*, 202. See Yen Chung-Huang, *Community and Politics: The Chinese in Colonial Singapore and Malaysia* (Singapore: Times Academic, 1995), and Yen Chung-Huang, 'Early Chinese Clan Organizations in Singapore and Malaya, 1819–1911', *Journal of Southeast Asian Studies*, 12, 1 (1981), 62–86, for an overview of Chinese community leadership.

replaced by looser economic leadership through the funding of temples and hospitals.[113] As demonstrated by Clement Liew, Chinese leader-mediators did not wield absolute control over the whole Chinese population.[114] Over time the Straits Chinese became dominant. An early example of this was Tan Tock Seng, a Hokkien merchant born in Malacca and founder of the hospital named in his honour, who was the first non-European appointed a Justice of the Peace in 1846.[115] Of course, Straits Chinese also enjoyed the advantage of British subjecthood. As described by Mark Frost, the Straits Chinese formed a 'settled, gentry-official class, co-opted by the colonial state as intermediaries'.[116] Even as European involvement in trade between the Straits Settlements and China increased, the trade remained reliant on the knowledge, skills and connections of Chinese intermediaries.[117]

It was the commercial success of the Chinese merchant elite that specifically distinguished them in the minds of colonial observers. As emphasised by Syed Alatas, colonial observers in Singapore intertwined notions of race, class and economic productivity.[118] The embrace of Western economic relationships and the value placed on individual property rights marked the Chinese merchant elite, to British observers, as particularly civilised. For example, the Chinese merchant community played a vital role in lobbying and raising money to fund the British Navy's suppression of piracy in Southeast Asia.[119] The Chinese merchant elite aligned with the wider merchant community and British colonial authorities. British praise of Chinese merchant elites was informed by shared economic interests. Colonial observers of Chinese merchants noted how 'the indolent air of the Asiatic was thrown aside', with the implication that by assimilating with British commercial practices Chinese merchants were perceived as having overcome the natural disadvantages of their racial heritage.[120] The *Singapore Chronicle* reprinted, and concurred with, John Dean's suggestion that the Chinese 'are keen, enterprising traders, extremely expert in their dealings ... I do not think they are exceeded by the natives of any country as a commercial people'.[121] Over time these multi-ethnic commercial alliances would be manifest in the make-up of the Chambers of Commerce and, as noted by Webster, the formation of 'a discrete economic and political identity'.[122] For all the criticisms of Chinese migrant labourers,

113 Frost, 'Emporium in Imperio', 44.
114 Liew, 'Ordo ab Chao at the Far End of India', 142.
115 Pan, *The Encyclopaedia of the Chinese Overseas*, 202.
116 Frost, 'Emporium in Imperio', 41.
117 Kuhn, *Chinese among Others*, 63.
118 Alatas, *The Myth of the Lazy Native*, 19.
119 *Singapore Chronicle*, 21 March 1833.
120 Robert Gouger, ed., *A Letter from Sydney, the Principal Town of Australasia* (London: Joseph Cross, 1829), 213.
121 *Singapore Chronicle*, 24 February 1831.
122 Webster, 'The Development of British Commercial and Political Networks in the Straits Settlements', 901.

colonial observers recognised that the success of British colonial rule in Singapore was contingent on the active role of a large Chinese population.

Colonial discourse specifically attributed Singapore's success to the combination of Chinese industriousness and British governance. Straits Chinese were particularly successful as they were connected to several communities simultaneously and were able to 'switch identity' in order to prosper in Singapore's competitive business environment.[123] Indeed the Chinese elite certainly appear to have utilised the connections made possible through both British subjecthood and their existing ties to southern China, combining European capital investment and the cheap labour procured by the credit-ticket system. John Crawfurd, though he praised Chinese enterprise, emphasised the importance of liberal British governance in Singapore's development. He attributed economic prosperity to 'British leadership combined with the energy of Chinese settlers'.[124] The Anglo-Chinese 'combination' was deemed particularly effective in managing the production of plantation crops. Crawfurd specifically praised the 'free enterprise of Europeans, and the skill and economy of the Chinese cultivator' in developing Singapore's pepper industry.[125] The idea that British rule enabled the potential of the Chinese, as merchants and labourers, was an important part of qualifying the praise for the Chinese community whilst maintaining British supremacy. Such racial hierarchies were created and used as a justification of colonial rule.

Singapore as an Imperial Template

Could the combination of British governance and Chinese economic activity in Singapore, which British contemporaries considered such a success, have been as effective in a different colonial context? The British merchant Gordon Forbes Davidson clearly thought it could. Davidson saw Singapore as a model that he could apply elsewhere. Importantly, after spending more than a decade in colonial Southeast Asia, Davidson attempted to establish a system of Chinese migration to New South Wales, which was explicitly based on the example of Singapore. An examination of Davidson's account of his time in Southeast Asia shows the impact of this experience on his ideas about labour and race.

Unlike the colonial governors and administrators, little is known about Gordon Forbes Davidson and he is rarely mentioned in historical literature. Tony Ohlsson has made brief reference to Davidson's New South Wales Chinese migration scheme, and Davidson was an associate of the American

[123] Frost, *Singapore*, 94–6; Webster, 'The Development of British Commercial and Political Networks in the Straits Settlements', 912.
[124] C. M. Turnbull, *A History of Singapore, 1819–1988* (Singapore: Oxford University Press, 1989), 109.
[125] Crawfurd, *History of the Indian Archipelago, Vol. I*, 485.

firm Russell & Co., but this is where the historiographical coverage ends.[126] He mainly dealt with private traders like Jardine Matheson, the infamous China-trade opium dealers, through his Singapore firm Clark, Davidson & Co.[127] The frequency with which his letters appear in the Jardine Matheson archive reveals a close commercial relationship with the firm, particularly in the early 1830s, and strong connection with James Matheson himself as letters frequently passed between the two. Davidson traded mainly spices (specifically cinnamon) but also opium, silk and rice through Jardine Matheson.[128] The main source of information about Davidson's time in Asia is his 1846 book *Trade and Travel in the Far East*, but an extensive search also yields letters in various archives, information on ancestry websites linked to his later life in Australia, and multiple articles relating to him in newspapers from Singapore, Australia and Britain.[129] From this trail it can be deduced he lived in Hull when in Britain, with a variety of business interests, including a steam mail company, a telegraph company, a cotton mill company and later a Chinese labour migration scheme to Australia.[130] Using these sources, we can build a chronology of Davidson's movements. He lived in Java (1823 to 1826), Singapore (1826 to 1835), Sydney (1836 to 1839), Macao (1839 to 1842) and Hong Kong (1842 to 1844). Davidson operated outside of official imperial structures and was symbolic of the new breed of private trader operating within the China trade after the removal of the East India Company monopoly in 1833.[131]

Gordon Forbes Davidson's ideas about colonisation were informed by his experience in Asia. In his writing in *Trade and Travel in the Far East* he continuously, in line with contemporary colonial ideas of racial hierarchy, linked ideas about labour and economic utility to race.[132] Davidson regularly equated

126 Tony Ohlsson, 'The Origins of a White Australia: The Coolie Question, 1837–43', *Journal of the Royal Australian Historical Society*, 97, 2 (2011), 204; Sibing He, 'Russell and Company in Shanghai, 1843–1891: U.S. Trade and Diplomacy in Treaty Port China', Paper presented to 'A Tale of Ten Cities: Sino-American Exchange in the Treaty Port Era, 1840–1950', Hong Kong University (23–24 May 2011).

127 Davidson was the lead partner in the firm; G. F. Davidson (Singapore) to Jardine, Matheson & Co. (Canton), 1 May 1833, in MS JM/B6/6, Jardine Matheson Archive (Cambridge University Library).

128 Numerous letters between 5 July 1829 and 21 November 1844, in MS JM/B6, Jardine Matheson Archive (Cambridge University Library).

129 G. F. Davidson, *Trade and Travel in the Far East; or recollections of twenty-one years passed in Java, Singapore, Australia, and China* (London: Madden and Malcolm, 1846).

130 Davidson's various projects and activities in Hull can be traced in numerous newspaper articles: *Leeds Times*, 2 August 1845; *Hull Packet*, 3 July 1846, 16 July 1846.

131 The influx of such traders has been described by Cheong as bringing 'chaos' to the Canton system: W. E. Cheong, *Mandarins and Merchants: Jardine Matheson & Co., a China Agency of the Early Nineteenth Century* (London: Curzon Press, 1979), 265.

132 Davidson's book was published to generally positive reviews in London in 1846; in particular in the *London Morning Post*, 23 January 1846.

industriousness and mercantilism with notions of civilisation.[133] These ideas about the relationship between labour and race were formulated during his time in Java and Singapore in the 1820s and fitted within the colonial notions of native laziness. Contemporary European observers within Southeast Asia identified clear racial divisions between Chinese and Malay residents, founded on their proficiency as a labour force. This context shaped Davidson's view of race as connected to economic activity. It was Davidson's experience in multiple colonies in Southeast Asia that shaped his view of Chinese labourers and informed his later attempts to establish a scheme of Chinese migration to New South Wales.[134]

In his book, Davidson's narrative began with his experiences from his arrival in Java in 1823. Whilst Davidson described Java as a 'lovely and magnificent island', he was struck by what he perceived as the laziness of the indigenous population.[135] Residing in Batavia from 1823 to 1826, Davidson's account of his time there was littered with such comments as 'the inhabitants of Java are … rather lazy withal' and 'the lazy Javanese labourer'.[136] The label of lazy fitted well within existing contemporary attitudes to the indigenous inhabitants of Southeast Asia. In *The Myth of the Lazy Native* Alatas discusses how the idea of natives being lazy was developed by European observers in the early nineteenth century across Malaysia, the Philippines and Indonesia.[137] These ideas evolved from a reluctance of indigenous peoples to form a labour force in plantation systems of high intensity production. For example, the inhabitants of Java, whom Davidson expected to act as a colonial labour force, were unlikely to enter into contract work on tobacco, rubber or coffee plantations as they were already agricultural smallholders in a pre-existing subsistence economy.[138] British capitalists like Davidson interpreted native resistance to labour on European-owned plantations as laziness. In fact, Davidson went as far as to assert that forced labour in Java was justifiable: 'I object in toto to slavery in any form; but I confess I do not think the slaves of Java would be benefitted, were their liberty given them tomorrow.'[139] Davidson directly linked an unwillingness to labour to inferiority and even justified slavery. By contrast a willingness to labour reflected positive stereotypes, or a higher position in Western concepts of civilisational hierarchy.

From 1826, Davidson lived in Singapore, where he observed the inter-actions between British colonial authorities, Chinese labourers, Chinese merchant elites and Malay inhabitants. Chinese labourers impressed Davidson with their work ethic: 'a tight curb on a China-man will make him

---

[133] Davidson, *Trade and Travel in the Far East*, 145.
[134] Davidson's 1837 migration scheme to New South Wales is discussed fully in Chapter 4.
[135] Davidson, *Trade and Travel in the Far East*, 2.
[136] Ibid., 8, 34.
[137] Alatas, *The Myth of the Lazy Native*, 1.
[138] Ibid., 1–31.
[139] Davidson, *Trade and Travel in the Far East*, 36.

do a great deal of work; at the same time, he has spirit enough to resist real ill treatment'.[140] Importantly this extract reflects the intermediate role of the Chinese labourers. Davidson saw the Chinese as both compliant and resistant to exploitation. In contrast to other racial groups, the Chinese were able to avoid becoming slaves. In contrast, Davidson was unimpressed by the indigenous population: 'the original Malay inhabitants of this Island are now the most insignificant, both as to numbers and as to general utility'.[141] Similarly, mixed-race Eurasian migrants to Singapore from Malacca were also dismissed by Davidson as 'a bad breed certainly, and the men I speak of seem to possess all the *devilry* of both races … their employments … are not quite so creditable to their characters'.[142] Davidson's continual use of words like 'employment', 'utility' and 'work' when constructing racial stratifications shows how his time in Singapore caused him to identify race and labour as mutually constitutive. This was consistent with a British imperial world view that emphasised 'hard work' as a mark of civilisation and godliness.[143]

It is important to emphasise that Davidson's observations of Singaporean society engaged with contemporary colonial discourse. For example, John Crawfurd wrote of the 'Indian islanders' that they were 'of slow comprehension and narrow judgement' and added that 'all their intellectual faculties are in general feeble'.[144] Colonial correspondences often repeated this view, with a minute for the attention of the Governor of India explaining:

> There is, however, a great difference between the Chinese and the Malays as regards the desire for the education of their children. The Chinese will make some sacrifice in order to his children being taught to read and write, but the Malay is wholly indifferent to it and will neither pay for nor make the slightest effort to obtain such an advantage for his children.[145]

Over the nineteenth century this perception, that the indigenous Malay inhabitants were not 'improvable' through education, grew stronger.[146] Thus the indigenous population was lost to the civilising mission of Empire compared to Chinese and Indian immigrants. This colonial view was so strong that an anti-elite view of the 'real Malay' as a commoner informed later Malay

[140] Ibid., 47.
[141] Ibid., 48.
[142] Ibid., 96.
[143] Specifically linked to the idea of a 'Protestant work ethic'; see Peter Harrison, '"Fill the Earth and Subdue It": Biblical Warrants for Colonization in Seventeenth Century England', *Journal of Religious History*, 29, 1 (2005), 3–24.
[144] Crawfurd, *History of the Indian Archipelago, Vol. I*, 37; Crawfurd's accounts are an essential part of tracing and charting the early history of colonial Singapore.
[145] C. Beadon, Secretary to the Govt. of India, Home Department (Singapore), 11 February 1858, in CO 273 (2) (National Archives).
[146] See Chapter 3 for a full exploration of the concept of colonial 'improvement'.

identity.[147] Like his contemporaries, Davidson saw the presence of the British Empire in Southeast Asia as simultaneously profitable and necessary, especially given the ineffectiveness of the indigenous population.

Davidson's time in Singapore had provided him with a template for supplying colonial labour. He saw the low cost, civilisational standing, tendency for hard work and large population as appealing aspects of the Chinese labour pool. By contrast, the decline of indigenous populations was both inevitable and, bearing in mind Davidson's economic interests, desirable. Additionally, the removal of the East India Company Charter, which allowed an increased and unregulated exchange of capital, information and people between the British Empire in Asia and China, created a fertile ground for Chinese labour migration experiments in the 1830s and 1840s. Empire-wide factors that increased the demand for cheap, yet voluntary, labour provided opportunities for entrepreneurs like Davidson to replicate colonial Singapore.[148]

Despite the official prohibition of emigration from China, Singapore proved that emigration from China was taking place. The *Canton Register* noted with interest that:

> Emigration although strictly forbidden by the law of China, is still practiced to a very considerable extent; and we observe in the *Singapore Chronicle* that the arrival lately of four junks, brought upwards of 1600 passengers, the greater proportion of whom we conclude to remain on the Island.[149]

The rapid development of Singapore, based on the integration of existing migration systems and European capital, demonstrated that Chinese migrant labour was a viable solution to colonial labour shortages. By the mid-1830s Crawfurd observed that the '[Chinese] government, in favour at least of male inhabitants, had relaxed the rigour of its prohibitory law against natives leaving the country'.[150] As described by Ulrike Hillemann, contact zones like Singapore were essential in the formulation of perceptions of China and the Chinese.[151] Importantly, in developing colonies like Singapore, the use of Chinese migrants as replacement labour served as a process of 'internal colonialism' that was used to pacify resistant or autonomous indigenous subjects.[152] The opportunity provided by the vast pool of cheap and reliable

---

[147] Lian Kwen Fee, 'The Construction of Malay Identity across Nations: Malaysia, Singapore, and Indonesia', *Journal of the Humanities and Social Sciences of Southeast Asia*, 157, 4 (2001), 865.

[148] See Chapter 4 for a discussion of the Colonial Land and Emigration Commission and the trans-imperial concerns about labour shortages.

[149] *Canton Register*, 24 May 1828.

[150] Hugh Murray and John Crawfurd et al., *An Historical and Descriptive Account of China, Vol. II* (Edinburgh: Oliver & Boyd, 1836), 369.

[151] Hillemann, *Asian Empire and British Knowledge*, 1–16.

[152] James C. Scott, *The Art of Not Being Governed: An Anarchist History of Upland Southeast Asia* (New Haven: Yale University Press, 2009), 40.

labour in China was not lost on British merchants, colonialists and imperial planners. The development of Singapore in the 1820s showed that an Anglo-Chinese society could be successful. In this context success was defined in terms of generating profit for British and Chinese merchant elites, whilst remaining politically stable. This was a notion of success in which the financial, political and social status of Chinese labourers themselves was largely irrelevant. By the 1830s various British actors attempted to repeat this success and experiment with Chinese labour under British rule in different colonies.

Conclusion

The colonial experience in Singapore demonstrates how colonial observers understood and interpreted pre-existing systems of Chinese migration in the context of colonial development. It also demonstrates the importance of racial stratifications in discussions of China and the Chinese. Chinese migrants were essentialised as either cheap labourers or wealthy merchants. Both groups were economically essential, and at the same time representations of them tangled with colonial ideas about civilisation and racial hierarchy. We will see in Chapter 2 how in John Crawfurd's contribution to the free trade debates he emphasised his expertise and experience in Asia when critiquing his opponents. Crawfurd connected his ideas about free trade and the role of the East India Company to the ideas about the Chinese character that he had formed whilst a colonial administrator in Singapore. Similarly, Gordon Forbes Davidson based his perceptions of different Asian communities on his experiences in Asia over a lengthy trading career. Metropolitan power structures attributed these colonial figures with a level of expertise, which was important because it ensured the replication of the notions of racial hierarchy from the contact zone of Singapore in other colonial contexts.

In subsequent chapters many of the issues seen in early colonial Singapore will re-emerge. The idea of a distinctly Chinese character evolved over the 1830s and 1840s. The changes to Anglo-Chinese relations occurring over this period created a fertile ground for the development of a racial discourse surrounding Chinese labour and the practical conditions to facilitate new systems of migration. Singapore demonstrated how Chinese labour migration took place, and confirmed that such migration was desirable. The new framework of Anglo-Chinese relations, with China opened to foreign trade in 1842, served to energise the development of British colonial control in Asia and provide a space for experimentation with migration. For British observers in Asia the effectiveness of Chinese labour was undoubted and applicable to new, diverse, colonial contexts. Crucially, the notion of a Chinese character underpinned assumptions about issues like trade and migration. These ideas did not stay in the colony. Colonial observers shared the Singapore model in Britain and across the British Empire.

Chapter 2

THE CHINESE CHARACTER: RACE, ECONOMICS, COLONISATION

'The Civilized World Versus China' was how the *Canton Register* described growing animosity between the Western merchant community and the Canton authorities in 1835.[1] The British opium trading firm Jardine Matheson owned this newspaper and its editorial line reflects the widely accepted decline of Western perceptions of China. The dominant historical narrative has been that a positive view of China, and by extension the Chinese, in the sixteenth and seventeenth centuries had transformed to a negative and critical attitude by the early nineteenth century.[2] The seventeenth and early eighteenth centuries were the height of Western fascination with Chinese institutions, society and culture. The praise of influential thinkers such as Gottfried Leibniz and Voltaire, as well as the fetish for Chinese architecture and Chinese consumer products, are all evidence of European reverence towards the civilised Celestial Empire.[3] In the late eighteenth century a combination of commercial and diplomatic frustration led to a transformation of how people in Britain perceived China more broadly. The failure of the Macartney Embassy (1792–94) was the key moment at which British reverence began to morph into disdain.[4] The formation and circulation of a Western perception of an archetypal Chinese character over the 1830s, in the build-up to the First Opium War (1839–42) between Britain and China, complicates this narrative. As seen in Singapore, colonial observers perceived Chinese migrants as economically valuable, rather than generally positively or negatively. The popularisation of the Singapore model of Chinese migration took place in the wider context of worsening Anglo-Chinese relations.

---

[1] *Canton Register*, 27 January 1835.
[2] Hillemann, *Asian Empire and British Knowledge*, 7, identifies this shift in British perceptions of China as occurring between 1763 and 1840. See also John S. Gregory, *The West and China since 1500* (New York: Palgrave Macmillan, 2003), 1–3.
[3] Gregory, *The West and China since 1500*, 45–8; Roberts, *China through Western Eyes*, 1. Regarding architecture, see William Chambers' Pagoda at Kew Gardens, built in 1762, as an example.
[4] For an overview of the Embassy's significance see Williams, 'Anglo-Chinese Caresses'.

This chapter will chart the spread and prominence of the idea of a distinctly Chinese racial character through the 1830s and 1840s. This marks a shift from examining the individual agents in the contact zone of Singapore to a broader discussion about the Chinese as a racial category across the British Empire and in Britain itself. Crucially, the wider discussion about China and Chinese migrants in the context of Anglo-Chinese conflict helped formulate images of a simultaneously industrious and duplicitous Chinese character that would prosper under British authority and instruction. British perceptions of a useful Chinese character and Chinese despotism could co-exist once the Chinese population was separated and distinguished from the Qing Empire.[5] The rhetoric of a Chinese people living under a Manchu yoke was popularised in the 1830s as Western firms who wanted China's restrictions on foreign trade lifted – such as the opium traders Jardine Matheson and Dent & Co. – justified their violation of Chinese laws and advocated military action against the Chinese authorities. This distinction between the Chinese people and the Qing dynasty was also useful in advocating labour migration to the British Empire as a form of liberation. Consequently, ideas about a Chinese character were often contradictory. China experts were able to articulate stereotypes about Chinese colonists who were industrious and obedient under European instruction, but innately deceitful and sinful when granted political power.[6]

First, this chapter explores the role of John Crawfurd in the removal of the East India Company monopoly of the China trade in 1833. We see here how Crawfurd was able to present himself as a China expert based on his experiences in Singapore and how his philosophy intertwined ideas about the Chinese as a racial category with his advocacy for liberal free trade economics. Second, the broad historical development of notions of a Chinese character is explored. This requires the examination of the common tropes attributed to China and the Chinese, which had developed over centuries of contact, but interacted with specific trends in publishing on racial and national 'character' in the 1820s and 1830s.[7] Third, the way that these ideas were mobilised in the

---

5 This process has been identified in texts such as Gregory, *The West and China since 1500*, 72–126, and Gabaccia and Hoerder, *Connecting Seas and Connected Ocean Rims*, 198.
6 Additionally opium and gambling addiction were commonly identified as innately Chinese traits.
7 See Kitson, *Forging Romantic China*, for more on eighteenth-century 'Chinoiserie' and 'Sinology'. Note also there is a broad range of literature on the role of publishing in moving ideas and information from colonies to the metropole. Some good examples include: John M. Mackenzie, *Propaganda and Empire: The Manipulation of British Public Opinion, 1880–1960* (Manchester: Manchester University Press, 1984); Simon Potter, *News and the British World: The Emergence of an Imperial Press System, 1876–1922* (Oxford: Oxford University Press, 2003); Simon Potter, ed., *Imperial Communication: Australia, Britain and the British Empire, 1830–1850* (London: University of London, 2005); Melodee Beals, 'The Role of the Sydney Gazette in the Creation of Australia in the Scottish Public Sphere', in Catherine Feely and John Hinks, eds, *Historical Networks in the Book Trade* (Abingdon: Routledge, 2017), 148–70.

changing context of the 1830s, particularly by China-coast merchants in the build-up to the First Opium War, is examined. Here we see how in advocating the liberation of the Chinese population from despotic Qing governance, in order to further their own economic agenda, the Western merchant community inadvertently made the case for Chinese migration and the Singapore model of Chinese colonisation under British leadership. By the end of the 1830s, the creation of an archetypal Chinese character, and the opening of China to the West in the First Opium War, provided a rationale for the use of Chinese migrant labour in the British Empire.

The China Expert and the 'Opening' of the China Trade

Whilst Singapore flourished economically, the East India Company Charter Act of 1833 was the final nail in the East India Company's commercial coffin.[8] The 1833 Act removed the East India Company monopoly of the China trade, which effectively de-regulated the 'country traders' – private companies that traded Indian products, most infamously opium, in China under licence from the East India Company – and created the space for new commercial networks on the China coast.[9] Anglo-Chinese trade was profitable for both the British state and the East India Company. The tea trade accounted for sixteen per cent of Britain's total customs revenue by the 1830s and was worth £4 million per annum to the East India Company.[10] Additionally, the sale of Indian opium in China, which had reversed the trade deficit of the China trade by creating a new import market, gave the East India Company a profit of £2.7 million in 1832.[11] Yet these profits were contingent on the 'Canton system' of trade regulation, which confined British trade to government-controlled merchants at Canton and had been in operation since 1757.[12] Not only was British trade regulated but British attempts to establish European-style diplomatic relations with China before 1833 had ended in failure. Debate in Britain over how Anglo-Chinese trade

---

[8] For more on the new role of the East India Company post-1833 see Anthony Webster, *The Twilight of the East India Company: The Evolution of Anglo-Asian Commerce and Politics, 1790–1860* (Woodbridge: Boydell Press, 2009).

[9] Alain Le Pinchon, ed., *China Trade and Empire: Jardine, Matheson & Co. and the Origins of British Rule in Hong Kong, 1827–1843* (Oxford: Oxford University Press, 2006), 5; British opium firms like Jardine Matheson were 'country traders'.

[10] Steve Tsang, *A Modern History of Hong Kong* (London: I.B. Tauris, 2007), 5; Philip Lawson, *The East India Company: A History* (London: Longman, 1993), 157.

[11] Lawson, *The East India Company*, 19; Glenn Melancon, *Britain's China Policy and the Opium Crisis: Balancing Drugs, Violence and National Honour, 1833–1840* (London: Ashgate, 2003), 1–6.

[12] Le Pinchon, *China Trade and Empire*, 10; Julia Lovell, *The Opium War: Drugs, Dreams and the Making of China* (London: Picador, 2011), 2. The regulations included various restrictions on the movements and personal lives of European merchants, but most importantly the restriction of trade to the state-sanctioned Hong merchants at Canton, which was believed to limit the volume of British imports.

and diplomacy should be reformed was contingent on the evidence of select China experts. Not only did the changes of 1833 open up space for private commercial expansion, but they were also the product of debates that became infused with ideas about the Chinese character.

It is hard to overstate the importance of individuals recognised as China experts in the changes of 1833. The pivotal role of John Crawfurd in the debates over the East India Company monopoly underlines the implications of the Anglo-Chinese experience in Singapore. The use of Crawfurd's individual story provides an entry point into complicated strands of imperial history, which have been the focus of entire texts in their own right. Here, Crawfurd offers an insight into vast debates about monopoly and free trade in Britain and Asia. Individuals formed key nodes within networks of empire, often moving from place to place. Historians have used specific individuals to connect imperial locales. These individuals act as case studies, which can physically move around the British Empire and are unrestricted by time or place.[13] Crawfurd's long career in Asia validated his expertise. After being posted to Penang by the East India Company in 1808, he served the Company during the British occupation of Java from 1811 to 1816, before returning to India. Crawfurd's experience of Penang and Java ultimately qualified him for his role in Singapore, but also meant he was selected for diplomatic missions on behalf of the Governor-General of India to Burma and Siam. By the time of Crawfurd's return to Britain in 1827 his wealth of experience meant that he was in demand by lobbying groups, such as the provincial East India Associations.[14]

During his time in Asia, John Crawfurd became a student of the nations and cultures he experienced. His impressive list of multi-volume publications reinforced his credentials as an expert on Asian cultures and societies, which would be utilised in the debates over the East India Company monopoly.[15] Specifically Crawfurd's first-hand experience in the contact zone of Singapore gave him a status of expertise that could be deployed against his metropolitan rivals.[16] In the first instance, his contributions to parliamentary select committees over a prolonged period legitimised his opinions, which were based on

[13] Catherine Hall, *Civilising Subjects: Metropole and Colony in the English Imagination 1830–1867* (Chicago: University of Chicago Press, 2002).

[14] See Yukihisa Kumagai, *Breaking into the Monopoly: Provincial Merchants and Manufacturers' Campaigns or Access to the Asian Market, 1790–1833* (Boston: Brill, 2013); and Yukihisa Kumagai, 'Kirkman Finlay and John Crawfurd: Two Scots in the Campaign of the Glasgow East India Association for the Opening of the China Trade, 1829–1833', *Journal of Scottish Historical Studies*, 30, 2 (2010), 175–99, for more on Crawfurd's connection to the East India Associations in their campaign against monopoly.

[15] The following works were also purchased by the East India Company and used for educational purposes: John Crawfurd, *History of the Indian Archipelago, Vols I–III* (Edinburgh: Archibald Constable, 1820); John Crawfurd, *Grammar and Dictionary of the Malay Language* (London: Smith, Elder, 1852).

[16] Hillemann, *Asian Empire and British Knowledge*, 106–49.

direct personal experience in Asia. After giving evidence to the House of Lords Select Committee on the East India Company in 1830, Crawfurd sat on the 1840 Select Committee on the trade with China. A variety of non-governmental groups made use of and helped to build his status and reputation as an expert in Britain. For instance, in 1828 Crawfurd became a lobbyist on behalf of the merchants of Calcutta and Singapore; his *View of the Present State and Future Prospects of the Free Trade and Colonisation of India* was published by the Central Committee on the East India and Chinese Trade in 1829; and 600 copies of his *Notes on the Settlement or Colonization of British Subjects in India* were ordered by the Glasgow East India Association.[17] He went on to write his most significant pro-free trade tract, *Chinese Monopoly Examined*, in 1830. On his return to Britain, Crawfurd became part of a network of merchants, lobbyists and regional East India and China Associations that aimed to remove the East India Company monopoly of the China trade.

John Crawfurd's career overlapped with the 'information revolution' that Zoë Laidlaw and Christopher Bayly have highlighted as a key feature of both imperial and colonial governance in the 1830s and 1840s.[18] Whilst metropolitan figures such as Robert Montgomery Martin collated colonial statistics to interpret and disseminate knowledge about the Empire, such information was supplemented by the direct colonial experience of those who had imperial careers.[19] In this environment the role of the expert and their specialised knowledge was recognised by both lobbyists and policy makers. Histories of Crawfurd's role in Britain have detailed his collaboration with provincial merchants and his later role as the first president of the Straits Settlement Association in 1868.[20] He was widely recognised by his contemporaries as an authority on the 'Indian Archipelago', and the fields of ethnography, commerce and colonial politics in particular.[21] Crawfurd's importance in Britain was influenced by the success of Singapore, where his role in the colony's early history was significant. In the 1921 multi-volume history *One Hundred Years of Singapore* Crawfurd was an essential source on the development of early colonial Singapore, providing commentary ranging from law and crime to education and land reform.[22] Crawfurd's writing provided the historical record of much of colonial Singapore's early administration. The

---

[17] Kumagai, *Breaking into the Monopoly*, 95–6.

[18] Zoë Laidlaw, *Colonial Connections, 1815–1845: Patronage, the Information Revolution and Colonial Government* (Manchester: Manchester University Press, 2005), 169–200; C. A. Bayly, *Empire and Information: Intelligence Gathering and Social Communication in India, 1780–1870* (Cambridge: Cambridge University Press, 1996).

[19] Laidlaw, *Colonial Connections*, 185–9.

[20] Yukihisa Kumagai, 'The Lobbying Activities of Provincial Mercantile and Manufacturing Interests against the Renewal of the East India Company's Charter, 1812–1813 and 1829–1833' (Ph.D. thesis, University of Glasgow, 2008), 105; Webster, 'The Development of British Commercial and Political Networks in the Straits Settlements', 914.

[21] Turnbull, 'Crawfurd, John (1783–1868)'.

[22] Braddell et al., *One Hundred Years of Singapore*.

1833 Charter Act connected Crawfurd's colonial and metropolitan lives. Crawfurd's experiences in Asia meant that his ideas about race influenced his advocacy of free trade and simultaneously provided legitimacy for his criticism of the East India Company. The environment created by the Charter Act was ultimately conducive to new systems of emigration from the China coast in the 1830s.

The 1833 Charter Act was ostensibly about trade, but the debates that circulated around it also grappled with ideas about race, character and civilisational hierarchy. John Crawfurd's role particularly highlights the cross-over between notions of free trade and emerging hierarchies, which emphasised notions of Chinese civilisational superiority over other racial groups in Asia. Tomotaka Kawamura's work demonstrates how the two main groups that benefited from the decline of the East India Company, Anglo-Indian agency houses and British provincial industrialists, were both connected to Crawfurd.[23] Due to these connections Crawfurd argued vehemently against the East India Company monopoly of the China trade. The extent to which Crawfurd's criticisms of the East India Company's management of the trade drew on his experiences in Asia, and his ethnographic observations, underlined the importance of debates about the China trade in shaping perceptions of the Chinese as a racial group in this period.

From his work with the Glasgow East India Association from 1828, to his role as the first president of the Straits Settlement Association in 1868, Crawfurd dedicated himself to advocating reforms that would benefit the Anglo-Indian agency houses. Specifically, these were reforms for the liberalisation of trade with China.[24] His record in Singapore suggests that he was already a convert to free trade liberalism, but as an additional incentive, Robert Bickers has noted that Crawfurd was on a 'handsome Bombay retainer' for his advocacy.[25] It is worth noting that notions of free trade, particularly in Asia, were essential to the ideological underpinnings of the Empire. Commercial freedom was one of the markers of civilisational superiority that legitimised imperial expansion.[26] In 'orientalist' fashion, the representation of the British Empire as an empire of freedom set it in contrast to Asian despotism and

---

[23] Tomotaka Kawamura, 'The British Empire and Asia in the Long Eighteenth Century', *Global History and Maritime Asia*, 17 (2010), 15.

[24] Kumagai, *Breaking into the Monopoly*, 107; Kumagai, 'The Lobbying Activities of Provincial Mercantile and Manufacturing Interests against the Renewal of the East India Company's Charter', 105; Webster, 'The Development of British Commercial and Political Networks in the Straits Settlements', 914.

[25] Bickers, *The Scramble for China*, 76. Crawfurd received a salary of £1,500 from free trade interests in Calcutta: Kumagai, 'Kirkman Finlay and John Crawfurd', 184.

[26] This fits very much with Gallagher and Robinson's 'imperialism of free trade': John Gallagher and Ronald Robinson, 'The Imperialism of Free Trade', *The Economic History Review*, 6, 1 (1953), 1–15. For more on how this worked in terms of Anglo-Chinese exchange, see Brian Stanley, '"Commerce and Christianity": Providence Theory, the Missionary Movement, and the Imperialism of Free Trade, 1842–1860', *The Historical Journal*, 26, 1 (1983), 71–94.

tyranny. The liberal embrace of empire saw issues such as humanitarianism and commercial freedom connected under the auspices of colonial improvement and the broader narrative of a 'civilising mission'.[27] In fact, Gareth Knapman's biography of Crawfurd demonstrates how Crawfurd's experiences in Asia were central to his support for liberal economic policy and the primacy of economic freedom.[28] Crawfurd's earlier role as a colonial administrator, his later role as a free trade advocate and his ideas about race were compatible and connected.

The arguments Crawfurd deployed in his critique of the East India Company monopoly sat within the standard rhetorical narratives of contemporary free trade advocates. The influence, or even dominance, of Adam Smith's *Wealth of Nations* in early nineteenth-century notions of political economy and, crucially, debates over the economic management of empire has been well acknowledged in the historiography.[29] Crawfurd and his allies – influenced by Smith – argued that the monopoly, whilst previously necessary, had run its natural course and reached its maximum profitability.[30] So dominant was this strain of economic thought that Philip Lawson suggests the decision to end the monopoly was tacitly agreed as early as 1825, and was merely confirmed by the committees and debates of the early 1830s.[31] Crawfurd's East India Company background was common amongst free trade campaigners, and he received support from prominent figures such as Joseph Hume and James Silk Buckingham, both of whom had their own histories, and grievances, with the East India Company.[32] In *Chinese Monopoly Examined* Crawfurd criticised the East India Company for limiting the Chinese tea trade as the only access point for Chinese tea into the British market.[33] Direct and quantifiable financial gain formed the basis of Crawfurd's case as he asserted that the 'advantages of a free intercourse with China' would be an additional '*one million sterling per annum*' in profit from the China trade.[34] However, Crawfurd's case was not purely economic. What distinguished

[27] Pitts, *A Turn to Empire*, 4–15.
[28] Knapman, *Race and British Colonialism in Southeast Asia*.
[29] Sarah Stockwell, ed., *The British Empire: Themes and Perspectives* (Oxford: Blackwell Publishing, 2008), 7; Boyd Hilton, *A Mad, Bad and Dangerous People? England 1783–1846* (Oxford: Oxford University Press, 2006), 21; Adam Smith, *An Inquiry into the Nature and Causes of the Wealth of Nations* (London: W. Strahan, 1776).
[30] Lawson, *The East India Company*, 157.
[31] Ibid., 158.
[32] Miles Taylor, 'Joseph Hume and the Reformation of India, 1819–1833', in Glenn Burgess and Matthew Festenstein, eds, *English Radicalism, 1550–1850* (Cambridge: Cambridge University Press, 2007), 285–309. In contrast to Crawfurd, Buckingham was not favourably regarded by the anti-monopoly movement, mainly due to his desire to remove the entirety of the East India Company's administration; for more on the contrast between Crawfurd and Buckingham, see Kumagai, *Breaking into the Monopoly*, 97–9.
[33] John Crawfurd, *Chinese Monopoly Examined* (London: James Ridgeway, 1830), 75.
[34] Ibid., 89. Italicisation in original text.

Crawfurd from contemporary critics of the East India Company was the significance of his experiences in Asia, and his emphasis on race as well as economic theory.

During the free trade debates, Crawfurd used his experience in Asia to present himself as an expert. In his tenure as Resident of Singapore, Crawfurd was notable for legislative measures that stimulated commercial growth.[35] As we have seen, he had legalised gambling, reduced duties on various products, kept Singapore a free port and enforced strict punishments for piracy.[36] It was Crawfurd's experience and success in Singapore that qualified him to give evidence to the 1830 Select Committee. When providing evidence Crawfurd highlighted his expertise. For example, he emphasised his knowledge of cotton cultivation across 'the Island of Java, and to considerable parts of Cochin China, and some parts of Siam and Ava; I refer also to some of the provinces of Bengal'.[37] Similarly, in Crawfurd's writing on the monopoly debate he continually referred to his own expertise in contrast to his metropolitan adversaries' lack of knowledge. It is important to note that not only did others recognise Crawfurd as an expert but he cultivated a self-image of supreme wisdom on issues relating to the British Empire in Southeast Asia. A lack of experience or knowledge was used to undermine opponents. Crawfurd aggressively argued that a pro-monopoly article in the *Quarterly Review* made 'vulgar pretensions to knowledge', had 'neither the capacity nor the inclination to supply' information about Chinese commerce and must have been using a map 'constructed before the age of Marco Polo'.[38] Crawfurd was fully aware of the value of his experience and his residence in Asia. To legitimise his arguments against the East India Company monopoly he invoked experiences that his critics did not share.

John Crawfurd's ideas about Singapore's different racial groups had heavily influenced his commercial policy as the British Resident. This also had an impact on his anti-monopoly writing and signalled a significant departure from the economic arguments that he shared with Hume and Buckingham.[39] As a colonial administrator Crawfurd felt strongly that the imposition of British, or Western, concepts on indigenous populations was vital to their civilisational development. In his *History of the Indian Archipelago* he wrote that 'the nations of the East, in point of civilization, continue unchanged – they seem rapidly to advance to a certain state of improvement, and then to continue in all ages as

---

[35] Webster, 'The Development of British Commercial and Political Networks in the Straits Settlements', 901.

[36] Braddell et al., *One Hundred Years of Singapore*, 80, 290–2.

[37] Parliamentary Papers, *Report from the Select Committee of the House of Lords appointed to inquire into the present state of the affairs of the East India Company, and into the trade between Great Britain, the East Indies and China; with the minutes of evidence taken before the committee*, 1830 (646), 345.

[38] Crawfurd, *Chinese Monopoly Examined*, 8 and 19.

[39] Taylor, 'Joseph Hume and the Reformation of India, 1819–1833', 285–309.

the same unchangeable semi-barbarians'.[40] As seen in Chapter 1, an example of the interplay between liberal colonial economic policy and different racial groups was Crawfurd's decision not to extend the colonial licensing system to gambling as it was an amusement which 'the most industrious of them (the Chinese) are accustomed to resort to'.[41] Crawfurd's commercial policies in Singapore had been influenced as much by his assumptions about different racial groups, and their needs, as by economic ideology.

The importance of notions of civilisation, development, skill and hierarchy in Crawfurd's free trade writing is most evident in his *View of the Present State and Future Prospects of the Free Trade and Colonisation of India*, published in 1829. In this text Crawfurd drew a comparison between the 'superior skill of the Chinese' and the 'unskillfulness of the Indians'.[42] Crawfurd's writing was infused with specific criticisms of 'the Indians' as a 'timid, often effeminate, and, as a nation, a feeble race of semi-barbarians' who were 'inferior to Europeans and to Chinese in real skill and intelligence'.[43] The repeated reference to Indian barbarism was set in contrast to British and Chinese civilisation, reflecting similar hierarchies to those seen in Singapore. Crucially the critique of the East India Company was not a critique of British imperialism in India, which, in Crawfurd's view, was entirely necessary. Crawfurd's experience in Southeast Asia clearly informed his equation of Chinese and Europeans as superior racial groups. Lamenting the Qing Empire's controls on emigration Crawfurd appeared to compare the effect of British imperialism with Chinese immigration as a bearer of progress. He remarked that 'to it [Chinese migration] we owe more than half the prosperity of all the countries in which it has occurred; such is the efficacy of a little infusion of civilization into semi-barbarous communities'.[44] That a text ostensibly about the reform of the East India Company contained so many allusions to the civilisational superiority of Chinese migrants over host communities was indicative of the pervasive influence of Crawfurd's time in Southeast Asia. This conceptual dichotomy, between civilised Chinese migrants and uncivilised Indian locals, would be particularly pertinent in the recruitment of Chinese tea cultivators for Assam, which is examined in Chapter 3.

The role played by Chinese communities in colonial commercial networks informed praise of Chinese civilisation. For Crawfurd an aptitude for trade was a sign of racial superiority. In his *History of the Indian Archipelago* Crawfurd identified Chinese mercantilism as something comparable to earlier stages of European commercial development: 'the Chinese, indeed, carry the

---

[40] Crawfurd, *History of the Indian Archipelago, Vol. II*, 39.
[41] Braddell et al., *One Hundred Years of Singapore*, 56.
[42] John Crawfurd, *View of the Present State and Future Prospects of the Free Trade and Colonisation of India* (London: James Ridgway, 1829), 19.
[43] Ibid., 68.
[44] Ibid., 70.

principle of the mercantile system to an extreme, which would have excited the admiration or envy of the European politicians of the early part of the last century'.[45] Crawfurd routinely used terms such as 'industry' and 'ingenuity' in his praise of Chinese settlers, whom, along with Europeans, he classed as 'improvers'.[46] Of course, not only could an aptitude for trade be used to form civilisational hierarchies, but the idea that the Chinese were pre-disposed to trade also assuaged fears that the removal of the East India Company monopoly would jeopardise Anglo-Chinese trade. Importantly, Crawfurd was not asserting Chinese equality with the British, but their superiority over other Asian races, as suggested in his Select Committee evidence: 'Chinese skill and capital resemble very much European skill and capital; I take European skill and capital however, to be as much superior to Chinese skill and capital, as Chinese skill and capital are superior to Hindoo skill and capital'.[47] For Crawfurd, racial hierarchies reflected and dictated commercial realities. Concepts of racial hierarchy Crawfurd had developed in Singapore and Southeast Asia heavily informed his understanding of trade and commerce and were present throughout his anti-monopoly writing. This had the added effect of further disseminating stereotypes and perceptions of a Chinese character, which was superior to comparable Indian personality traits and more suited to British colonial rule.

Crawfurd was part of a growing group of imperial careerists who were identified as China experts by metropolitan bodies, such as parliamentary Select Committees, and promoted as experts by lobbying organisations. As outlined by P. J. Marshall, British India provided an opportunity for figures 'to win reputations for themselves as transmitters of knowledge to a curious and expectant Europe'.[48] The East India Company Charter renewal acted as a particular stimulus to metropolitan interest in the experience of imperial careerists like Crawfurd. It was the philosophy of liberal thinkers, like John Stuart Mill, that Indian policy should be constructed from the advice of experts in India, rather than emerging from metropolitan political processes.[49] Within this framework of Indian governance, Crawfurd's experience amongst the Chinese migrants in Singapore was seen as particularly significant during debates over the future management of the China trade.

Other Select Committee witnesses also drew on experience of Chinese migration in Asia. Sir Ralph Rice, who had spent seven years as a court

---

[45] Crawfurd, *History of the Indian Archipelago, Vol. III*, 171.

[46] Crawfurd, *Chinese Monopoly Examined*, 27; Crawfurd, *Journal of an Embassy from the Governor-General of India to the Courts of Siam and Cochin China, Vol. I*, 26.

[47] Parliamentary Papers, *Report from the Select Committee of the House of Lords appointed to inquire into the present state of the affairs of the East India Company*, 349.

[48] P. J. Marshall, 'British-Indian Connections c.1780 to c.1830: The Empire of the Officials', in Michael J. Franklin, ed., *Romantic Representations of British India* (London: Routledge, 2006), 47.

[49] Ibid., 48. Mill was writing on Indian policy during his career with the East India Company, from 1823 to 1858.

recorder on Penang, similarly emphasised the contrast between the indigenous population and Chinese immigrants.[50] In giving evidence to the 1830 Select Committee, Rice identified a comparable hierarchy in which the Malay population was the most 'uncivilised' and prone to violent criminality, whilst the Chinese population had a tendency to steal but were simultaneously 'admirable merchants, most excellent in every respect'.[51] Various witnesses made reference to the perceived character traits of the Chinese, such as American merchant Joshua Bates who referred to Chinese commercial success in Singapore, or Judge William Malcolm Fleming who bemoaned Chinese opium addiction.[52] As outlined by Kumagai, the make-up of witnesses reflected the mobilisation of opposition to the East India Company monopoly engineered by private interest groups in Asia and Britain.[53]

Notably, John Crawfurd's status as an expert on China and the British Empire continued and built beyond the 1833 charter renewal. For example, in giving evidence to the 1847 Select Committee on Britain's commercial relations with China, Crawfurd recalled his experience of the Chinese population. Both the question and answer reveal the enduring imperial interest in Chinese migrant labour:

> From your intercourse with the Eastern Archipelago, have not you found the Chinese great emigrants, willing to apply themselves to labour, and willing to transfer themselves to other countries?—They are very well conducted, and very industrious, and very useful colonists. There are no people in the world more easy to manage, I think, and who can behave better when they are well treated. I might mention one curious example of it: I was engaged in negotiating a treaty with the native princes, Malays, who were not quite so respectable a people as the Chinese, either in point of morals or industry. They were rather restive, and our whole military force consisted only of 100 sepoys. The chief Chinese merchants came to me, and told me, that if I had any apprehension at all that the military force was not quite strong enough, they were perfectly ready to come and protect the British settlement, and that they had 2,000 of the best young men at my service. Their services, however, were not required.[54]

Crawfurd's re-telling of the importance of Chinese support in establishing British control of Singapore demonstrates the longevity of the narrative of Anglo-Chinese success in Singapore in discussions of China and Chinese labour.

[50] Parliamentary Papers, *Report from the Select Committee of the House of Lords appointed to inquire into the present state of the affairs of the East India Company*, 85.
[51] Ibid., 87.
[52] Ibid., 375 and 66.
[53] Kumagai, *Breaking into the Monopoly*.
[54] Parliamentary Papers, *Report from the Select Committee on Commercial Relations with China; together with the minutes of evidence, appendix, and index*, 1847 (654), 2544.

John Crawfurd's experiences in Southeast Asia allowed him to assert himself as more qualified than his metropolitan, monopolist opponents, and informed and connected his ideas about free trade and the Chinese as a racial group. Crucially, metropolitan policy makers deemed Crawfurd's experience of Chinese migration in Southeast Asia as relevant to the legislative management of trade between Britain and China. British imperial and economic growth in Southeast Asia meant that observers in London connected Chinese migration and Anglo-Chinese trade as imperial issues. Observation of Chinese migration to Singapore, and the meanings attached to migrants, informed perceptions of the Qing Empire and Britain's China policy.

The Chinese Character

In 1836 the opium trader James Matheson wrote that the Chinese were 'to be spoken of much in the same spirit as one would speculate concerning the suppositious tenants of the moon'.[55] This sense of mystery summarises centuries of Western efforts to define, explain and understand China and the Chinese. Aside from a cursory acknowledgement of Marco Polo's 'discovery' of China, it is common in histories of Sino-Western relations to identify the sixteenth century as a starting point of significant interaction and exchange.[56] In particular the inroads made by Portugal, with the acquisition of a permanent base on the China coast at Macao in 1557, opened up opportunities for missionary endeavour. The activities of Jesuit missionaries involved both the attempted conversion of the Chinese populace to Christianity and the transmission of knowledge of China to a Western audience. Early publishing on China was consequently dominated by biblical scholarship. In the century or so after the establishment of the Catholic mission in China in 1583, European missionaries are estimated to have composed and published 450 works in Chinese, 330 of which were religious texts.[57] This early missionary impact was minimal in terms of Chinese conversion, but it was significant in igniting a Western fascination with understanding and extracting knowledge from China. By the 1760s Christianity had been outlawed in China – the Qianglong Emperor was wary of the alternative moral authority offered by the Pope – and Chinese interactions with the West were regulated through the Canton system.[58] Aside from relations with Russia, all official economic and political exchange between China and the West was channelled and mediated

---

[55] James Matheson, *The Present Position and Prospects of the British Trade with China* (London: Smith, Elder and Co., 1836), 3.

[56] Gregory, *The West and China since 1500*, 5. For an overview of British knowledge of China over this period see Rosalind Ballaster, *Fabulous Orients: Fictions of the East in England, 1662–1785* (Oxford: Oxford University Press, 2005).

[57] Peter Burke and R. Po-Chia Hsia, *Cultural Translation in Early Modern Europe* (Cambridge: Cambridge University Press, 2007), 39.

[58] Gregory, *The West and China since 1500*, 34.

through the thirteen Hong merchants, who were chosen by and ultimately answerable to the Qing authorities.[59] The system also limited Western residence in China to Canton and Macao.[60] As a result, Canton, much like Singapore, became a contact zone in the late eighteenth century and would remain a key site of exchange throughout the 1830s.

Much recent scholarship has been concerned with British 'perceptions', 'views' and 'representations' of China and the Chinese from the late eighteenth century onwards.[61] In particular the work of Hao Gao on Britain's diplomatic overtures has emphasised how these events led to a greater interest in Sinology and the conceptualisation of 'the Chinese'.[62] Yet histories of Anglo-Chinese relations have rested on the oversimplifications and assumptions of the decline theory. As seen in Singapore, distinctions – whether of class, language or regional origin – were essential to the conceptual formation of a Chinese character. Crucially for Anglo-Chinese relations, the industrious Chinese populace and despotic Qing Empire were separated, allowing for the framing of British aggression as ultimately benevolent and morally imperative. Though many of the characteristics attributed to the Chinese were contradictory – for example, some authors simultaneously praised honesty in business transactions whilst critiquing innate deceitfulness – the central point of emphasis was that perceptions of the Chinese character not only validated British military and economic aggression, they also provided a case for the use of Chinese migrants as colonial labourers.

In Britain the language of an archetypal national character was becoming increasingly common in the late eighteenth and early nineteenth century. The writings of John Crawfurd, discussed in the previous chapter, show that attempts to essentialise the Chinese as a racial group predated the 1830s. However, the 1830s was a decade of particular significance due to an increase in English-language publishing on China. Print literature was essential to the definition of racial, ethnic or national groups beyond 'local' geographical spaces.[63] Within these publications the fact that different communities were

---

[59] For an overview of the Co-hong system see Paul Van Dyke, *Life and Enterprise on the China Coast, 1700–1845* (Hong Kong: Hong Kong University Press, 2005).

[60] Westerners could reside permanently in Macao and could only stay in Canton temporarily during the trading season. Western women were not allowed to stay in Canton at all as Qing officials sought to discourage permanent foreign residence.

[61] Jeng-Guo Chen, 'The British View of Chinese Civilization and Emergence of Class Consciousness', *The Eighteenth Century*, 45 (2004), 193–205; Berg, 'Britain, Industry and Perceptions of China', 269–88; Tsao, 'Representing China to the British Public in the Age of Free Trade'.

[62] Hao Gao, 'Prelude to the Opium War? British Reactions to the "Napier Fizzle" and Attitudes towards China in the Mid Eighteen-Thirties', *Historical Research*, 87, 237 (2014), 491–509; Hao Gao, 'The Amherst Embassy and British Discoveries in China', *History*, 99, 337 (2014), 568–87.

[63] Benedict Anderson, *Imagined Communities: Reflections on the Origin and Spread of Nationalism* (London: Verso, 1983), 1–7.

evaluated by their level of culture or civilisation was an important condition for the formulation of a Chinese character and its potential value to the British Empire. Specifically, the civilisational, and connected commercial, potential of Chinese migrants was emphasised by those arguing for the colonial use of Chinese labour.[64] Moreover, the role of British self-identity, cast as the most civilised nation, in perceptions of China highlights the importance of British imperialism as a context for the formation of the Chinese character.

As the British Empire's territorial possessions in Asia increased in the late eighteenth century, it encountered a variety of indigenous populations and migrant communities in a variety of contexts. Defining and categorising these different Asian groups was a particular obsession of British ethnographers in the early nineteenth century. The specialist journals of the period carried articles on the history and nature of different Asian nations – such as the *Oriental Herald* (established in the 1820s), the *Chinese Repository* (established in the 1830s) and the *Journal of the Royal Asiatic Society* (with its first volume in 1834). Figures who sought to define the Chinese character were carriers and disseminators of knowledge about a range of Asian nations. For example, John Crawfurd's *History of the Indian Archipelago* included sections on the 'Language and Literature of the Malays', 'Language and Literature of the Celebes' and the 'Ancient History of Java'.[65] Texts such as Crawfurd's *Journal of an Embassy from the Governor-General of India to the Courts of Siam and Cochin China* and the missionary Charles Gutzlaff's *Journal of a Residence in Siam* defined, in the Western imagination, Asian kingdoms and peoples into similar categories to European empires and nations.[66] Alongside these ethnographic texts the imperial information revolution saw various metropolitan actors taking an interest in Britain's Asian colonies.[67] The definition of a Chinese character was part of a wider British interest in the categorisation of new colonial subjects.

Colonial observers also formed perceptions of Chinese character in a wider context of declining Anglo-Chinese diplomatic and commercial relations. The frustration of the Macartney Embassy is a good example of how wider diplomatic events shaped British attempts to understand China. The most famous texts to emerge directly from the Embassy were Aeneas

---

64   Chapter 3 demonstrates this explicitly.
65   Crawfurd, *History of the Indian Archipelago, Vols I–III.*
66   Crawfurd, *Journal of an Embassy from the Governor-General of India to the Courts of Siam and Cochin China*; Charles Gutzlaff, *Journal of a Residence in Siam: and of a Voyage Along the Coast of China to Mantchou Tartary* (Canton: Chinese Repository, 1832).
67   Bayly, *Empire and Information*, 8. The works of Robert Montgomery Martin sought to categorise and provide a statistical analysis of Britain's imperial possessions: Robert Montgomery Martin, *A History of British Possessions in the Indian and Atlantic Oceans* (London: Whittaker & Co., 1837); Robert Montgomery Martin, *Statistics of the Colonies of the British Empire: From the Official Records of the Colonial Office* (London: W.H. Allen and Co., 1839). For a full account of Martin's work see Frank H. H. King, *Survey Our Empire! Robert Montgomery Martin (1801–1868): A Bio-Bibliography* (Hong Kong: University of Hong Kong, 1979).

Anderson's *A Narrative of the British Embassy to China* (1795) and Sir George Staunton's *An authentic account of an Embassy from the King of Great Britain* (1797). Staunton – whose son Thomas was an interpreter for the Embassy and would later advocate military action against China as an MP – showed a particular interest in understanding the Chinese character.[68] His account of the Embassy includes various attempts to describe unique Chinese characteristics, such as extracts on the 'character of civil and military officers', 'thoughts of a person long resident in China, as to the character of the people and government in that country', 'trait in character of Chinese', and the 'character of Chinese men'.[69] Scholars have emphasised how Macartney and other members of the mission observed a China in decline. Macartney referred to China as 'an old, crazy, first rate man-of-war'.[70] Such observations have been identified as the starting point of a re-evaluation of China's position in the world.[71] The Embassy also confirmed the superiority of British technology and, consequently, British civilisation.[72] The failure of the Macartney Embassy was followed by similar diplomatic failures by Lord Amherst (1816) and William Napier (1834), which again provided more accounts of a tyrannical Qing Empire in decline.[73] As Anglo-Chinese trade grew, and the British state became increasingly concerned by the lack of diplomatic progress, questions about who the Chinese were and what delineated their character became increasingly interesting to metropolitan and imperial audiences.

Early nineteenth-century missionary texts on China are notably diverse. Charles Gutzlaff, who features in this chapter, is a good example of a missionary who disseminated knowledge about China to a wider audience. Similarly to Gutzlaff, the missionary Robert Morrison (who worked as a translator for the East India Company and edited the Jardine Matheson-owned newspaper the *Canton Register*) also wrote widely. In doing so he went well beyond the brief of his missionary role. An accomplished linguist, Morrison became best known for his *Grammar of the Chinese Language*, which the East India Company published, and as a pioneer of Chinese language teaching

[68] Julia Lovell, *The Great Wall: China Against the World* (London: Atlantic Books, 2006), 4–9.

[69] Sir George Staunton, *An authentic account of an Embassy from the King of Great Britain* (London: G. Nicol, 1797), x–xvii. Similar efforts to use diplomatic missions to evaluate the civilisational status and nature of a 'closed' nation can be seen in US exchange with Japan in the 1850s: see Jeffrey A. Keith, 'Civilization, Race, and the Japan Expedition's Cultural Diplomacy, 1853–1854', *Diplomatic History*, 35, 2 (2011), 193.

[70] Helen H. Robbins, *Our first ambassador to China: an account of the life of George, Earl of Macartney, with extracts from his letters, and the narrative of his experiences in China, as told by himself, 1737–1806, from hitherto unpublished correspondence and documents* (London: John Murray, 1908), 386.

[71] Chen, 'The British View of Chinese Civilization and Emergence of Class Consciousness', 193–205.

[72] Berg, 'Britain, Industry and Perceptions of China', 270.

[73] Gao, 'The Amherst Embassy and British Discoveries in China'; Gao, 'Prelude to the Opium War?'; Glenn Melancon, 'Peaceful Intentions: The First British Trade Commission in China, 1833–5', *Historical Research*, 73 (2000), 33–47.

in Britain.[74] Morrison's interest in learning the Chinese language came from a broader philosophy of immersive mission promoted by the London Missionary Society. It was commonly accepted that in order to improve the chances of conversion, Western missionaries required as much knowledge about China and the Chinese as possible.[75]

Missionaries disseminated the information and knowledge they collected and as a result played a vital role in discussions of the Chinese character. For example, William Milne's 'Account of a Secret Association in China, Entitled the Triad Society' articulated many of the tropes commonly deployed to denigrate Chinese labourers in Singapore as subversive gambling and opium addicts.[76] Often critiques of the Chinese in missionary literature were set alongside critiques of contemporary merchants. The London Missionary Society missionary Walter Henry Medhurst admonished the 'sinful condition' of the Chinese in the same chapter that he 'appealed' to the 'opium merchant'.[77] One of the most important missionary authors was Elijah Bridgman, the first American missionary to China, who edited the regular title the *Chinese Repository* and collaborated with missionary colleagues from varied backgrounds.[78] Missionaries – though often semi-autonomous and morally conflicted, as they balanced access to unsaved souls against the evils of opium addiction – were at the forefront of defining the attributes of the Chinese character over the eighteenth and nineteenth centuries.

Whilst missionaries were critical in shaping perceptions of the Chinese, growing political and commercial interest in China in the 1830s meant that the Chinese character was increasingly open to definition by different Western actors. British territorial expansion in Asia opened up avenues for colonial officials to be established as experts, as seen by the example of John Crawfurd in Singapore.[79] Crawfurd's experience in Asia and his connections to both metropolitan and colonial power brokers meant that his opinions on the Chinese – whether given through publications, personal letters or

[74] R. K. Douglas, 'Morrison, Robert (1782–1834)', rev. Robert Bickers, *Oxford Dictionary of National Biography*, Oxford University Press, 2004; online edn, May 2007, www.oxforddnb. com/view/article/19330 (accessed 30 September 2018).

[75] Edwin J. Van Kley, 'Europe's "Discovery" of China and the Writing of World History', *American Historical Review*, 76 (1971), 358–85. This was standard practice for the London Missionary Society: see Christopher Allen Daily, 'From Gosport to Canton: A New Approach to Robert Morrison and the Beginnings of Protestant Missions in China' (Ph.D. thesis, SOAS, 2009), for more on the methods used by the London Missionary Society.

[76] Milne, 'Account of a Secret Association in China, Entitled the Triad Society', 241. For the importance of these stereotypes and their connection to opium consumption, see Lovell, *The Opium War*.

[77] Walter Henry Medhurst, *China: its State and Prospects* (Boston: Crocker & Brewster, 1838), 67.

[78] Bickers, *The Scramble for China*, 36; Jessie Gregory Lutz, *Opening China: Karl F. A. Gutzlaff and Sino-Western Relations, 1827–1852* (Cambridge: William B. Eerdmans, 2008), 151.

[79] Crawfurd, *History of the Indian Archipelago, Vols I–III*; Hugh Murray and John Crawfurd et al., *An Historical and Descriptive Account of China, Vol. I* (Edinburgh: Oliver & Boyd, 1836).

evidence to parliamentary Select Committees – were influential.[80] Experts from contact zones in Asia were increasingly appropriated by metropolitan authors. Robert Montgomery Martin's *British Relations with the Chinese Empire* (1832) was a prime example, as Martin dedicated an entire chapter to John Crawfurd's 'opinions of the Chinese', which reflected the perceived significance of Crawfurd's first-hand experience in Asia.[81] Crawfurd and Martin were not impartial observers, but heavily committed to the expansion of British imperial control and trade across Asia. Authors like Crawfurd were more directly connected to imperial power structures and systems of colonial rule than their missionary contemporaries.[82] Wider debates about national character, the increased economic significance of Anglo-Chinese relations and the growing number of China experts in Asian contact zones all contributed to developing notions of Chinese character over the 1830s.

Authors with different backgrounds and interests understood China through different analytical frameworks. However, the 1830s and 1840s also saw a degree of standardisation with an increase in the number of texts that utilised the specific vocabulary of character. In this period the *Chinese Repository* repeatedly ran sections on the 'Chinese national character' and the indexes contained similar terminology, including references to the 'Chinese, their national character' and 'the character of Chinamen'.[83] One of the first texts with a titular reference to character was the British missionary and diplomat George Tradescant Lay's *The Chinese as They Are: Their Moral, Social and Literary Character*, which was published at the height of the Opium War in 1841.[84] That Lay sought to engage with numerous aspects of character reflects the various uses and adaptations of racial character as a concept. Charles Gutzlaff suffixed character with 'religion', whilst for the later Governor of Hong Kong, John Francis Davis, 'manners' defined character.[85] Character meant different things to different observers, yet it was a useful shorthand to generalise personality traits and attach them to specific racial categories. The language of character was so pervasive that in 1831 outgoing East India Company Select Committee President Charles Marjoribanks wrote a *Brief Account of the English Character*, which was translated into Chinese by Robert Morrison and was distributed on voyages along the China coast by Charles

[80] Kumagai, *Breaking into the Monopoly*, 93–113; Webster, *The Twilight of the East India Company*.
[81] Robert Montgomery Martin, *British Relations with the Chinese Empire in 1832* (London: Parbury, Allen & Co., 1832).
[82] See Chapter 1 for an overview of Crawfurd's writing on the Chinese in Asia and his background.
[83] *Chinese Repository*, Vol. I (1833), Vol. X (1841), Vol. XI (1842).
[84] George Tradescant Lay, *The Chinese as They Are: Their Moral, Social and Literary Character* (London: William Ball & Co., 1841).
[85] Charles Gutzlaff, *A Sketch of Chinese History, Ancient and Modern, Vol. I* (London: Smith, Elder and Co., 1834), 43–54; John Francis Davis, *The Chinese: a general description of the empire of China and its inhabitants* (New York: Harper & Brothers, 1836), 240.

Gutzlaff and Hugh Hamilton Lindsay.[86] The distribution of the tract on these voyages indicates the role of newly empowered private interests in aggressively challenging both Chinese and British authorities. For example, the opium trader William Jardine endorsed Gutzlaff's involvement in exploration aboard the *Lord Amherst*.[87] Additionally, Lindsay distributed Marjoribanks' pamphlet in contravention of the instructions of his successor, John Davis.[88] The tract highlighted English desire for trade, which was evidenced by the distance that ships travelled to China; emphasised that there was no desire for conquest, given that Britain already had a large empire; and cited assistance to shipwrecked Chinese sailors and Chinese merchants as evidence of English kindness.[89] In detailing the English character Marjoribanks also praised the commercial character of the Chinese: 'the people of China are highly intelligent, industrious, and prosperous'.[90] By the 1830s the need to understand and essentialise the Chinese character was acknowledged by various Western observers, and especially by British imperial actors and stakeholders. Moreover, the notion of character was not merely a useful interpretative concept, but it was used actively in Anglo-Chinese interactions as a tool to try to engender changes in policy in both Britain and China.

Liberating China

The discussion of Chinese migrants in Singapore and Chinese character in the East India Company Charter debate took place alongside increasing agitation by British merchant firms on the China coast. After the charter renewal had removed the East India Company monopoly of the China trade in 1834, the 'country trading' firms expanded their smuggling activities, which were illegal under Qing regulations. Over the 1830s, free from the limiting effect of the East India Company, these firms engaged in an aggressive 'information war' that involved sponsoring publications that criticised the insularity of the Qing state.[91] An important, but often overlooked, theme of this literature is that in arguing for China to be opened to Western trade it also advocated for the free movement of Chinese emigrants.[92] This section will give an insight into literature produced by British merchants on the China coast. The specific

[86] Robert Bickers, 'The Challenger: Hugh Hamilton Lindsay and the Rise of British Asia, 1832–1865', *Transactions of the Royal Historical Society*, 6th series, 22 (2012), 147–50.

[87] Bickers, *The Scramble for China*, 27.

[88] For more on the conduct of Lindsay during this voyage, see Bickers, 'The Challenger'.

[89] Ting Man Tsao, 'Representing "Great England" to Qing China in the Age of Free Trade Imperialism: The Circulation of a Tract by Charles Marjoribanks on the China Coast', *Victorians Institute Journal*, 6, www.nines.org/exhibits/Representing_Great_England?page=2 (accessed 30 September 2018).

[90] Ibid.

[91] Chen, 'An Information War Waged by Merchants and Missionaries at Canton'.

[92] As mentioned in Chapter 1, Chinese emigration was technically prohibited until 1860.

focus is on the largest opium-trading firm Jardine Matheson, who published an English-language newspaper, the *Canton Register*, and maintained an extensive publication network. Even within this network many of the character traits discussed in contemporary publications were seemingly contradictory. Jardine Matheson's publications described the Chinese as both hardworking labourers and lazy opium addicts; or commercially astute and trustworthy, yet fundamentally deceitful. Despite these inconsistencies, the characteristics ascribed to the Chinese had significant consequences. Ideas about character were important in creating a distinction between the Chinese people and the Qing Empire. This divide was used both to promote the economic intrusion of Britain's informal empire into China and to advocate the use of Chinese migrant labour in the British Empire.

Chapter 1 demonstrated how British colonial administrators praised the relative industriousness of the Chinese, in comparison to indigenous peoples. For those interested in sourcing cheap and effective migrant labour the fact that Chinese migrants embraced a contractual employer–employee relationship, unlike many indigenous groups, was an overwhelmingly positive trait. Eulogies of Chinese labour were commonplace in English-language publications. For example, articles in the *Canton Register* praised Chinese ingenuity in 'agricultural labour' and 'irrigation' in order to feed such a large population.[93] Chinese traits were identified as useful to British modes of production in Asian colonies. The *Chinese Repository* detailed how China's 'increasing numbers taught them the necessity of labour' but simultaneously lamented that 'in olden times they were far more sincere, honest, and less corrupted than at present'.[94] Much praise of the Chinese was tempered, in that it suggested they were merely less savage than other groups, rather than virtuous in their own right: 'piracies were committed on the coast of China more frequently than even in the waters of the Indian Archipelago. But the desperadoes of this country are not as bloodthirsty as the Malays, and therefore fewer people were killed and less ravages committed.'[95] Moreover, the common trope of an innate predilection for addiction – which, according to Jardine Matheson, was the cause of the opium crisis – was extended to include gambling as a racial character trait: 'all classes of persons, coolies, servants, shopmen, gentlemen of town and country, officers civil and military, old men and boys, engage in gambling'.[96] In the 1830s many of these negative stereotypes became connected to an idea of an archetypal Chinese character. Crucially, the vices

---

[93] *Canton Register*, 14 July 1835.
[94] *Chinese Repository*, Vol. I (1833), 262. The *Repository* was a missionary journal published in Canton by American Protestant missionary Elijah Coleman Bridgman and was regularly co-edited by Charles Gutzlaff.
[95] *Canton Press*, 20 January 1838.
[96] *Canton Register*, 13 October 1835.

of the Chinese were redeemable because of their embrace of Western-style economic and labour relationships.

Jardine Matheson provide a good example of the importance of the influence of economic relationships on perceptions of the Chinese character. The firm simultaneously maintained a friendly relationship with Hong merchants and Chinese employees, known as compradors, whilst holding Qing officials in contempt. The *Canton Register* regularly articulated this distinction, which often critiqued Chinese officials and defended Chinese merchants. However, members of the firm did not make such distinctions clear when addressing a British audience. Matheson began his 1836 book *The Present Position and Prospects of the British Trade with China* by describing 'the Chinese – a people characterised by a marvellous degree of imbecility, avarice, conceit, and obstinacy'.[97] Throughout the book, which emphasised the perceived oppression of Western merchants by Chinese officials, Matheson made repeated reference to the Chinese character. For example, he explained that the poor policy of the East India Company was based on 'an utter ignorance of the real character of the Chinese' which was 'mercenary and rapacious'.[98] Matheson also attributed Chinese imperial policy to the 'far-sighted cunning and inflexible pertinacity of the Chinese character'.[99] Resistance to the opium trade, and reluctance to liberalise trade with the West in general, motivated Matheson's critique. He chastised the 'policy of this extraordinary people, to shroud themselves' and complained at how the Chinese 'consider all other inhabitants of the earth … as barbarians'.[100] In writing for a metropolitan audience Matheson made little effort to differentiate between the Chinese people and the Qing Empire as his China-coast newspaper did.

The distinction between the government and population was crucial on the China coast. A positive review of James Matheson's book from the rival Canton newspaper the *Canton Press* explained that the difficulties faced by the merchants were the fault of the government and not the population: 'the Chinese Empire has, ever since the first European adventurers made their appearance on the coasts of China, restricted the intercourse between them and its own subjects'.[101] The merchants at Canton continually emphasised the desire of China's 'subjects' to trade. Of particular use to Western authors were the northern, Manchu origins of the ruling Qing dynasty, which allowed the imperial elite to be portrayed as a foreign ruling power with the true (Han) Chinese living under their 'yoke'.[102] The use of the term 'yoke'

---

97 Matheson, *The Present Position and Prospects of the British Trade with China*, 1.
98 Ibid., 9.
99 Ibid., 11.
100 Ibid., 15.
101 *Canton Press*, 13 August 1836.
102 Harrison, *China*, 33–51. Most famously John Scarth referred to the 'Tartar yoke' in John Scarth, *British Policy in China: is our war with the Tartars or the Chinese* (London: Smith, Elder and Co., 1860), 9.

invoked a developing mythology of Britain's own historical development. The growth of democracy in the nineteenth-century British Empire was framed as a reclamation of Anglo-Saxon freedoms from Norman tyranny.[103] Articles on Chinese history appeared frequently in journals like the *Chinese Repository* and provided a historical context for the perceived despotism of the Qing Empire: 'it is now about one hundred and eighty years since the Tartars obtained the government of the whole Chinese dominions ... they imposed certain regulations which were viewed by the conquered either as highly disgraceful or oppressive'.[104] Western awareness of the diversity of religion, language and culture in nineteenth-century China was most commonly expressed in critiques of the Qing. A virtuous Chinese population victimised by cruel foreign rulers legitimised the Western merchant's contravention of Chinese laws and formed part of the justification of the Opium War as a war of liberation.

The salvation of the Chinese population from the despotism of the Qing Empire was deemed particularly important because the Chinese people were already civilised. A letter to the editor of the *Canton Register* articulated this: 'now if you disapprove of the state of mean submission and ignorance in which the Chinese are placed ... you have no alternative ... but to reclaim them from the alarming degree of civilization in which they already stand'.[105] The idea that China's historical civilisation was in jeopardy was a common theme of Western writing.[106] For example, for Walter Henry Medhurst, China exhibited 'many traces of civilization' but at the present time 'possesses as much civilization as Turkey now, or England a few centuries ago'.[107] For missionaries like Medhurst, China's once great civilisation was now in decline. Qing China, in spite of the civilisational potential of its population, was moving backwards. The 'reclamation' of Chinese civilisation could be interpreted as the opening of China to Western trade or religion; as a justification for war; or to promote emigration into the British Empire. These different openings demonstrated the various routes to civilisational salvation.

The conclusion of many British observers was that if the Chinese were more civilised than other Asian racial groups, but inhibited by a despotic government and some innate character flaws, they would be able to prosper under British rule. Chinese despotism should not just be removed, it should also make way for British civilisation.[108] The *Canton Register* invoked the most

[103] Reginald Horsman, 'Origins of Racial Anglo-Saxonism in Great Britain before 1850', *Journal of the History of Ideas*, 37, 3 (1976), 388.
[104] *Chinese Repository*, Vol. I (1833), 328. Such criticism of the 'Tartars' could also be found in the writing of Lord Macartney, which was not published at the time of the Embassy.
[105] *Canton Register*, 15 December 1835.
[106] Specifically the belief that 'knowledge' and 'civilisation' in China were decreasing under the Qing was articulated in letters to the *Canton Register*, 8 March 1832.
[107] Medhurst, *China*, 87.
[108] Hillemann, *Asian Empire and British Knowledge*, 106–49.

British of symbols, John Bull, to criticise the authoritarian Qing Empire in an article titled 'Happiness of the Chinese'. The *Register* asked, 'what would John Bull think of being sentenced to be pilloried for two or three months; beaten with a hundred cudgel blows, and transported three years, for killing an ox in order to eat it?'[109] In an article titled 'Barbarism – Civilisation', the *Register* invoked the global progress of the Anglo-world as evidence that the Chinese must convert to British notions of governance and international relations:[110]

> By what right are the aborigines of North America and New Holland driven from their indisputable homes by the governments of the United States and Great Britain? By no other than that barbarism must vanish before civilisation, ignorance succumb to knowledge: such appears to be a law of nature, or rather, the will of God![111]

The comparison of the Chinese with 'the aborigines of North America and New Holland' shows the importance of notions of civilisation as a justification for British, and more broadly Western, imperialism. These notions underwrote Jardine Matheson's challenge of Qing authority. Such a comparison simultaneously emphasised the perceived contrast in terms of civilisation between the Chinese and indigenous colonial populations. The specific problem in the case of China was the Qing dynasty's despotic rule: 'the intrigue and deceit of the Chinese, and the rude courage of the Tartar, seem to unite in what may be considered the present national character of China'.[112] The prevailing argument of the 1830s was that to liberate the southern Han Chinese from their current rulers and place them under British rule would be mutually beneficial. The British Empire provided the context for the construction of new perspectives on China and the Chinese. These concepts of Chinese character as compatible with British authority were not just being discussed in newspapers and travel literature but were already tested in the contact zone of Singapore in the 1820s and 1830s.

Concepts of a homogeneous Chinese national character, or even a binary divide between Chinese people and state, were complicated by variations of language, class and geography. For the Western mercantile community, the Chinese merchant elites and Chinese compradors were particularly important groups in facilitating the China trade. They therefore attracted special praise in contrast to the Chinese populace as a whole. Economic necessity

---

109   *Canton Register*, 25 March 1834.

110   For more on the concept of an 'Anglo-world' see James Belich, *Replenishing the Earth: The Settler Revolution and the Rise of the Anglo-World, 1783–1939* (Oxford: Oxford University Press, 2009).

111   *Canton Register*, 30 December 1834. This extract also points to the influence of notions of civilisation and improvement in post-enlightenment Scotland as discussed in Richard J. Grace, *Opium and Empire: The Lives and Careers of William Jardine and James Matheson* (Montreal & Kingston: McGill-Queen's University Press, 2014).

112   *Chinese Repository*, Vol. I (1833), 328.

motivated this praise, but class distinctions and a mutual understanding of commercial respectability were also important. Hugh Hamilton Lindsay – the aggressive free trade advocate, East India Company official, pamphleteer, and later MP – wrote of the Chinese merchant elite's 'high character' and suggested that 'it would be difficult to find, in any community of merchants, men more alive to the feelings of humanity'.[113] The close business relationship between merchants and 'respectable' Chinese was perhaps no better demonstrated than by the role of the Chinese buyers for Western firms, later known as compradors.[114]

Chinese compradors were employed by Western merchant houses to conduct sales and purchases from Chinese merchants. The responsibility of compradors implied a high level of trust as Western merchants often lacked the necessary linguistic abilities to properly monitor transactions or negotiate with Chinese business partners.[115] Jardine Matheson were particularly reliant on Chinese staff as they employed a house steward (or lead comprador), a provisions comprador, a cash comprador and an operational comprador, who as a group acted as a 'Chinese firm within a foreign firm'.[116] A good example of the closeness of these business relationships was the Western defence of comprador turned Hong merchant Aming in 1836. The Canton authorities tried and prosecuted Aming for his involvement in smuggling. The Western merchant community petitioned Chinese officials for his release, publicised his plight, and many prominent merchants visited him during his incarceration.[117] The close mutual interests of Western merchants and their Chinese employees and business partners meant that criticisms and negative tropes attached to the Chinese character or Qing officials often omitted these groups. This mirrored the symbiotic relationship between merchant elites in colonial Singapore.

More important than class difference or economic cooperation, particularly with regard to emigration, was Chinese regional and linguistic variations – though Western observers did not always identify such distinctions. For example, whilst recognised as a China expert, Charles Gutzlaff described China as the 'largest and most homogenous nation' in the world.[118] Many of Gutzlaff's contemporaries, and subsequent historians, have emphasised

---

[113] Hugh Hamilton Lindsay, *The Rupture with China and Its Causes; Including the Opium Question, and Other Important Details: In a Letter to Lord Viscount Palmerston, Secretary for Foreign Affairs* (London: Sherwood, Gilbert, and Piper, 1840), 4; see Bickers, 'The Challenger', for an overview of Lindsay's activities.

[114] For a discussion of the term 'comprador' see Kaori Abe, 'The City of Intermediaries: Compradors in Hong Kong, 1830s to 1880s' (Ph.D. thesis, University of Bristol, 2014).

[115] Solomon Bard, *Traders of Hong Kong: Some Foreign Merchant Houses, 1841–1899* (Hong Kong: Hong Kong Museum of History, 1993), 46.

[116] Wai Kwan Chan, *The Making of Hong Kong Society: Three Studies of Class Formation in Early Hong Kong* (Oxford: Clarendon Press, 1991), 55–7.

[117] C. Toogood Downing, *The Stranger in China* (Philadelphia: Lea & Blanchard, 1838), 127–31.

[118] Charles Gutzlaff, *China Opened, Vol. I* (London: Smith, Elder and Co., 1838), 286.

the significance of regional variations. As Fairbank and Gregory have high-lighted, China's regions are equivalent to European nation states in terms of geographical size, population, linguistic divergence and cultural identity, if not political autonomy.[119] The idea of China as a nation of nations is certainly tangible if we accept the primacy of language as a marker of national identity. For example, Chapter 1 showed how in the writing of Seah Eu Chin, the Chinese community of Singapore was a good example of this divergence as the Chinese in the colony were separated into six 'tribes' based on dialect groupings.[120] It is also important to stress that the identification of Chinese regional distinctions often took place in contact zones that were external to China.

Existing literature has underplayed the extent to which migration was essential to Western knowledge of regional difference. Chinese emigrants would form ethnic associations based on points of geographical origin in their adopted homelands.[121] Migrants of a shared dialect group would often relocate to the same destinations due to local and familial networks. Linguistically or regionally connected migrants would form a *qiaoxiang*, or 'emigrant community', which reflected the social structures of mainland China.[122] As the vast majority of emigrants were from southern China it was common for Western colonial observers to emphasise regional distinctions with the north.[123] One of the main regions of emigration, Fukien (Fujian province), was particularly singled out for praise by Western authors, in contrast to northern China. For example, Robert Mudie wrote of Fukien, 'the inhabitants of this province are remarkably industrious'.[124] Socio-economic practices, such as footbinding, were particularly useful as identifiers of regional difference and allowed for Western promotion of the perceived inherent character traits of southern over northern Chinese.[125] The acknowledgement of Chinese regional difference, based around concepts like 'industriousness', served the broader narrative of a Chinese population that could be separated conceptually from the Qing Empire. Ironically, the fact that China was an empire – with Taiwan, Mongolia and Tibet all politically attached to 'China proper'

---

[119] John King Fairbank, *The Great Chinese Revolution, 1800–1985* (New York: Harper & Row, 1986), 9; Gregory, *The West and China since 1500*, 21.

[120] Siah, 'The Chinese in Singapore', 284.

[121] Kuhn, *Chinese among Others*, 42.

[122] Pan, *The Encyclopaedia of the Chinese Overseas*, 27. The term *qiaoxiang* refers to both 'overseas Chinese townships' as well as areas in China that were affected by high levels of emigration and therefore received preferential treatment from the Chinese state: see Mette Thuno, *Beyond Chinatown: New Chinese Migration and the Global Expansion of China* (Copenhagen: NIAS Press, 2006), 13.

[123] These distinctions also fed into the undermining of the Manchu Qing dynasty as ruling with an illegitimate despotism over the southern Han Chinese.

[124] Robert Mudie, *China and its Resources, A Notice of Assam* (London: Grattan and Gilbert, 1840), 86.

[125] Harrison, *China*, 23.

over the 1600s – opened the Qing to criticism from agents of British impe-rialism.[126] The north-south distinction heavily fed into the idea that the Han Chinese of the southern regions required liberation from their despotic rulers.

The *Register*'s first major competitor, the American-owned *Chinese Courier and Canton Gazette*, was similarly critical of both Chinese and British trade regulations.[127] The American firm Russell & Co. funded the paper and it primarily criticised the East India Company monopoly, which was why the paper ceased publication in 1833 with the passing of the Charter Act.[128] Both Canton newspapers enthusiastically advocated Chinese emigration. In particular, emigration was described as a necessary solution to China's impending Malthusian crisis. An 1832 *Courier* article on the 'Chinese Poor' criticised the 'low price of wages and the overplus of working people, famine and inundation too often contribute to overwhelm the inhabitants of whole districts of the country'.[129] Similarly, in 1834 the *Register* published an editorial concerned with the surplus population of China. This article criticised the Qing Empire 'which caused them [the Chinese people] to abhor foreigners and to crowd under the protection of their native leaders'.[130] This criticism fitted with the firm's broad critique of the tyranny of the Chinese Emperor but was also connected to the issue of emigration. The *Register*'s owners and editors hoped that 'excess finds an outlet in emigration, we fondly hope the threatening evil may be averted from this empire'.[131] The firm's desire for China to open its borders advocated such an opening in both directions. In the pre-Opium War context of the 1830s a warning was offered for the cost of Chinese isolationism: 'if they do not advance with the world they will sooner or later fall a sacrifice to their stubbornness'.[132] Invoking Western notions of political economy, such as the theories of Malthus, allowed restric-tions on emigration to be seamlessly critiqued as part of a broader ideological attack on the isolationism of the Qing Empire.

The promotion of Chinese emigration also drew on knowledge of existing Chinese expatriate communities. Citing the *Singapore Chronicle*, which was a common source, the *Register* referred positively to Chinese emigration as early as 1828:[133]

---

[126] Patricia Buckley Ebrey, *The Cambridge Illustrated History of China* (Cambridge: Cambridge University Press, 2010), 227.
[127] From April 1832 the title was simply styled the *Chinese Courier*.
[128] Frank H. H. King, *A Research Guide to China-Coast Newspapers, 1822–1911* (Harvard: Harvard University Press, 1965), 46.
[129] *Chinese Courier*, 23 June 1832.
[130] *Canton Register*, 7 October 1834.
[131] Ibid.
[132] Ibid.
[133] The *Singapore Chronicle* was the first English-language newspaper in Singapore (1824) and benefited from the reciprocal re-printing of stories from the *Register*. John Crawfurd edited the *Chronicle* in the 1820s. For more on Singapore newspapers see C. M. Turnbull, 'The European Mercantile Community in Singapore, 1819–1867', *Journal of Southeast Asian History*,

> Although strictly forbidden by the law of China, [emigration] is still practised to a very considerable extent; and we observe in the *Singapore Chronicle* that the arrival lately of four junks, brought upwards of 1600 passengers ... over-population, which we imagine to be the case in many parts of China, this voluntary retirement must be very beneficial ... a large majority of these people are of the class of mechanics, carpenters, blacksmiths, and various other handicrafts, they have been found of the highest use.[134]

Again, the despotism of the Chinese government was highlighted, but the migration of Chinese workers to replace Malay labour was viewed as positively on the China coast as it was in Singapore. The *Courier* concurred with the *Register*. In a multiple issue report on 'Chinese Emigrants' from 1832 the *Courier* identified Chinese overpopulation as necessitating emigration and suggested – in line with the Opium War narrative of liberation – that migration benefited the Chinese people: 'where these emigrants are permitted to enjoy their rights of property and personal liberty, no fault is to be found with them, they are obedient, frugal, temperate, and industrious'.[135] This view of emigration further reflects the separation of the Qing Empire from the Chinese people, and underlines connection of this separation to the view of an industrious and economically productive Chinese character. As conflict with Chinese authorities intensified during the Opium War, the British Empire loomed increasingly large as a space in which the 'rights' and 'liberty' of the 'industrious' Chinese could be properly protected.

Conclusion

This chapter demonstrates how discussions about Chinese labour in Singapore took place in a broader context of British discussions about the Chinese character. This is not to say that the character traits ascribed to the Chinese were uniformly accepted – as the multiplicity of ideas and their inherent contradictions illustrate – but that the general concept that Chinese people would thrive if freed from despotism lent itself to the promotion of Chinese emigration into the British Empire. It was in the interests of China-coast missionaries and merchants alike to present the Qing Empire as a despotic entity from which liberation – either spiritual or economic – was necessary. The consequence of this rhetoric of liberation was the inevitable emigration of such 'money-loving a people as the Chinese' to British colonies.[136]

    Singapore also fulfilled an important role in the debates about the China trade as the colonial experience allowed figures like John Crawfurd to claim

---

     10 (1969), 14.

[134] *Canton Register*, 9 August 1828.

[135] *Chinese Courier*, 29 September 1832 and 6 October 1832.

[136] *Essex Standard*, 2 December 1842.

expert status. In turn, British merchant firms who operated on the China coast and had a vested interest in a more liberal economic relationship with the Qing Empire supported Crawfurd's critique of the East India Company monopoly and praise of the Chinese as an industrious people. The dominant anti-Qing narrative did confirm certain perceptions of Chinese character. Consequently, figures who promoted Chinese migration as a solution to labour shortages in the British Empire invoked this notion of character. Even when emigration was not explicitly discussed, it was still assumed to be part of the broader opening that needed to take place. Both trading restrictions on foreign merchants and controls on migration inhibited the innate, entrepreneurial tendencies of the Chinese people. Similarly, China's large population was a reason to both criticise the Qing as ineffective and advocate emigration as a pre-emptive solution to the predicted humanitarian crisis. Broad British discussions of China over the 1830s affected discourse on the necessity and desirability of Chinese emigration and Chinese labour in the British Empire.

What were the practical ramifications of these ideas about the Chinese character? The following chapters outline the movements of Chinese emigrants to new imperial destinations in the 1830s and 1840s. Importantly, as Western merchant firms circumvented Qing trade restrictions to sell opium they also facilitated the movement of Chinese labourers and artisans from southern China to British colonial possessions. At the same time, the economic needs of plantation colonies that were developing agricultural exports without recourse to recently abolished systems of slave labour drove the demand for migrant labour. These schemes drew on the belief that Chinese migrants possessed an innate racial character that was more economically productive than the alternatives and predisposed to thrive under British governance.

Chapter 3

CROSSING THE INDIAN OCEAN: CHINESE LABOUR IN SOUTH ASIA AND BEYOND

Perceptions of a Chinese character, one that was suited to provide a colonial labour force under British governance, had been developed in Singapore and disseminated by propaganda from Western merchants on the China coast. But what were the applications of the Chinese migrant labour beyond the limits of contact zones on the China coast or in Southeast Asia? Examining new experiments with Chinese labour migration in the 1830s and 1840s reveals the continuing construction of the Chinese character as a useful tool for colonial production. Chinese migrants were particularly desirable in different colonies that required skilled and unskilled, cheap and free labour. The timing of this phenomenon was crucial, with two connected changes re-shaping the British Empire's economic development from the 1830s. Parallel to the abolition of slavery in 1833, unremunerative British colonies underwent a rapid transformation into plantation-based 'resource pools'.[1] This process is neatly summarised by Alessandro Stanziani:

> Growing demand in the West for raw materials and other tropical products led British colonizers to set up modern plantations as agro-industrial enterprises in several colonies of the British Empire, including India. Sugar, coffee or tea emerged as the most profitable products in the Caribbean, Fiji, Mauritius, Mala and Ceylon, as well as in Assam, Bengal, the northern Himalayas and southern parts of colonial India.[2]

Without access to African slave labour or voluntary European colonists, such as those who populated Britain's settler colonies, the colonial administrators who tried to boost plantation agriculture and develop export economies

---

[1]   P. J. Cain and A. G. Hopkins, *British Imperialism: Innovation and Expansion, 1688–2000* (London: Longman, 2013), 102.

[2]   Alessandro Stanziani, *Labor on the Fringes of Empire: Voice, Exit and the Law* (Cham: Palgrave Macmillan, 2018), 8. Note that abolition had implications well beyond the West Indies: see Hideaki Suzuki, ed., *Abolitions as a Global Experience* (Singapore: NUS Press, 2016).

looked to Chinese migration to Singapore as a model. Crucially, the desire for Chinese labour was not purely economic but part of a broader ideology of colonial improvement. As in Singapore, economic necessity and ideas about race were intertwined.

This chapter brings together three case studies, which demonstrate the different ways in which colonial authorities sourced Chinese labour for new colonial settings. The first case study is the development of tea planting experiments in Assam in the 1830s. In order to develop tea plantations for the production of tea for export to Britain, colonial projects in Assam recruited Chinese tea cultivators from both China and Singapore. The second case this chapter examines is the repeated attempts to introduce Chinese colonists to Ceylon in a period notable for increased metropolitan and economic pressure on Indian Ocean plantation colonies. The governorship of James Alexander Stewart-Mackenzie is a central concern. In particular, this section focuses on labour shortages on the island and the desire of Stewart-Mackenzie to follow the model of Singapore and Assam by using Chinese labour as part of a programme of colonial improvement. The repeated efforts to introduce Chinese labourers into Ceylon in the late 1830s and early 1840s reflected the impact that the British concepts of Chinese character and Singapore had on labour migration. Finally, there is a discussion of the role of the Colonial Land and Emigration Commission – formed in January 1840 – in overseeing migration policy generally and filling colonial labour needs. The Empire-wide interest in labour and migration led to efforts to replicate existing systems of migration to new colonial destinations, such as Mauritius and the West Indies. Not only did these experiments lead to a confirmation of certain ideas about the Chinese character, they also influenced the formation of new racial hierarchies by comparing Chinese migrants with different indigenous communities. Ultimately these case studies demonstrate how ideas about Chinese character and colonisation, developed in Singapore, were tested, with varying degrees of success, in different plantation colonies over the 1830s and 1840s.

The Assam Project

The 1830s, a decade of tumultuous Anglo-Chinese diplomatic relations, were marked by British fears about the future supply of tea from China.[3] Politicians and tea merchants worried that an over-reliance on a single producer that lay outside direct colonial authority would leave Britain's tea supply, and

---

[3]   British concern over maintaining access to Chinese markets in the 1830s has been discussed in depth in the following articles: John M. Carroll, 'The Canton System: Conflict and Accommodation in the Contact Zone', *Journal of the Royal Asiatic Society Hong Kong Branch*, 50 (2010), 51–66; Gao, 'Prelude to the Opium War?'; Melancon, 'Peaceful Intentions', 33–47.

therefore Britain's import revenues and the East India Company's profitability, at risk.[4] Consequently, the discovery of wild tea plants in the Northeast Indian region of Assam provided scope for British-owned tea production and an opportunity to move away from commercial reliance on China. The drawback was that China and tea were 'synonymous' and that metropolitan consumers would be suspicious of new, Indian, tea.[5] This section will examine one of the solutions to this conundrum: the recruitment of Chinese tea cultivators to work on tea plantations in Assam.[6]

Like Singapore, the Assam tea plantations acted as a new contact zone in which colonial observers constructed and tested racial hierarchies. As Jayeeta Sharma suggests, the 'civilised' Chinese tea cultivators acted as a counterpoint to the 'savage' Assamese natives in the colonial mind-set.[7] The situation was, however, never quite so simple. A sense of mistrust informed attitudes towards Chinese cultivators and, despite colonial hierarchies that emphasised native laziness, indigenous peoples came to play an essential role in the production of Assam tea. Yet these narratives of racial superiority and stratification were connected to the recruitment of labour. As in Singapore, the recruitment of Chinese tea cultivators from the China coast in the 1830s fed into both the economic development of British imperialism in Asia and the ideologies of racial hierarchy that were used to justify colonial control.

Following the 'discovery' of wild tea plants in Assam in the 1820s, the East India Company established a Tea Committee in January 1834 under the direction of Governor-General of India William Bentinck to begin the experimental cultivation of tea in Assam.[8] In 1834, at the same time as the establishment of the Tea Committee, William Napier, the first 'Superintendent of the China Trade', was dispatched to Canton. Though Napier famously failed to aggressively establish a new diplomatic protocol, it must be emphasised that the primary concern of British foreign policy under Palmerston was not necessarily to overtly challenge the Chinese state, but to maintain and protect

[4] Nicholas Dirks, *The Scandal of Empire: India and the Creation of Imperial Britain* (London: Harvard University Press, 2008), 143.

[5] Jayeeta Sharma, 'Lazy Natives, Coolie Labour, and the Assam Tea Industry', *Modern Asian Studies*, 43, 6 (2009), 1289.

[6] This episode has been discussed by Jayeeta Sharma, *Empire's Garden: Assam and the Making of India* (London: Duke University Press, 2011); H. A. Antrobus, *The History of the Assam Company, 1839–1953* (Edinburgh: T. and A. Constable Ltd, 1957); Stan Neal, 'Opium and Migration: Jardine Matheson's Imperial Connections and the Recruitment of Chinese Labour for Assam, 1834–1839', *Modern Asian Studies*, 51, 5 (2017), 1626–55.

[7] Sharma, *Empire's Garden*.

[8] Antrobus, *The History of the Assam Company*, 5; Anonymous, *Assam: a sketch of its history, soil, and productions* (London: Smith, Elder and Co., 1839), 24. Of course, the idea of a 'discovery' is a Western misnomer; locals had long made use of the tea plant: S. K. Sharma and Usha Sharma, eds, *North-East India: Volume 5 Assam – Economy, Society and Culture* (New Delhi: Mittal, 2005), 40.

the tea trade from potential disruption.[9] The first line of the Tea Committee's 'proposition' neatly summarised their view that 'the commercial relations of this country with China have lately assumed a character of uncertainty'.[10] The tea trade's economic value meant its continuation was a priority for both Indian and British authorities – by the 1830s it brought £4 million per annum to the East India Company and provided seven per cent of Britain's public revenue in excise duties.[11] An Indian supply of tea would circumvent China, meaning any diplomatic breakdown over opium smuggling would not threaten the lucrative trade. In addition to the economic benefits of Indian tea production, the language used by Tea Committee members demonstrated an attitude of civilisational superiority that was ubiquitous in British imperial planning.[12] For example, the Tea Committee Secretary, the director of the East India Company's botanic garden at Calcutta, Nathaniel Wallich, made the case that it was imperative to not be 'dependent on the will and caprice of a despotic nation for the supply of one of the greatest comforts and luxuries of civilized life'.[13] Here Wallich implied not only that the cultivation and consumption of tea was a mark of civilisation, but that the Chinese state, as 'despotic', was inherently untrustworthy. For Wallich, the future of Britain's tea supply could not be left to the Chinese state or Assamese natives, but required the guidance and management of the civilised British.

As well as the need for Chinese expertise to both produce and provide marketable legitimacy for the tea, colonial concepts of racial hierarchy influenced the desire for Chinese labour. For John Crawfurd, the very existence of a Chinese tea industry and absence of an Indian tea industry was indicative of Chinese superiority. Writing in 1829, Crawfurd determined that the Chinese 'character' was 'peculiarly adapted to the tedious manipulation indispensable to the preparation of tea'.[14] By contrast Crawfurd lamented that 'not one pound of tea has ever been grown in our Indian possessions' in spite of the similar climatic conditions and the wild growth of the tea plant.[15] This failure was ascribed to the 'unskillfulness of the Indians in almost everything approaching to manufacturing', in contrast to the 'superior skill of the

---

[9]   Melancon, 'Peaceful Intentions', 33–47; Gao, 'Prelude to the Opium War?', 491–509.

[10] Proposition to the Honourable Directors of the East India Company to Cultivate Tea upon the Nepaul Hills, and such other parts of the Territories of the East India Company as may be suitable to its growth. By Mr. Walker, in Parliamentary Papers, *Tea Cultivation (India). Return to an order of the Honourable the House of Commons, dated 15 February 1839;—for, copy of papers received from India relating to the measures adopted for introducing the cultivation of the tea plant within the British possessions in India*, 1839 (63), 6.

[11] Lawson, *The East India Company*, 157.

[12] See Pitts, *A Turn to Empire* on the centrality of civilisational superiority as the guiding philosophy of imperial expansion.

[13] N. Wallich, 'Observations on the Cultivation of the Tea plant, for Commercial purposes, in the mountainous parts of Hindostan', Parliamentary Papers, *Tea Cultivation*, 15.

[14] Crawfurd, *View of the Present State and Future Prospects of the Free Trade and Colonisation of India*, 18.

[15] Ibid.,18.

Chinese'.[16] The cultivation of tea not only required specialist knowledge, but it implied skill and consequently a degree of civilisation. Colonial observers interpreted the lack of a pre-existing Indian tea industry as an indictment of Indian civilisation more generally. These were long-standing notions of comparative civilisation; there had been plans to establish a Chinese colony at Calcutta in 1783.[17] Importantly, as seen in Chapter 2, Crawfurd's opinion was that of a well-respected and experienced expert, with currency in both India and Britain.

While Crawfurd criticised the 'Indians' generally, other British observers maligned the population of Assam specifically. Jayeeta Sharma's work has discussed how colonial authorities perceived the Assamese as lazy and opium-addicted.[18] Opium, like tea, grew naturally in the region and addiction amongst the Assamese was seen to be such a problem that private opium cultivation was banned and the Indian Government was given a monopoly of opium production in the area in 1861.[19] Charles Bruce, who managed the Assam tea plantations, lamented how opium 'has degenerated the Assamese from a fine race of people to the most abject, servile, crafty and demoralized race in India'.[20] Not only was Assamese savagery emphasised by those on the ground, such as Bruce, but it was directly contrasted with Chinese civilisation in contemporary scientific discourse. Dr John McCosh, of the Bengal Medical Service, wrote accounts of the region's typography that both British and colonial newspapers and journals reprinted. Writing in the *Singapore Chronicle* he emphasised how Assam was 'thinly populated by strangling hordes of slowly procreating barbarians, and allowed to lie profitless in a primeval jungle', but not completely cut off from enterprising 'Chinese merchants, [who] by a short land journey across these mountains convey [sic] their merchandise on mules'.[21] The mountainous border between Assam in Northeast India and Yunnan in Northwest China was imagined as a line between savagery and civilisation. This division fits within the broad tradition of state formation in Southeast Asia discussed by James C. Scott. The Assamese 'hill tribes' were viewed as a 'barbarian periphery' that would either have to be changed or removed in order for the British to achieve their aim of commercial tea production.[22] In the context of the 1830s the Chinese were not only necessary

---

[16] Crawfurd, *View of the Present State and Future Prospects of the Free Trade and Colonisation of India*, 19.

[17] Richard B. Allen, 'Slaves, Convicts, Abolitionism and the Global Origins of the Post-Emancipation Indentured Labour System', *Slavery & Abolition*, 35, 2 (2014), 334.

[18] Sharma, *Empire's Garden*, 5.

[19] Sharma, 'Lazy Natives, Coolie Labour, and the Assam Tea Industry', 1297; the peculiar irony being that Chinese opium addiction had maintained the economic viability of the tea trade.

[20] George Thompson, *Report of a Public Meeting and Lecture at Darlington … on China and the Opium Question* (Durham: J. H. Veitch, 1840), 13.

[21] *Singapore Chronicle*, 6 August 1836; *Asiatic Journal*, Vol. 26, 1838.

[22] Scott, *The Art of Not Being Governed*, 1–40.

as tea cultivators with specific expertise, but were expected to provide an industrious, skilled and compliant labour force in contrast to native laziness and resistance.[23]

The Tea Committee decided that the initial experiment in tea production would require a limited number of Chinese experts 'employed to instruct the natives' under the direction of Charles Bruce in Assam.[24] This plan was partly modelled on the Dutch use of Chinese tea cultivators in Java and heavily influenced by existing systems of Chinese migration in the British Empire.[25] Governor-General Bentinck had travelled to Malacca and Singapore in 1829 to 'observe the Chinese character' and had been impressed.[26] Again, this elevation of character underlines how concepts of hierarchy factored into the Tea Committee's decision making. Bentinck later outlined his plan that an agent should be appointed to obtain Chinese tea cultivators and samples of Chinese tea plants.[27] On Bentinck's instruction, George J. Gordon, a former employee of the bankrupt Indian merchant firm Mackintosh & Co., was sent to the China coast in 1834 to procure Chinese tea seeds and tea cultivators.[28] With Gordon on an exploratory mission, Bruce preparing a tea plantation in Assam, and Wallich overseeing the whole operation from Calcutta, the Assam tea experiment began.

In June 1834, Gordon headed, aboard the *Water Witch*, to Canton with instructions to gather information about Chinese tea manufacturing as well as to acquire seeds, plants and tea makers.[29] He was sent to Canton with 'a recommendation from this Government to the British authorities at Canton … to procure for Mr Gordon any facilities or protection that may be found necessary', and to fund his endeavours an account for '20,000 to 25,000 dollars placed at his command'.[30] That quality, rather than quantity, was required was also emphasised in Gordon's instructions: 'It will be Mr Gordon's principal duty to bring round a select, rather than numerous, body of planters; men qualified to conduct every operation connected with the production of good tea.'[31] It was suggested that the project need not exceed fifty recruits. Gordon opted to recruit tea cultivators from the Bohea hills

---

[23] Hillemann, *Asian Empire and British Knowledge*, 128.
[24] W. H. Macnaughten to the Tea Committee, 18 April 1836, Parliamentary Papers, *Tea Cultivation*, 63.
[25] The Dutch experience is referred to in the correspondence of the Tea Committee: Tea Committee to C. Macsween, 15 March 1834, Parliamentary Papers, *Tea Cultivation*, 17.
[26] Douglas M. Peers, 'Bentinck, Lord William Henry Cavendish- (1774–1839)', *Oxford Dictionary of National Biography*, Oxford University Press, 2004; online edn, October 2009, www.oxforddnb.com/view/article/2161 (accessed 30 September 2018); Sharma, *Empire's Garden*, 35.
[27] *Assam*, 23.
[28] *Assam*, 24; W. C. Bentinck, 24 January 1834, Parliamentary Papers, *Tea Cultivation*, 6.
[29] Antrobus, *The History of the Assam Company*, 30.
[30] The Tea Committee to C. Macsween, 15 March 1834, Parliamentary Papers, *Tea Cultivation*, 17.
[31] Ibid.

(Wuyi Shan), a district notable for black tea production some 300 kilometres inland, after visiting several different tea districts. In doing so he relied on the opium trading networks of British opium merchants.[32] Gordon's notes on the subject reveal a hierarchy of Chinese tea cultivators as he explained that 'the inferiority of Ankoy tea arises from unskilful culture and preparation of the leaf … I made, therefore, no offer to the peasantry at Twa-Be, to accompany me to Bengal as planters'.[33] Gordon recruited the Bohea planters through a 'native agent', who remained un-named, and expected the arrival of his recruits at Canton in January 1835.[34] By March 1835 it had been realised that the tea plant in Assam was viable and Gordon was recalled from the China coast.[35]

With the help of Chinese tea cultivators, the first batch of Assam tea arrived in London in November 1838, where metropolitan experts inspected the tea and adjudged it to be of satisfactory quality. It was first auctioned (at an inflated price due to the high level of public interest) in January 1839.[36] The landing of the tea in Britain and the developing animosities with China meant that Assam tea and the Assam region were a hot topic of discussion in the British press in early 1839. In January various metropolitan and provincial titles remarked on the 'curiosity among commercial men to the first sale of the specimens'.[37] Additionally, on 15 February, the House of Commons ordered a 'Copy of papers received from India relating to the measures adopted for introducing the Cultivation of the Tea Plant within the British Possessions in India' from the East India Company.[38] The resulting Parliamentary Paper, which mainly comprised the correspondence to and from the Tea Committee, was published two weeks later by East India House, providing an insight into the development of Assam's tea plantations.[39] Most significantly, the Assam Company was formed at a meeting of London merchants on 14 February 1839, with an available capital of £500,000 in 10,000 shares of £50 each and with outspoken merchant and nobleman George Gerard de Hochepied Larpent as its Chairman.[40] The privatisation of the Assam tea plantations

[32] For a full discussion of this process see Neal, 'Opium and Migration'.

[33] The Tea Committee to C. Macsween, 15 March 1834, Parliamentary Papers, *Tea Cultivation*, 17.

[34] Ibid., 42. Bizarrely, Gordon also gave tea seeds to the widow of William Napier to plant in Scotland.

[35] Tea Committee, 12 March 1835, Parliamentary Papers, *Tea Cultivation*, 39.

[36] Antrobus, *The History of the Assam Company*, 265.

[37] *Yorkshire Gazette*, 19 January 1839; *The Era*, 13 January 1839.

[38] Parliamentary Papers, *Tea cultivation (India). Return to an order of the Honourable the House of Commons, dated 15 February 1839;—for, copy of papers received from India relating to the measures adopted for introducing the cultivation of the tea plant within the British possessions in India*, 1839 (63).

[39] This publication was approved by Robert Gordon, the Commissioner of the Board of Control, at the request of the Assam Company.

[40] Antrobus, *The History of the Assam Company*, 37. In this meeting of the Assam Company it was discussed that the East India Company had agreed to 'speedily make available' information on Assam: Minute book of the Assam Company, 12 February 1839–17 December 1845, in MS 9924/1 (London Metropolitan Archives).

had been planned from the outset, though the Assam Company did not take direct control of the tea plantations until early in 1840.[41]

Despite the success of the tea in Britain, there had been problems with the Chinese tea cultivators in Assam. Many of Gordon's secondary recruits had arrived in Assam dishevelled and impoverished (they thought their expenses were covered separately from their wages) and had to be compensated. For the 1839 recruitment Wallich approached the opium traders Jardine Matheson directly. By this point the firm had emerged as the dominant private merchant house on the China coast. Jardine Matheson made copies of contracts with twelve Chinese tea cultivators, which named James Matheson personally.[42] All of the contracts ran from 15 August 1839 for five years and were identical in structure.[43] Following the recruitment of the twelve tea cultivators in August 1839, Matheson explained to Wallich the difficulties caused by the start of the First Opium War. Matheson wrote that 'in these troublesome times … the attention of the Chinese Govt. has lately been drawn to the subject, and they have issued many severe proclamations against those who may aid or abet the emigration of their subjects'.[44] In the last round of Chinese recruitment to be conducted by the firm for the Assam experiment Matheson was able to recruit fourteen tea cultivators as well as eight lacquerers and box makers, meeting the requirements that had been outlined by Wallich. The firm's opium trading vessels the *Charlotte* and the *Red Rover* shipped recruits to Calcutta.[45] Unfortunately for the Tea Committee, the hostilities of the First Opium War, from early 1839, destabilised the firm's access to the tea cultivating regions of China.

Following the commercial success of the first Assam teas, the Assam Company began trading in 1839. The new Company took control of production in Assam in the first tea season of 1840.[46] The Assam Company, with its high levels of available capital, hired Dr Lumqua, a man of high esteem whose salary had been too expensive for the Tea Committee, to manage the Chinese workers in Assam and arrange further Chinese recruitment.[47] On the advice of Lumqua, a Chinese agent (styled Eekan or E-kan) was appointed

41 Antrobus, *The History of the Assam Company*, 269.
42 These contracts are still located in the Jardine Matheson Archive at Cambridge University Library.
43 Tea Cultivator Contracts, in MS JM/F11, Jardine Matheson Archive (Cambridge University Library).
44 James Matheson (Hong Kong) to Dr N. Wallich (Calcutta), 25 September 1839, in MS JM/C10, Jardine Matheson Archive (Cambridge University Library).
45 Matheson to Wallich, 25 September 1839, in MS JM/C10.
46 Wilson Gow and Stanton Gow, eds, *Tea Producing companies of India and Ceylon: showing the History and Results of those Capitalised in Sterling* (London: A. Southey & Co., 1897), 3.
47 Dr Lumqua's salary of 1,110 Rs. can be compared to the total labourers' advance of 20,586 Rs. prior to 31 December 1839, from *Report of the Bengal Branch of the Assam Company* (Calcutta: Samuel Smith & Co., 1840), 17.

to hire Chinese labourers from Penang and Singapore.[48] Eekan was able to recruit 216 labourers from Penang and 245 from Singapore but, in these easily accessible contact zones outside of China, he was 'not successful in finding any experienced artisans'.[49] Instead these recruits were intended to become apprentices under tea makers already in Assam who would develop into skilled tea artisans.

The Assam Company's Chinese recruitment from the Straits Settlements was vastly more problematic than the recruitment of Jardine Matheson. In February 1840 nine Chinese labourers, out of a group of 105 intended for Assam, were arrested and put on trial for assault at Bogra. Bruce warned that too many Chinese workers were arriving as he was still in the government's military service and could not devote the time to manage the plantation.[50] Eekan's shipment of Chinese labourers from Singapore arrived the next month. However, after fifty-seven labourers were arrested over an affray in which a local was killed at Pabna, the remainder of the 'gang' refused to move to Assam without a 'further advance of pay, and supplies of opium and provisions'.[51] After three months the group was completely abandoned in northern India. The Assam Company regretted 'that so many lawless characters should be let loose upon society'.[52] Reports of this episode attribute the failure to poor selection of workers by Eekan and the poor character of the Chinese from Penang and Singapore. Additionally, those who did reach the stations in Assam fell victim to fever – a common occurrence in the Assamese jungle. The failure of this scheme to source unskilled labour from Singapore cost the Assam Company vast amounts of money.[53] Further recruitment projects were also doomed by the death of Lumqua in August 1840 who, according to the 1841 Report of the Local Directors, had been 'a kind of Captain, with Magisterial powers, among his countrymen'.[54] As a result the Assam Company began to seek alternative forms of labour.

From early in the Assam Company's ownership and management of the Assam plantations the Company placed emphasis on the diffusion of specialist knowledge and abilities away from the specialist Chinese artisans. For example, the first annual report of the Assam Company remarked how one particular establishment had produced tea, despite consisting of 'only two Chinese black tea makers, with twelve native assistants'.[55] There was a growing realisation

---

[48] *Report of the Bengal Branch of the Assam Company*, 9.
[49] Ibid., 9.
[50] Ibid., 378; note the implication that the Chinese required British supervision.
[51] Assam Company, *Report of the Local Directors made to the Shareholders at a General Meeting, held at Calcutta, August 11th, 1841* (Calcutta: Bishop's College Press, 1841), 5.
[52] Ibid., 5.
[53] Ibid., 6.
[54] Ibid., 7; Harold H. Mann, *The Early History of the Tea Industry in North-East India* (Bengal Economic Journal, 1918), 24.
[55] Assam Company, *Report of the provisional committee made to the shareholders and a general meeting, held*

on the ground in Assam that the Chinese were becoming superfluous to tea production, and their numbers gradually decreased. J. P. Parker, Superintendent of the East Division, discussed how when seven Chinese tea makers were 'discharged' after refusing to relocate to a different division, leaving only two, the establishment was able to continue tea cultivation without them.[56] A contributing factor to the move away from Chinese recruitment was the employment of indigenous labour. In 1841 Charles Bruce noted how he was eventually able to induce the 'wild people' of the 'Naga tribes' to help in the labour of clearing the jungle.[57] The heavy financial cost of the failed Singapore recruitments turned the Company's attention to a local labour supply. The 1841 Assam Company Report noted that the 'Assamese are beginning to work, and for the important art of Tea manufacture, they seem peculiarly adapted, and likely to supply eventually all the labour that will be required'.[58] Once British supervisors like Charles Bruce possessed the knowledge of tea cultivation there was no need to pay more for Chinese cultivators. Evidently, demand for Chinese labour had limits; especially as the colonial experience over the 1830s had led to a more nuanced view of the indigenous peoples in Assam.

The 1841 report also explained that the tea of the 1839 season was 'made by Takelans, inhabitants of Assam; and their manufacture was considered, in every respect, as good as that of the Chinese artizan'.[59] The previously dismissed 'natives' were contributing their knowledge of tea preparation and providing skilled labour. As a result the difficult recruitment of Chinese specialists became increasingly unnecessary. A letter from a Mr Masters accompanying a tea invoice in late 1841 stated that 'the whole of it has been made without the aid of the Chinamen, and that only one person on the establishment had ever seen a Chinaman engaged in the manufacture'.[60] By 1842 there was no longer a necessity for the recruitment of Chinese artisans as their expertise was no longer required and had been replaced by cheaper, locally-sourced labour. Additionally, the Assam Company lacked the networks or resources to effectively manage large numbers of Chinese labourers, many of whom did not possess the necessary skills to cultivate tea. Luckily for the Assam Company, thanks to the diffusion of specialist knowledge in the 1830s, they no longer needed to recruit skilled Chinese labour. By the 1860s there

at the London Tavern, Bishopsgate Street, 31st January 1840 (London: Smith, Elder and Co., 1840), 6.

56 Assam Company, *Report of the Local Directors made to the Shareholders, at a General Meeting, Held at Calcutta, 6th October, 1842* (Calcutta: William Rushton and Co.), 1842; J. P. Parker (Upper Assam) to R. H. Buckland (Calcutta), 9 August 1842, in Assam Company, *Report of the Local Directors … 1842*.

57 Assam Company, *Report of the Local Directors … 1841*, 12.

58 Ibid., 18.

59 Ibid., 18.

60 Assam Company, *Report of the Local Directors … 1842*, 14.

were no Chinese tea cultivators or labourers left in Assam.[61] Instead, the Assam plantations relied on migrant labour from elsewhere in India. Between 1870 and 1900 almost 750,000 labourers arrived in Assam, with 250,000 coming from the Chota Nagpur States of Eastern India.[62] This labour force operated under a system of indenture contracts and the strict control of the planters, whose interests were protected by colonial legislation.[63] By the end of the nineteenth century Assam had been transformed into a patchwork of vast and profitable tea plantations. This process of economic development began with the recruitment of Chinese migrants based both philosophically and physically, in terms of onward migration, on the example of agricultural development in Singapore.

Transforming Ceylon

The British took control of the Dutch possessions on the island of Ceylon in 1795 in what was meant to be a 'temporary' response to the threat of French territorial expansion in the region.[64] By 1815 Ceylon was a British Crown Colony. This colonial unification was achieved by a series of wars with the inland Kandyan Kingdom, through which British control had been extended to the entire island. The unification of the island under British rule has been identified by histories of Ceylon as the starting point of the island as a modern colonial state.[65] Similarly to when the British seized control of Java from the Dutch in 1811, the new administration saw an opportunity to 'modernise' the island's economy and to break down traditional social hierarchies.[66] Once the Kandyan Kingdom's political authority in the island's interior was eroded, British colonial authorities turned their attention to Ceylon as an island of economic potential. However, the question of how to transform Ceylon into a plantation economy without an adequate supply of labour was a persistent problem over the 1820s and 1830s.[67] This section will examine attempts by Governor James Alexander Stewart-Mackenzie (1837–41) to introduce Chinese labour as part of Ceylon's economic transformation.

Developing a competitive export economy was a priority for British colonial administrators in Ceylon. In the late 1820s, Ceylon was the subject of

---

[61] Sharma, 'Lazy Natives, Coolie Labour, and the Assam Tea Industry', 1324.

[62] Hugh Tinker, *A New System of Slavery: The Export of Indian Labour Overseas, 1830–1920* (London: Oxford University Press, 1974), 50.

[63] Sharma, 'Lazy Natives, Coolie Labour, and the Assam Tea Industry', 1307.

[64] To maintain consistency with the primary source documents this book uses 'Ceylon' over the postcolonial name 'Sri Lanka'.

[65] Alicia Schrikker, *Dutch and British Colonial Intervention in Sri Lanka, 1780–1815: Expansion and Reform* (Leiden: Brill, 2007), 4.

[66] Donald W. Fryer and James C. Jackson, *Indonesia* (London: Ernest Benn, 1977), 47–9.

[67] John D. Rogers, 'Early British Rule and Social Classification in Lanka', *Modern Asian Studies*, 38, 3 (2004), 626.

a Commission of Eastern Inquiry led by William Colebrooke, who resided on the island from 1829 to 1831.[68] The Commission's report, published in 1833, had some significant implications for the colonial government and led to clashes with Governor Sir Robert Wilmot-Horton.[69] The key disagreement was over the Commission's suggestion that the colony had to become financially independent. In contrast, Wilmot-Horton believed that Britain ought to retain as many colonies as possible, even if it meant a significant expense to the metropole. For Wilmot-Horton the civilising mission of empire was more important than its economic utility. Colebrooke's other recommendations included checks on the executive powers of the Governor, the centralisation of the island's judicial system and integrating the different communities (including both settled-Dutch and indigenous populations) into the colonial legislative council. That the Colonial Office endorsed the Commission's report meant that Wilmot-Horton was compelled to increase production and exports, to pay for infrastructure spending, whilst the impending abolition of slavery created a labour crisis. Simultaneously, colonial observers in Ceylon in the late 1830s and early 1840s described a period of 'coffee mania' during which there was sizeable private investment in coffee plantations, heightened by anticipated impact of abolition on West Indian coffee production.[70] By the mid-1830s, British metropolitan and colonial administrators were committed to transforming Ceylon's economy.[71]

Whilst colonial authorities focused on the economy, colonial observers were also concerned with documenting the island's history and contemporary racial composition.[72] Many nineteenth-century accounts of the island drew heavily on Robert Knox's seventeenth-century *Historical Relation of the Island of Ceylon in the East Indies*, which laid the foundations of British understanding of the Kandyan Kingdom and the racial divisions of Ceylon.[73] Simon Casie Chitty – a linguistic expert and the first Singhalese member of the legislative council – in his version of the 1831 census, distinguished these groups and the

---

[68] Laidlaw, 'Investigating Empire', 757; C. A. Harris, 'Colebrooke, Sir William Macbean George (1787–1870)', rev. Lynn Milne, *Oxford Dictionary of National Biography*, Oxford University Press, 2004, www.oxforddnb.com/view/article/5867 (accessed 30 September 2018); Lieut.-Col. Colebrooke, *Report on the Administration of the Government of Ceylon* (24 December 1831), in Parliamentary Papers, *Slave trade (East India).—Slavery in Ceylon. Return to an order of the Honourable the House of Commons, dated 1 March 1838*, 1837–38 (697).

[69] Vijaya Samaraweera, 'Governor Sir Wilmot-Horton and the Reforms of 1833 in Ceylon', *The Historical Journal*, 15, 2 (1972), 209–28.

[70] Roland Wenzlhuemer, 'Indian Labour Immigration and British Labour Policy in Nineteenth-Century Ceylon', *Modern Asian Studies*, 41, 3 (2007), 577.

[71] Frank Broeze, ed., *Gateways of Asia: Port Cities of Asia in the 13th–20th Centuries* (London: Routledge, 2010), 191.

[72] This can be compared to the work of John Crawfurd in Southeast Asia, as discussed in Chapter 1.

[73] Robert Knox, *An Historical Relation of the Island of Ceylon in the East Indies* (London: Royal Society, 1681).

European settlers according to whether they were located in the Singhalese Districts, Malabar Districts or the Kandyan Provinces.[74] The racial composition of Ceylon was considered important by colonial authorities for two reasons. First, the British were aware that before their conquest of the island's interior the different communities and regions had been independent and autonomous. They were also aware that despite the unification of the island, Ceylon remained a 'plural society'.[75] Second, given the pressures put on colonial finances by the Colebrooke Commission and the resulting necessity for a cheap, productive labour force, the capacity of the native population to fulfil this need was subject to debate. In keeping with the dismissive attitude seen across the Empire in Asia, Governor Wilmot-Horton was also resistant to Colebrooke's recommendations for indigenous representation on the legislative council.[76] Despite acknowledgement of entrenched differences within Ceylon's population, some colonial observers still dismissed the native population as a whole. British resident Sampson Brown summarised such a view in the *Ceylon Magazine*: 'I have had some rather long chats about the natives and their moral character. They certainly are a most repelling race: there's no making anything of them as yet, and I doubt if we ever shall.'[77] The views of Wilmot-Horton and Sampson Brown reflect the dismissive attitude of British colonial observers to the different racial groups of Ceylon, specifically played out in decisions around political representation and alternative forms of indigenous authority.

In addition to the dismissal of the 'natives and their moral character', colonial governors also faced pressures around labour shortages, particularly as Ceylon was affected by the abolition of slavery in the 1830s. Slaves in Ceylon were often sourced domestically and scholarly literature on Indian Ocean slavery has been focused on imported slaves from the East Coast of Africa. Though slavery in the Indian Ocean predated European involvement, the movement of slaves to Ceylon vastly increased under Portuguese and Dutch colonial governance as European capital and networks led to the increased importation of un-free labourers.[78] Under British governance the institution of slavery on the island was gradually eroded. In 1816 an Executive Act declared, 'all children who may be born of slaves from and after the 12th of August 1816 inclusive, shall be considered free'.[79] There were limits to the extent of British abolitionism in Ceylon. In taking control of

---

[74] Simon Casie Chitty, *The Ceylon Gazetteer* (Ceylon: Gotta Church Mission Press, 1834), 48.

[75] Broeze, *Gateways of Asia*, 200.

[76] Michael Roberts, 'Problems of Social Stratification and the Demarcation of National and Local Elites in British Ceylon', *The Journal of Asian Studies*, 33, 4 (1974), 553.

[77] Sampson Brown, 'Life in the Jungle, or letters from a planter to his cousin in London', *Ceylon Magazine*, 11, 17 (1842), 234.

[78] Richard B. Allen, 'Satisfying the "Want for Labouring People": European Slave Trading in the Indian Ocean, 1500–1800', *Journal of World History*, 21, 1 (2010), 73.

[79] Parliamentary Papers, *Slave trade (East India)*.

Kandy the British had gained access to the region with the greatest 'economic potential', specifically from agriculture.[80] In 1833, when the British Empire abolished slavery, slave numbers in Ceylon were already on the decline due to earlier legislation. A dispatch from the Colonial Secretary Baron Glenelg to Governor Stewart-Mackenzie in 1837 gave the total figure at that time of 27,397 slaves.[81] That is not to say that the British authorities were entirely opposed to forced labour. Wilmot-Horton's administration used the *Rajakaria* – which was the government right to extract labour from land tenants as rental payment – to complete the Colombo–Kandy Road before abolishing the system.[82] By the late 1830s, Ceylon was on a trajectory of transformation into a post-slave plantation economy that would rely on free labour. Where this labour would come from was not clear. For Governor Stewart-Mackenzie, Chinese migrant labour was the preferred solution.

James Alexander Stewart-Mackenzie departed Britain to take up his governorship in July 1837. Upon arrival he had to operate within the framework of the Colebrooke Commission's recommendations and the policies of Governor Wilmot-Horton. The Colebrooke Commission had two major legacies for Stewart-Mackenzie. First, it had limited the executive power of the Governor by making the executive council answerable to the legislative council and by establishing an independent judiciary.[83] Second, the Commission had set out expectations of the Colonial Office that limited the autonomy of the Governor in managing the island economy. It decreed that the colony would become economically self-sufficient, whilst ending compulsory labour and dismantling government monopolies.[84] The Commission's reforms also stressed that the colonial government should disregard social and cultural differences between racial groups, but pursue what metropolitan planners believed to be universal ideas of civilisation and progress. To this end three 'Ceylonese' seats were created on the legislative council in 1835.[85] The main policy issues that Stewart-Mackenzie faced all related to change: the transformation of the island economy into a profitable, privatised plantation system; the complete abolition of slavery and other forms of compulsory labour; and, to borrow a phrase from his advisor Simon Casie Chitty, the improvement of the 'native character'.[86] These different challenges can be grouped under

[80] Wenzlhuemer, 'Indian Labour Immigration and British Labour Policy in Nineteenth-Century Ceylon', 575.

[81] Parliamentary Papers, Slave trade (East India), 598.

[82] Lennox A. Mills, *Ceylon under British Rule, 1795–1932* (London: Oxford University Press, 1933), 73.

[83] Rogers, 'Early British Rule and Social Classification in Lanka', 643; Vijaya Samaraweera, 'The Ceylon Charter of Justice of 1833: A Benthamite Blueprint for Judicial Reform', *The Journal of Imperial and Commonwealth History*, 2 (1974), 274.

[84] Rogers, 'Early British Rule and Social Classification in Lanka', 639.

[85] Rogers, 'Early British Rule and Social Classification in Lanka', 639–43. These were seats specifically reserved for 'non-European' residents.

[86] Chitty, *The Ceylon Gazetteer*, 257.

the umbrella notion of colonial improvement, that underpinned the Assam project. In Jayeeta Sharma's work on interactions between the British state and Assamese tribes, the 'improving regime' encompassed both economic productivity in the form of tea production and missionary activity to 'elevate the character of the people'.[87] Similarly, Stewart-Mackenzie's main concern was to bring about economic improvement or 'modernisation', which was simultaneously distinct from, and connected to, notions of moral or intellectual improvement.

Due to the Colebrooke Commission and changing Colonial Office expectations, Ceylon was under metropolitan pressure to become an efficient and profitable 'resource pool' for the Empire.[88] Following the privatisation of the Dutch cinnamon monopoly, the development of coffee plantations in Ceylon in the late 1830s was an all-consuming economic project.[89] In 1837 the English import duty on Ceylon coffee was reduced to the same level as West Indian coffee, which led to a vast increase in investment in coffee cultivation.[90] The boom of private investment transformed the island. In 1834 the colonial government sold forty-nine acres of Crown land for coffee cultivation, yet by 1841 the annual sales figure was 78,685 acres with a total capital investment in coffee cultivation of around £3 million between 1837 and 1845.[91] The prospects of coffee cultivation seemed so bright that the 'Governor [Stewart-Mackenzie] and the Council, the Military, the Judges, the Clergy, and half of the Civil Servants' were amongst the buyers.[92] The coffee plantations were not sustained long-term – they were replaced by commercial tea cultivation from the 1880s onwards – but their proliferation in the 1830s exacerbated existing labour shortages.[93] Contemporary writers noted how the labour supply and the capital available for labour were not equivalent to the demand created by the new coffee plantations – in addition the cost of agricultural labour in Ceylon quadrupled over the 1830s.[94]

Migrant labour from India was the obvious solution to Ceylon's shortage, particularly as India was already an exporter of labour and the passage was so quick. The Indian Ocean colony of Mauritius saw the first large-scale importation of Indian 'coolie' labourers as indentured labourers, and the

---

[87] Jayeeta Sharma, 'Old Lords and "Improving" Regimes', in Sharma, *Empire's Garden*, 119–47. See also Peter Marshall on 'intellectual' and 'moral' improvement: Marshall, 'British-Indian Connections c.1780 to c.1830', 52.

[88] Cain and Hopkins, *British Imperialism*, 102.

[89] Wenzlhuemer, 'Indian Labour Immigration and British Labour Policy in Nineteenth-Century Ceylon', 577.

[90] G. C. Mendis, *Ceylon under the British* (New Delhi: Asian Educational Services, 2005; first published 1952), 66.

[91] Ibid., 66.

[92] Mills, *Ceylon under British Rule*, 229.

[93] Rhoads Murphey, 'Colombo and the Remaking of Ceylon: A Prototype of Colonial Asian Port Cities', in Broeze, *Gateways of Asia*, 201.

[94] Lieut. de Butts, *Rambles in Ceylon* (London: W. H. Allen & Co., 1841), 185.

colony would act as a model for the later migration of indentured Indian labourers to the West Indies and around the Empire.[95] However, a spate of cases in which Indian labourers were killed in attempting to avoid passage to Mauritius in 1838 was a cause for concern to both the Colonial Office and the Indian Government, and led to the system's suspension.[96] Act XIV of 1839 enacted by the Government of India prohibited all private Indian emigration pending further investigation.[97] A 'Petition of the Planters, Merchants, Traders and other Inhabitants of the Island of Mauritius' from May 1839 claimed to have recruited upwards of 20,000 'native Indian labourers' in the four years between 1835 and 1839.[98] Ceylon was harmed by such prohibition of Indian emigration due to the fears about onward migration to colonies like Mauritius. This ordinance specifically aimed to prohibit migrants entering into contracts for other colonies, where they might be subject to abuse.[99] Although emigration was managed by the Indian Government from the 1840s to protect against abuses, only Act XIII of 1847 repealed the prohibition with respect to Ceylon due to concerns over coercive onward migration to other destinations.[100] Over the long term, Indian labour – whether seasonal, indentured or convict – did fill Ceylon's needs.[101]

This period of uncertainty over Indian labour was the context in which Stewart-Mackenzie took control. The Colonial Office expected him to engineer significant economic change, using effective, cheap and voluntary labour, without using Indian immigrant labour. Boosting productivity in the colony, a requirement that had been emphasised by the Colebrooke Commission, was a top priority. Stewart-Mackenzie repeatedly corresponded with the Indian government and Colonial Office on the necessity of steam-powered boats for transport and the implementation of advanced agricultural techniques and technologies.[102] As well as coffee cultivation, Stewart-Mackenzie was also

---

95 Northrup, *Indentured Labour in the Age of Imperialism*, 14; see Irick, 'Chi'ing Policy towards the Coolie Trade', 3, for more on the origins of the term 'coolie'.

96 Parliamentary Papers, *Mauritius. Copies of correspondence addressed to the Secretary of State for the Colonial Department, relative to the introduction of Indian labourers into the Mauritius; and of the report of the Commissioners of Inquiry into the present condition of those already located in that colony*, 1840 (331), 13.

97 Nancy Gardner Cassels, *Social Legislation of the East India Company: Public Justice versus Public Instruction* (New Delhi: Sage, 2011), 210.

98 Parliamentary Papers, *Mauritius*, 7.

99 The Secretary of the Government of India to Colonial Secretary for Ceylon (Fort William), 29 June 1839, in 'Papers regarding the employment of Indian indentured labourers overseas, correspondence of the government of Ceylon with the Government of India', IOR/F/4/1846/77642, Boards Collection (British Library).

100 Repeal of Act XIV of 1839 respecting emigration to Ceylon, IOR/Z/E/4/19/C671, Boards Collection (British Library).

101 Allen, 'Slaves, Convicts, Abolitionism and the Global Origins of the Post-Emancipation Indentured Labour System', 335.

102 James Alexander Stewart-Mackenzie (Queen's House Colombo) to G. Baillie (Agent for the Island of Ceylon, London), 17 February 1838; James Alexander Stewart-Mackenzie

interested in sugar production, and appealed to London for equipment as 'we are greatly in want of the most powerful machinery'.[103] Stewart-Mackenzie maintained his personal and political networks in London, and his native Scotland, through his correspondences from Ceylon. His letters gave his views on metropolitan political issues as well as support and resources for his projects in Ceylon. The developing of the colony's production technologies formed part of a wider drive by Stewart-Mackenzie to improve the productivity of the colony and, by extension, its inhabitants.

An examination of executive and legislative council proceedings, and Ceylon's *Government Gazettes*, reveals Stewart-Mackenzie's interest in improving the 'natives'. Such sources display his scepticism about the indigenous capacity for self-representation. Stewart-Mackenzie wrote to London, as his predecessors did, to warn against admitting locals to the civil service.[104] In his first full-length speech to the legislative council, Stewart-Mackenzie promoted legislation which had been 'calculated to improve the morality and reduce crime among the lower orders generally'.[105] Improving the 'moral' character of the colony's inhabitants was a priority. A Government Ordinance of 1840 enacted fines or, failing that, hard labour for 'promiscuous Gaming, at cockfighting, or with any Table, Dice, Cards or other Instrument for Gaming', or for being 'convicted a third time or more often of being idle and disorderly'.[106] As in Assam, the perceived Asian predilection for opium and gambling addiction was also identified by British observers in Ceylon.[107] Notably, as in colonial Singapore, morality and industriousness were equated by colonial authorities in Ceylon. Legislation was announced by Stewart-Mackenzie's administration in November 1839 'for the Punishment of Idle and Disorderly Persons and Rogues and Vagabonds' and was followed in 1840 with an 'Ordinance for the better regulation of Servants, Labourers and Journeymen Artificers under Contracts for Hire and Service'.[108] Such measures can be compared to similar vagrancy legislation in the Cape Colony, which was aimed at forcing the Khoikkhoi peoples into labour relationships that benefited Western production owners.[109] Across the British Empire, and in Britain

---

(Queen's House Colombo) to Bentinck, 12 March 1838; James Alexander Stewart-Mackenzie (Queen's House Colombo) to Brickham, M.D., 25 January 1839, in GD46/9/6, Mackenzie Papers (National Archives of Scotland).

[103] James Alexander Stewart-Mackenzie (Queen's House Colombo) to William Fairburn (Mill Bank, London), 25 April 1840, in GD46/9/6, Mackenzie Papers (National Archives of Scotland).

[104] Sujit Sivasundaram, *Islanded: Britain, Sri Lanka, and the Bounds of an Indian Ocean Colony* (London: University of Chicago Press, 2013), 291.

[105] Ceylon Legislative Council (1839–41), 5 December 1839, CO 57/8 (National Archives).

[106] Ceylon Legislative Council (1839–41), 27 October 1840, CO 57/8 (National Archives).

[107] C. G. Uragoda, 'History of Opium in Sri Lanka', *Medical History*, 27 (1983), 69–76.

[108] Ceylon Government Gazettes (1839), CO 58/18 (National Archives); Ceylon Government Gazettes (1840), CO 58/19 (National Archives).

[109] Elizabeth Elbourne, 'Freedom at Issue: Vagrancy Legislation and the Meaning of Freedom

itself, legislative efforts were simultaneously made to punish unemployment and limit workers' rights. In Ceylon, the design of both pieces of legislation was to prevent workers from leaving employment, through enforcing proper contracts, and, ultimately, to deter 'idleness'. As in the colonial context of Singapore, notions of moral improvement informed the economic activity of the indigenous population.

In this context of restricted Indians and lazy natives, Governor Stewart-Mackenzie turned to China. Histories of Chinese migration and colonial Ceylon have omitted Stewart-Mackenzie's attempts to source Chinese labour through his connections to the China-coast opium traders Jardine Matheson.[110] Stewart-Mackenzie's attempts to acquire Chinese labour for Ceylon provide an opportunity to trace the influence of Chinese migrations to Singapore and Assam. Stewart-Mackenzie's first attempt to source 'Chinese with capital' was an attempt to replicate the Chinese merchant elite of Singapore. In this context the Chinese would fulfil a role of 'economic improvement' in which they would act as a collaborative force with colonial authorities. As in Singapore, such figures could also act as philanthropic moral improvers who subsidised schools, temples and hospitals. The second attempt to acquire Chinese migrants – in the form of skilled Chinese tea cultivators – was more focused on knowledge transfer, as in Assam. As merchants and tea cultivators the Chinese would act as agents of economic improvement and would play a role in the transformation of Ceylon into a lucrative plantation colony.

Stewart-Mackenzie's first enquiries into using Chinese migrant labour in Ceylon began at the very start of his governorship. James Matheson directed Stewart-Mackenzie's initial enquiries to Alexander Lawrie Johnstone – the prominent Singapore merchant and lead partner in A. L. Johnstone & Co. – 'respecting Chinese emigrants to Ceylon'. Johnstone responded by stating that 'I do not think there is any probability of Chinese with capital emigrating to Ceylon. But I have little doubt they might be induced to go over as labourers.'[111] From this response, it can be deduced that Stewart-Mackenzie had specifically been seeking 'Chinese with capital', presumably as investors in cinnamon and coffee cultivation as in Singapore. Johnstone, drawing on his own experience in Singapore, elaborated that although unlikely, it would be preferable for Stewart-Mackenzie to attract self-employed Chinese migrants, rather than labourers:

in Britain and the Cape Colony, 1799 to 1842', *Slavery & Abolition: A Journal of Slave and Post-Slave Studies*, 15, 2 (1994), 117.

[110]   For more on Governor Stewart-Mackenzie's connection to James Matheson, see Stan Neal, 'Imperial Connections and Colonial Improvement: Scotland, Ceylon and the China Coast, 1837–1841', *Journal of World History*, 29, 2 (2018), 213–38.

[111]   James Matheson (Canton) to James Alexander Stewart-Mackenzie (Ceylon), 11 April 1838, in MS JM/C5, Jardine Matheson Archive (Cambridge University Library).

The Chinese would be found most useful to the colony, their improvement would be infinitely greater when they were interested themselves, than working as labourers for others ... All the cultivation in the interior of Singapore Island has been made by Chinese.[112]

In this correspondence, the language of 'improvement' is present and important to both Stewart-Mackenzie and Johnstone. That Matheson turned to Johnstone's expertise demonstrated an acknowledgement of the success of Chinese emigration to Singapore. It also demonstrated a personal rather than commercial connection between the largest British merchant house in Canton and Singapore's premier firm, A. L. Johnstone & Co., which prospered in the Straits Settlements until its closure in the 1890s.[113] We can see here the influence of Singapore and the China coast (see Chapters 1 and 2), in the demand for Chinese labour in a plantation colony that otherwise had few links to China.

Matheson's involvement in recruiting Chinese labourers for Assam also allowed him to claim personal expertise on the topic of Chinese emigration. He found space in the form of a lengthy 'additional memoranda' to share his own expertise on Chinese emigration.[114] Matheson gave Stewart-Mackenzie an overview of the 'great numbers' of Chinese who emigrated annually to 'Singapore, Malacca and Penang'.[115] He also weighed up the positives of Chinese migration to Ceylon, such as the cheap price of sustenance given by Ceylon's 'rice' production, against possible negatives, such as the sojourning nature of Chinese migration that limited settlement.[116] Matheson's recommendation for a system of emigration was for Chinese migrants to be landed in Ceylon by British and Portuguese vessels passing from China to Bombay. Furthermore Matheson foresaw that to give this plan 'stability', it would be

Found advisable to hold out encouragement for some families to remove from the Straits of Malacca, who would serve as managers for new operations. Some individuals of good character accustomed to intercourse with the English, would be also desirable to act as overseers and interpreters.[117]

Note that Matheson, even with his access to migrants direct from China, suggests turning to the Straits Settlements as a source of Chinese managers, with experience of collaboration with colonial authorities. As seen in previous

[112] Matheson to Mackenzie, 11 April 1838.
[113] Roland Braddell et al., *One Hundred Years of Singapore, 1819–1919, Vol. II* (London: John Murray, 1921); W. H. Read, *Play and Politics: Recollections of Malaya by an Old Resident* (London: Wells Gardner, Darton & Co., 1901).
[114] Notably this 'memoranda' was enclosed in this private letter, it was not written for a wider audience.
[115] Matheson to Stewart-Mackenzie, 11 April 1838.
[116] Ibid.
[117] Ibid.

chapters, the notion of 'good character' is significant. Judging by the comments of both Matheson and Johnstone, the focus of Stewart-Mackenzie's request appeared to be for a moneyed class of Chinese migrants who would comply with British colonial authority to create a plantation economy, as in Singapore. As seen in Chapter 1, a community leader like Seah Eu Chin – who was a notable figure in colonial Singapore as a major employer and plantation owner – would have been exactly the type of migrant Stewart-Mackenzie was looking to attract, alongside a larger labouring population. In late 1838, Stewart-Mackenzie suggested to Matheson that his 'memoranda' had been 'interesting' and pledged to forward any future news on the subject.[118]

Governor Stewart-Mackenzie next approached James Matheson over the issue of Chinese migration in February 1840. Stewart-Mackenzie was now specifically interested in facilitating tea cultivation in Ceylon. The timing of this project was important. The Tea Committee successfully sold the first batch of Assam tea in London in 1839, but the problems with the Assam Company's recruitment of Chinese labour were not known publicly until late 1840. Stewart-Mackenzie was acting during a period of optimism about the prospects of Chinese tea cultivation in Assam. He asked Matheson for the 'acquirement of the common labourer who would look after a tea plantation about to be established'.[119] Despite having grandiose plans for a system of tea cultivation that would provide 'employment for a very large number', Stewart-Mackenzie initially requested 'good labourers' numbering '50 to 100'.[120] As well as Chinese tea cultivators, Matheson was also asked for a 'large supply of tea seed … packed in boxes with light sand' and, in contrast to the 1838 correspondence, Stewart-Mackenzie specified that these migrants need be 'single men, and in the prime of life, stout and able bodied'.[121] This request for Chinese tea cultivators for Ceylon, using the resources of James Matheson on the China coast, was an almost direct replication of the Assam experiments of the 1830s. Stewart-Mackenzie's request for 'stout and able bodied' men was also reminiscent of the language of systematic emigration and colonisation in general. This appeal came just six months after James Matheson had agreed the final contracts with tea cultivators for Assam. In this instance the specific pressures on Governor Stewart-Mackenzie to create a plantation economy – rather than a vague desire for colonial improvement – necessitated his interest in procuring Chinese tea cultivators.

Ultimately, however, Stewart-Mackenzie's plans for Chinese-managed tea cultivation went unrealised. Stewart-Mackenzie was a divisive figure in

118 James Matheson (Canton) to James Alexander Stewart-Mackenzie (Ceylon), 24 September 1838, in MS JM/C5, Jardine Matheson Archive (Cambridge University Library).
119 James Alexander Stewart-Mackenzie (Ceylon) to James Matheson (Canton), 7 February 1840, in MS JM/B1/9, Jardine Matheson Archive (Cambridge University Library).
120 Ibid.
121 Ibid.

Ceylon due to his role in religious and educational reforms, and the Colonial Office reassigned him as High Commissioner to the Ionian Islands in 1841.[122] As such, Stewart-Mackenzie informed Matheson that he would be returning to Europe in April 1841, expressing 'regret' that he was unable to undertake the 'cultivation of tea'.[123] In anticipation of this news Matheson had already delayed transporting tea cultivators to Ceylon.[124] With his letter Matheson enclosed copies of the contracts signed by tea cultivators as part of the Assam experiment. Because of the problems with Chinese migrants in Assam in 1840 he warned Stewart-Mackenzie that 'you have considerable risk of finding them not qualified, a point we have no means of ascertaining here'.[125] In addition to the problem of unqualified recruits in Assam, we can see here the limiting effects of the Opium War on access to labour from China. In response, Stewart-Mackenzie was 'well satisfied' that Matheson had not sent the Chinese cultivators he had recruited because he would not be able to oversee the project personally.[126]

Stewart-Mackenzie's later correspondence with Matheson provides further evidence of the conceptual link between economic development and colonial improvement, similar to that seen in Assam. As seen in his ordinances as Governor, Stewart-Mackenzie was particularly interested in discouraging 'idleness' amongst the island's population. In his letter to Matheson expressing regret at his failure to institute Chinese-run tea cultivation on the island, Stewart-Mackenzie explained his self-appointed task as Governor: 'to improve and advance the mental resources of the varied population of the island'.[127] This quest gives a clue as to why Stewart-Mackenzie, like colony-builders in Singapore in particular, had initially sought to introduce 'Chinese with capital' to Ceylon as investors and colonists. By contrast, the request for Chinese tea cultivators, as in Assam, was born out of necessity. Notably, Stewart-Mackenzie had not sought a few overseers but a significant number of 'good labourers'. His two different attempts to source Chinese labour, born of different motivations and circumstances, show how he deemed Chinese migrants to be useful in the economic transformation of Ceylon. Despite the abandonment of the tea planting project, Stewart-Mackenzie left a legacy for large-scale tea cultivation in Ceylon.

Although Stewart-Mackenzie failed to establish a Chinese-run tea industry in Ceylon, tea cultivation did eventually prosper and surpassed the 'coffee

[122] Sivasundaram, *Islanded*, 301.
[123] James Alexander Stewart-Mackenzie (Pavilion Rundy) to James Matheson (Canton), 20 April 1841, in MS JM/B6/9, Jardine Matheson Archive (Cambridge University Library).
[124] James Matheson (Macao) to James Alexander Stewart-Mackenzie (Ceylon), 9 January 1841, in MS JM/C5, Jardine Matheson Archive (Cambridge University Library).
[125] Ibid.
[126] James Alexander Stewart-Mackenzie (Ceylon) to James Matheson (Canton), 16 May 1841, in MS JM/C5, Jardine Matheson Archive (Cambridge University Library).
[127] Stewart-Mackenzie to Matheson, 20 April 1841.

mania' that had gripped investors in the late 1830s. The development of the Ceylon tea industry followed on from the success of Assam. The Ceylon Agricultural Society was founded in 1841 and, by the 1870s, Ceylon had established a reputation as a centre of 'scientific agriculture'.[128] The 'Belfast Chameleon' Sir James Emerson Tennent, one of the primary chroniclers of the colony's development over the nineteenth century, remarked that, 'should it ever be thought expedient to cultivate tea in addition to coffee in Ceylon, the adaptation of the soil and climate has thus been established, and it only remains to introduce artisans from China to conduct the subsequent processes'.[129] In the 1860s a small number of Chinese artisans were brought to Ceylon and the suitability of Ceylon as a centre for tea production was firmly established amongst the colonial planting community.[130] By the 1880s tea production vastly outstripped coffee cultivation in Ceylon.

Imperial Labour Shortages and Chinese Migration in the 1840s

The issues Stewart-Mackenzie faced in Ceylon were both local and imperial in nature. Notions of colonial improvement – whether economic, moral or intellectual – were not confined to Ceylon and Assam. Metropolitan observers increasingly attached these ideas to issues of colonisation and labour migration across the British Empire. The creation of the Colonial Land and Emigration Commission resulted from both the growing interest in centralised imperial colonisation policy and an Empire-wide labour shortage. The Colonial Land and Emigration Commission became increasingly aware of the possibility of using Chinese labour in new colonies to address labour shortages on an imperial scale. Zoë Laidlaw's *Colonial Connections* highlights the 'information revolution' taking place in the Empire, which made use of the 'blue books' compiled annually by colonial governors from 1822.[131] New information available in the metropole greatly informed calls for a more organised migration policy to meet the chronic labour needs of a range of colonies – crucially Australia, Mauritius and the West Indies – and potentially introduce Chinese migrant labour.

One of the loudest and most consistent voices calling for an improved system of colonisation was that of Edward Gibbon Wakefield. Wakefield's primary concern was that free migrants, not slaves or convicts, should be introduced to the Australian colonies by the imperial government in

128 T. J. Barron, 'Science and the Nineteenth-Century Ceylon Coffee Planters', *The Journal of Imperial and Commonwealth History*, 16 (1987), 9–17.
129 J. Emerson Tennent, *Ceylon: an account of the island physical* (London: Longman, 1859), 251; Jonathan Jeffrey Wright, '"The Belfast Chameleon": Ulster, Ceylon and the Imperial Life of Sir James Emerson Tennent', *Britain and the World*, 6, 2 (2013), 196.
130 Barron, 'Science and the Nineteenth-Century Ceylon Coffee Planters', 18.
131 Laidlaw, *Colonial Connections*, 171.

London.[132] He disseminated his ideas through texts such as *Letter from Sydney, the Principal Town of Australasia* and *Sketch of a Proposal for Colonising Australia,* and in 1830 Wakefield established the National Colonization Society.[133] This Society became influential in the Colonial Office. For example, Robert Torrens chaired the Society and became a Colonial Land and Emigration Commissioner in 1840. Having helped to float the South Australian Land Company in 1832, Torrens was a supporter of 'self-supporting colonization', which encouraged peasant proprietorship, and was able to exert his influence through the Colonial Land and Emigration Commission.[134] The clout of Wakefield's supporters of free labour and assisted emigration meant that their ideas affected imperial policy. By the beginning of the 1840s, the Empire in Asia and Australasia was a tempting field for state-managed colonisation.[135]

As the Colonial Office took measures to increase voluntary migration, specifically to Australian colonies, a framework to manage the bureaucracy of emigration became increasingly necessary. For example, Thomas Frederick Elliot, one of the original three Commissioners, worked with the London Emigration Committee from 1831 and was Agent-General for Emigration from 1837. Elliot's management of emigration, originally focused on South Australia, soon broadened.[136] The growing involvement of the Colonial Office in migration led to the creation of the Colonial Land and Emigration Commission by the Colonial Secretary Lord John Russell in January 1840.[137] The Commission consisted of three members – Thomas Elliot, Robert Torrens and E. E. Villiers – who were appointed to serve as 'the connecting link between the disposal of Crown Lands and the conveyance of immigrants'. They were also engaged in distributing funds designated by the Colonial Office for the promotion of emigration.[138] Elliot, who had strong expertise in the field of emigration, became the Chairman of the Colonial Land and Emigration Commission and took the lead on Empire-wide migration policy.[139]

[132] David J. Moss, 'Wakefield, Edward Gibbon (1796–1862)', *Oxford Dictionary of National Biography*, Oxford University Press, 2004; online edn, May 2007, www.oxforddnb.com/view/article/28415 (accessed 30 September 2018).

[133] Ibid.

[134] Peter Moore, 'Torrens, Robert (1780?–1864)', *Oxford Dictionary of National Biography*, Oxford University Press, 2004, www.oxforddnb.com/view/article/27565 (accessed 30 September 2018).

[135] W. P. Morrell, *British Colonial Policy in the Age of Peel and Russell* (London: Frank Cass & Co., 1966), 5.

[136] Ibid., 10.

[137] Ibid., 10.

[138] Fred H. Hitchins, *The Colonial Land and Emigration Commission, 1840–78* (Philadelphia: Philadelphia University Press, 1931), 308.

[139] Margaret Ray, 'Elliot, Sir Thomas Frederick (1808–1880)', *Oxford Dictionary of National Biography*, Oxford University Press, 2004; online edn, January 2008, www.oxforddnb.com/view/article/41086 (accessed 30 September 2018).

Insight into the work of the Commission can be best gained from the 'General Reports'. The 1842 report gives some insight into the scope of the Commission's early activities.[140] Reports on the 'Disposal of Lands' in the colonies covered Antipodean colonies, such as New South Wales, Van Diemen's Land, Western Australia and New Zealand; Central and North American possessions, including Nova Scotia, Newfoundland and the West Indies; and 'additional colonies', such as the Cape of Good Hope, Ceylon and the Falkland Islands.[141] Importantly, though the desire to manage issues of labour on an imperial scale was stimulated by the specific issues of the abolition of convict transportation and slavery, the institutions that emerged dictated policy beyond these specific colonial contexts. The 'Disposal of Lands' supplemented the third section, 'Emigration', as land available in the colonies was the primary method of inducing free migration. The 'Emigration' section gave an overview of migration levels to the colonies, and emigration levels from the United Kingdom, and discussed legislation for the regulation of and encouragement of migration.[142] The scope of the Colonial Land and Emigration Commission's work over the 1840s became increasingly broad – encompassing control over the disposal of Crown lands and emigration, as well as the collection and dissemination of information.[143]

In response to the imperial labour crisis the Colonial Land and Emigration Commission sought more information on China as a possible source of immigrants. To discover more, the Colonial Land and Emigration Commission drew on existing information about Chinese migrant labour and the expertise of British observers from across Britain's Asian Empire. Indeed, Elliot had already compiled much information detailing his involvement in Australian migration on the 'Capabilities of the Chinese to become good emigrants to the colony of New South Wales'.[144] The 1843 General Report included a 'Proposal to obtain emigrants from the Straits of Malacca' for British plantation labour in the West Indies. This was based on the contemporary accounts of the competence of Chinese labour and the 'number of emigrants who arrived at Singapore in 1842 and 1843'.[145] The work of the Colonial Land and Emigration Commission was essential in identifying Chinese labourers as

---

[140] Though their work began in 1840, the first General Report was not published as a Parliamentary Paper until 1842.

[141] Parliamentary Papers, *Colonial Land and Emigration. General Report of the Colonial Land and Emigration Commissioners*, 1842 (567).

[142] Ibid., 2.

[143] Laidlaw, *Colonial Connections*, 192. By 1849 the report covered many of the same issues, but with an increasing interest in cross-colonial migration: Parliamentary Papers, *Colonial Land and Emigration Commission. Ninth general report of the Colonial Land and Emigration Commissioners*, 1849 (1082).

[144] Parliamentary Papers, *Capabilities of the Chinese to become good emigrants to the colony of New South Wales*, 1838 (389), 49.

[145] Parliamentary Papers, *Colonial Land and Emigration Commission. Report*, 1843 (621), 32–3.

a suitable source of replacement labour for former slave-holding colonies.[146] For information on the utility of the Chinese in the Straits Settlements, Elliot turned to the expertise of John Crawfurd. In response to a list of questions about the nature of Chinese labour from the Commission, Crawfurd extolled the virtues of the Straits Chinese.[147] Importantly for the planned scheme, Crawfurd assured Elliot that the Chinese would be able to fulfil the requirements of the plantation system as they were 'a sort of ambidextrous people who can turn their hands to anything'.[148] It was the knowledge of experts like Crawfurd, coupled with the experience of Chinese colonists in the Straits Settlements, which provided metropolitan planners with a possible solution to the Empire-wide labour shortage.

Like Singapore, another British colony, Mauritius, became a template of the utility of Chinese labour in developing plantation colonies. Using Chinese labourers on Mauritian sugar plantations was a possibility from the beginning of British rule. Robert Townsend Farquhar, who served as Governor of Mauritius from 1810 to 1817 and again between 1820 and 1823, was the first colonial administrator to experiment with Chinese. Farquhar had witnessed the economic benefits of using Chinese emigrant communities as Lieutenant-Governor of Penang in 1804.[149] Between 1788 and 1810 the Chinese population in Penang increased from 537 to 5,088.[150] As a result of his time in Penang, Farquhar wrote *Suggestions for counteracting any injurious effects upon the population of the West India colonies from the abolition of the slave trade* in 1807, in which he advocated a scheme for encouraging Chinese labourers to migrate to the West Indies as a replacement for African slave labour.[151] This suggestion led to the establishment of a Select Committee to report into the possibility of using Chinese labourers in the West Indies in 1811. The committee ultimately decided against the scheme due to concerns over its practicality in terms of distance.[152] Disappointed by the committee's decision, Farquhar dispatched a Chinese immigrant in Mauritius (Hayme) to recruit more Chinese labourers for the colony in 1821.[153] Notably, despite

[146] Northrup, *Indentured Labour in the Age of Imperialism*, 10.
[147] Parliamentary Papers, *Emigration. West Indies and Mauritius.* Correspondence relative to emigration of labourers to the West Indies and the Mauritius, from the west coast of Africa, the East Indies, and China, since the papers already laid before the House, 1844 (530), 269–71.
[148] Ibid. 270.
[149] For more on Farquhar's time in Penang see Anthony Webster, 'British Expansion in South East Asia and the Role of Robert Farquhar, Lieutenant-Governor of Penang 1804–5', *The Journal of Imperial and Commonwealth History*, 23, 1 (1995), 1–25.
[150] Hussin, *Trade and Society in the Straits of Melaka*, 185–7.
[151] G. B. Smith, 'Farquhar, Sir Robert Townsend, first baronet (1776–1830)', rev. Lynn Milne, *Oxford Dictionary of National Biography*, Oxford University Press, 2004, www.oxforddnb.com/view/article/9180 (accessed 30 September 2018).
[152] Parliamentary Papers, Report from the committee appointed to consider of the practicability and expediency of supplying our West India colonies with free labourers from the east.
[153] Ly-Tio-Fane Pineo Huguette, *Chinese Diaspora in Western Indian Ocean* (Mauritius: MSM, 1985), 69.

Farquhar's experience, he was reliant on a Chinese intermediary already resident in Mauritius. Hayme returned in 1826 with a select group of carpenters – Whampoo, Hankee, Nghien, Hakkim and Ahim – and in 1829 the Planter's Association recruited a small group of agricultural labourers, meaning that by 1830 the Chinese community in Mauritius numbered twenty-six.[154] Huguette's work on Chinese communities in the Indian Ocean projects an average of twelve new Chinese arrivals per year over the course of the 1830s. As such, by the time the Indian Government suspended Indian indentured emigration in 1839, the planters of Mauritius were already familiar with the systems through which they could acquire Chinese labourers.

Between 1837 and 1843 more than 3,000 Chinese labourers arrived in Mauritius, with most shipments coming from the Straits Settlements of Penang and Singapore.[155] However, the colonial blue books for Mauritius show that the population of 'labourers, natives of China and the Malay Coast' dropped from 1,470 in 1843 to 566 in 1844.[156] The explanation for this drop-off was that the Colonial Office refused to extend the bounty system that supported the importation of Indian labourers to Chinese labourers. A dispute regarding bounty payments for the 103 Chinese labourers who had arrived in Mauritius from Singapore aboard the *Dona Carmelita* demonstrates this.[157] Rather than supporting the importation of additional Chinese labour, the Colonial Office used the bounty money to encourage Indian labourers already in Mauritius to sign extended contracts instead of taking return passages back to India.[158]

Though short-lived, this Chinese migration to Mauritius served as a template for new colonial projects. Specifically, after the cession of Hong Kong to Britain in 1842, British merchants replicated systems of Chinese indentured labour in the West Indies.[159] One of the main challenges facing the imperial planners and colonial planters was filling the labour shortage created by abolition.[160] The challenge was to secure a workforce that was both

154 Marina Carter and James Ng Foong Kwong, *Forging the Rainbow: Labour Immigrants in British Mauritius* (Port Louis: S. N., 1997), 4; Huguette *Chinese Diaspora in Western Indian Ocean*, 23–73.

155 Marina Carter and James Ng Foong Kwong, *Abacus and Mah Jong: Sino-Mauritian Settlement and Economic Consolidation* (Boston: Brill, 2009), 33. Chinese arrival figures from 'An Overview of the History of Indenture', *Aapravasi Ghat World Heritage Site*, www.aapravasighat.org/English/Resources%20Research/Documents/History%20of%20Indenture.pdf (accessed 7 September 2018). Original figures available from PE 159, *Register of Chinese Immigrants*, 1843 (Mauritius National Archives).

156 Mauritius Blue Book (1843), CO 172/69 (National Archives); Mauritius Blue Book (1844), CO 172/70 (National Archives).

157 Giquel & Co. (Port Louis, Mauritius) to the Hon. W. Staveley, 18 August 1842, in 'Correspondence relative to Emigration of Labourers to the West Indies and the Mauritius, from the West Coast of Africa, the East Indies, and China', *Sessional Papers of the House of Lords, Vol. IX* (House of Lords, 1844), 210.

158 Ibid.

159 This is discussed in detail in Chapter 5.

160 Hitchins, *The Colonial Land and Emigration Commission*, 309.

cheap and productive. The Colonial Land and Emigration Commission saw Chinese labourers as a solution in the similar plantation context of the West Indies. Lord Stanley received copies of the agreements entered into by Chinese labourers in Mauritius from the Colonial Land and Emigration Commission when he was determining the details for state-managed indentured agreements between Chinese migrants and the West India Committee.[161] The Colonial Land and Emigration Commission Report of 1843 praised Chinese migrants as 'by far the most industrious and most hardy of oriental labourers'.[162] Additionally, when the Colonial Land and Emigration Commission's *Colonization Circular* of 1843 gave the bounty rules for Chinese emigration to the West Indies it was suffixed by John Crawfurd's 'paper on Chinese labourers' which detailed the terms of Chinese labour migration to the Straits Settlements and recommended Chinese labour.[163] Again, Crawfurd praised the Chinese as 'entrepreneurial' and superior to Bengali and Malay labour, but cautioned that they would expect to be well paid and advised that the colonial government pay for their importation.[164] It is notable that even after having returned to Britain from Singapore permanently in 1827 Crawfurd's expertise was invoked by the Colonial Land and Emigration Commission sixteen years later. The Colonial Land and Emigration Commission saw Chinese labour migration to the Straits Settlements, and subsequently Mauritius, as something replicable in the post-slave economy of the West Indies.

This new system of labour importation resulted from the abolition of slavery, and the subsequent reluctance of freed slaves to take work as waged labourers on their former plantations. The British state was therefore desperate to assist the West Indian planters in sourcing labour to maintain the colony's economic output. There had been a solitary, unrepeated, experiment with 200 Chinese contract labourers in 1806, and the report on the possibility of Chinese labour as a replacement for slave labour, instigated by Farquhar, in 1810. However, the 1840s saw a new wave of interest in solving the labour crisis in the West Indies.[165] The practicalities of using both Chinese and Indian labour were explored repeatedly in Colonial Office correspondences, Colonial Land and Emigration Commission reports and select committee reports.[166] The 1843 annual report included material on the prospect of intro-

---

[161] Parliamentary Papers, *Emigration. West Indies and Mauritius*, 245.

[162] Parliamentary Papers, *Colonial Land and Emigration Commission Report of 1843*, 41–2.

[163] Colonial Land and Emigration Commissioners, *Colonization Circular* (30 October 1843), 34–3.

[164] Ibid., 37–8.

[165] Parliamentary Papers, *Report from the committee appointed to consider of the practicability and expediency of supplying our West India colonies with free labourers from the east*; L. L. Walton, *Indentured Labour, Caribbean Sugar: Chinese and Indian migrants in the British West Indies, 1838–1918* (Baltimore, Maryland: The John Hopkins Press, 1993), 42.

[166] Parliamentary Papers, *Emigration. West Indies and Mauritius*; Parliamentary Papers, *Report from the Select Committee on West India Colonies*, 1842 (479); Parliamentary Papers, *West Indies. Copies or extracts of correspondence relative to the labouring population in the West Indies*, 1845 (642).

ducing Chinese labour in the West Indies, with the note 'character of these labourers' in the margins.[167] The report concluded that an experiment with Chinese labour was worth a try, again drawing on economic necessity and notions of the Chinese character as superior to the alternatives:

> But seeing the numerous motives for wishing to satisfy in every proper way the demand for labour in the West Indies, and considering that the more intelligent the class of people introduced, as well as the better able to protect their own interests, the more beneficial it must be to all concerned, it seems very desirable that the present experiment should be tried, and that it should be practically ascertained whether China may be added to the fields from which to attempt to furnish means for the successful cultivation of sugar by free labour.[168]

Based on the available information, Lord Stanley permitted the immigration of Chinese labourers to the West Indies from 1843 provided that the government regulate the system through licences to avoid the types of abuses seen in the Indian indenture system. Additionally, Stanley stipulated that labourers had to be procured from the British Straits Settlements, under the watchful eye of British authorities, as opposed to the Chinese treaty ports. The uptake of the licence system, with applications to bring 2,850 Chinese labourers to the West Indies, demonstrates that Chinese labour was in demand.[169] Abolition had not led to a significant decrease in the number of coffee plantations in the West Indies, which was an anticipated response to emancipation that would have mitigated some of the demand for imported labour.[170]

Ultimately, this scheme for Chinese immigration to the West Indies never took place. The scheme's failure was concisely summarised in the Colonial Land and Emigration Commission's 1845 report: 'We learn that no Chinese emigrants have been procured from Singapore to go to the West Indies. We believe that they had plenty of employment on the spot.'[171] Singapore's success as a migrant destination prevented this scheme for onward migration. However, the lifting of the ban on Indian emigration shortly after the licences were agreed meant there was no Chinese immigration to the West Indies until an order for 5,000 labourers from the newly established British firm Syme, Muir & Co. in 1849.[172] In the 1850s a regular system of Chinese emigration to the West Indies emerged. Emigration agent James T. White travelled from

---

[167] Parliamentary Papers, *General report of the Colonial Land and Emigration Commissioners*, 1843 (621), 32.

[168] Ibid.

[169] Licenses granted for the conveyance of Chinese Labourers from the British settlements in the Straits of Malacca to Jamaica, British Guiana and Trinidad, 6 March 1844, CO129/4 (National Archives).

[170] John M. Talbot, 'On the Abandonment of Coffee Plantations in Jamaica after Emancipation', *Journal of Imperial Commonwealth History*, 43, 1 (2015), 38–9.

[171] Parliamentary Papers, *Fifth general report of the Colonial Land and Emigration Commissioners*, 1845 (617), 22.

[172] For more on this experiment and the firm Syme, Muir & Co., see Chapter 5.

Calcutta to the Chinese treaty port of Amoy to oversee the government-managed emigration system directly from the China coast. Chapter 5 details this process, but it is important to emphasise that the drive for colonial economic development – exemplified by the transformation of Assam, Ceylon and Mauritius – played a pivotal role in the extension of systems of Chinese migration to new destinations in the British Empire.

Conclusion

Plans to use Chinese migrant workers in Assam, Ceylon, Mauritius and the West Indies in the late 1830s and early 1840s both built on and modified existing systems of Chinese labour migration. The Assam project was dependent on Chinese expertise, reinforced the classification of the Chinese as racially superior to the indigenous population and drew on Chinese labour pools in Singapore. The development of a plantation economy in Ceylon was directly modelled on the experiment with tea cultivation in Assam and James Alexander Stewart-Mackenzie looked to introduce both Chinese merchants and Chinese labourers, as was seen in Singapore. Likewise migration to Mauritius was informed by Robert Townsend Farquhar's experience in the Straits Settlements and was used as a model for much-discussed systems to replace African slave labour in the West Indies. A growing metropolitan interest in race and labour migration influenced the replication of Chinese labour systems in different colonies. The involvement of the Colonial Land and Emigration Commission was an example of the interplay between imperial and colonial concerns. Preconceptions about the possible impact of Chinese migration in these new colonial destinations demonstrated the impact of ideas about Chinese character that colonial observers developed and disseminated over the 1820s and 1830s in contact zones like Singapore. Ideas about Chinese character intersected with broad imperial conversations about labour and race.

The examples discussed in this chapter demonstrate the different factors that stimulated interest in Chinese labour. The transition to plantation economies based on 'free' labour was a major catalyst for a serious pan-imperial examination of the possibilities of sourcing labour from new locations. Additionally, the specific limits placed on Indian emigration meant that demand for Chinese labour, perceived to be a cheap and reliable alternative, increased. Stewart-Mackenzie's interest in colonial improvement and his legislative commitment to dissuading 'idleness' demonstrated a clear connection between a propensity to labour and the relative value of different racial groups. Crucially, the economic issues Stewart-Mackenzie faced in Ceylon reappeared in other colonies. As demonstrated by the increasingly broad brief of the Colonial Land and Emigration Commission, imperial planning prioritised issues of 'economic improvement'. Theorists, such as Wakefield, advocated assisted emigration from Britain as an ideal approach to colonisation. However, the realities of supplying cheap, effective labour for a vast and distant range of colonies meant that Chinese labour emerged as a solution.

Although these attempts to establish Chinese migration schemes ultimately failed to produce consistent long-term results they remain significant for two reasons. First, they show the belief in the Chinese as agents of colonial improvement in the British Empire even as positive views of the Qing Empire declined, particularly during the transformation to plantation agriculture. Second, they demonstrate how wider imperial conditions, specifically the growing focus on productivity and corresponding labour crisis (which persisted into the 1840s), led to an increased interest in the potential of Chinese labourers as colonists for the British Empire. As Chapter 4 demonstrates, these wider imperial conditions were not limited to plantation colonies, but also reached Britain's white settler colonies. After all, it was not a coincidence that alongside Mauritius and the West Indies, the Colonial Land and Emigration Commission had a strong focus on sourcing labour for the Australian colonies.

Chapter 4

FROM SINGAPORE TO SYDNEY: RACE, LABOUR AND CHINESE MIGRATION TO AUSTRALIA

From the 1830s onwards various British colonies struggled with labour shortages, but there was one continent where this issue of labour coincided with racial anxieties and explicit racial prejudice: Australia. The development of Indian Ocean colonies, which relied on Asian indentured labour over the nineteenth century, has been characterised as a separate process from the development of Britain's white settler colonies. This chapter demonstrates how the colonial model of Singapore influenced Chinese migration, and discussions about Chinese migrants, in Australia. Again, the Australian example demonstrates the importance of wider imperial changes in the demand for labour and debates about racial hierarchy. The suspension of convict transportation to New South Wales in 1840 exacerbated pre-existing labour shortages, which created demand for Chinese migrant labour. In New South Wales, there was a broader interest in using cheap Asian labour to address labour shortages. Tony Ohlsson and Rose Cullen have examined how debates over the introduction of indentured labour from India fed into broader anxieties about race and labour in colonial New South Wales.[1] This chapter examines the use of Chinese migrant labour in this context of labour shortages and white settler opposition to Asian immigration.

The proposed Chinese immigration schemes stoked developing racial anxieties amongst the white settler population. There is a wealth of literature on Chinese exclusion in Australia in the context of racist anti-immigration movements across the white settler colonies of the British Empire and the United States of America.[2] Histories of exclusion focus on the second half

---

[1] Ohlsson, 'The Origins of a White Australia', 203–17; Rose Cullen, 'Empire, Indentured Labour and the Colony: The Debate over "Coolie" Labour in New South Wales, 1836–1838', *History Australia*, 9, 1 (2012), 84–109.

[2] The best example of this literature, which places Australia in a broader context, is Lake and Reynolds, *Drawing the Global Colour Line*.

of the nineteenth century as political and economic turmoil in southern China and the prospect of gold in Australia and California stimulated mass migrations. An estimated 55,000 Chinese migrants left China for Australian colonies between 1851 and 1875.[3] In response, over the second half of the nineteenth century Australian colonies introduced a series of immigration controls aimed at restricting Chinese immigration. This culminated in the Immigration Restriction Act (1901) as the first policy of the newly federated Australia. The dominant explanation for proliferation of immigration controls in colonial Australia is that negative racial stereotypes were popularised in response to mass migrations from China. Critics of Chinese immigration presented the Chinese as a social and economic threat to white settler society. We can see this pattern of an exclusionary response to immigrants, based on negative stereotypes, in the present day. However, this chapter demonstrates that negative stereotypes about the Chinese were circulating in colonial Australia before Chinese immigrants even arrived. The racial politics of Australia were pre-configured to oppose Chinese immigration. Importantly, both supporters and critics of Chinese immigration could draw on Singapore as an example of the Chinese as desirable colonists or a threat to the moral development of settler colonies.

In Chapter 1 we saw how Gordon Forbes Davidson viewed Singapore as a colonial model. This chapter explores Davidson's attempt to establish a scheme to bring Chinese migrant labour from Singapore to New South Wales in 1837. In the Australian context, he advocated Chinese migrants as a voluntary, non-convict, solution to labour shortages and as a replacement for the unproductive indigenous population. In doing so he both applied ideas about racial hierarchy and labour developed in Southeast Asia, and drew upon existing tropes of Aboriginal inferiority. It is also important to acknowledge that the failure of this scheme was due to both Davidson's personal failings and a hostile reception from white settlers in New South Wales. Davidson's proposal revealed anxieties about the potential of Chinese migrant labour that would develop into full-scale political action against Chinese immigration in the second half of the nineteenth century. Building on the Davidson example, this chapter also examines the ways in which Singapore continued to shape Australian discourse about Chinese immigration during the mass migrations from China in the 1850s onwards. Whilst histories of racial exclusion in Australia in the second half of the nineteenth century emphasise connections between the white settler colonies, this chapter demonstrates how Singapore, and the Singapore model of Chinese migration, informed ideas about race, labour and colonisation in colonial Australia.

---

[3]   Pan, *The Encyclopaedia of the Chinese Overseas*, 62.

Race and Labour in Colonial New South Wales

As outlined in Chapter 1, little is known about Gordon Forbes Davidson and he is rarely mentioned in histories of Singapore or Sydney.[4] His career in Asia and Australia was varied and sporadic. He lived in Java (1823–26), Singapore (1826–35) and Australia (1836–39), whilst at the same time travelling to major trading ports in Southeast Asia, India and the China coast. Importantly, as a mobile figure, who was primarily interested in making a profit, Davidson also connected ideas about race and labour in different colonial contexts. In recent decades, historians of the British Empire have emphasised the centrality of creating knowledge to the imperial project and the significance of information transfer between different colonies.[5] Moreover, it has been increasingly common to use individual life stories to reveal the hidden and complex themes of empire that a lack of primary sources can obscure. Such personal approaches, as found in *Colonial Lives across the British Empire*, illustrate how the overlaps and connections between individuals can be used to explore the intertwined strands of imperial history.[6] As individuals formed key nodes within networks of empire they have also been successfully used to connect imperial locales – such as Birmingham, Australia and Jamaica in Catherine Hall's *Civilising Subjects* – and can act as case studies that are not limited to a fixed time or place, but can physically move and transcend geographical limitations.[7] Gordon Forbes Davidson's colonial lives offer an insight into attitudes towards race, labour and colonisation, and connect two very different colonial contexts.

Gordon Forbes Davidson's experiences in Southeast Asia were crucial for the formation of his ideas about colonisation, race and labour. In his book *Trade and Travel in the Far East* he continuously, in line with contemporary colonial ideas of racial hierarchy, linked ideas about labour and economic utility to race.[8] Davidson regularly equated industriousness and mercantilism with notions of civilisational development. These ideas about the relationship between labour and race were formulated during his time in Java and Singapore in the 1820s and fitted within the colonial notions of 'the lazy

---

[4] Tony Ohlsson has made brief reference to Davidson's New South Wales Chinese migration scheme. See Ohlsson, 'The Origins of a White Australia', 204. Also, Sibing He has discussed Davidson's American connections: see 'Russell and Company in Shanghai, 1843–1891'.

[5] Good examples include Laidlaw, *Colonial Connections*; and James Hevia, *The Imperial Security State: British Colonial Knowledge and Empire-Building in Asia* (New York: Cambridge University Press, 2012).

[6] David Lambert and Alan Lester, eds, *Colonial Lives across the British Empire: Imperial Careering in the Long Nineteenth Century* (Cambridge: Cambridge University Press, 2006).

[7] Hall, *Civilising Subjects*.

[8] Davidson's book was published to generally positive reviews in London in 1846, in particular in the *London Morning Post*, 23 January 1846.

native'.[9] As in Singapore, the Chinese community in Java played an important role, that of a cheap and productive workforce, in the colonial economy. Contemporary European observers within Southeast Asia identified clear racial divisions between Chinese and Malay residents, founded on their proficiency as a labour force.[10] This tradition shaped Davidson's view of race as connected to economic activity. It was Davidson's experience in multiple contexts in Southeast Asia that shaped his view of Chinese labourers and informed his later attempts to establish a scheme of Chinese migration to New South Wales.

Early in 1836 Gordon Forbes Davidson moved to New South Wales and his account of his first three years' residence demonstrated an acceptance of many of the contemporary prejudices and concerns in the colony. On arrival Davidson was impressed: 'landing in Sydney, the traveller from India is ready to exclaim, surely this is not a town some seventeen thousand miles from England! Everything reminds him of home.'[11] Glad to be in an 'English' town, Davidson was struck by the shortage of suitable workers as he remarked that 'labour is so much cheaper in Britain than it is in Australia', and was unimpressed by British and Irish migrants who 'generally are very difficult to satisfy in the matter of rations'.[12] The solution to this shortage was not to be had through further convict transportation. As Davidson's initial excitement subsided, he concurred with growing criticism of convict transportation as damaging to the colony's moral character.[13] In a tirade against drunkenness Davidson asked, 'what better conduct, however, can be expected from men, nine-tenths of whom either are or have been convicts?'[14] Davidson's criticism of the role of convicts, or freed convicts, reflected the contemporary discussions about convict transportation and its moral implications.

The movement away from transportation, and consequently away from convict labour, threatened Australia's pastoral economy. Opposition to transportation in the 1830s was framed in terms of opposition to slavery and forced labour, as well as moral depravity.[15] The 1837 Select Committee on Transportation, presided over by the radical MP William Molesworth,

---

9   This term is taken from the title of Alatas, *The Myth of the Lazy Native*. See Chapter 1 for more on this.

10   Alatas, *The Myth of the Lazy Native*, 1.

11   Davidson, *Trade and Travel in the Far East*, 120.

12   Ibid. 187–202.

13   For an overview of the complexity and evolution of the debate around convict transportation, see David Andrew Roberts, 'Beyond 'the Stain': Rethinking the Nature and Impact of the Anti-Transportation Movement', *Journal of Australian Colonial History*, 14 (2012), 205–79.

14   Davidson, *Trade and Travel in the Far East*, 122.

15   For more on the way that Molesworth's anti-transportation drew on anti-slavery discourse, see Isobelle Barrett Meyering, 'Abolitionism, Settler Violence and the Case against Flogging: A Reassessment of Sir William Molesworth's Contribution to the Transportation Debate', *History Australia*, 7, 1 (2010), 1–18.

recommended that the convict transportation system be abolished.[16] The system was believed to be both ineffective in reforming convicts and a contributing factor to the social ills of the colony. In contrast to metropolitan condemnation of convict transportation, colonial opinion was divided over a system that provided cheap and reliable labour.[17] By 1840 convict transportation to New South Wales had been ended, though versions of the system continued to Van Diemen's Land and Western Australia.[18] In addition to the ending of convict transportation, the increased demand for cheap manual labourers in 1830s Australia was caused by the rapid growth of land ownership in the colony as freed convicts took up smallholdings on the edge of existing settlements.[19] As the labour force of the colony gradually became employers they exacerbated New South Wales' existing shortages by creating excess demand for labour.[20] An indication of the necessity to prevent the proliferation of land ownership was the replacement of government land grants with land sales in 1831. Despite the establishment of a 'bounty system', funded using revenue from land sales, to induce voluntary migrants from Britain, an alternative source of imported labour was still necessary.[21]

Davidson was also dismissive of the prospects of an Aboriginal workforce. He warned of the payment of indigenous labourers that it 'must not be given them, however, till their work is done: give it beforehand, and not a hand's turn will they do, but decamp at once to enjoy their dinner'.[22] Much of Davidson's writing on New South Wales was concerned with descriptions of Aboriginal culture and customs. Particularly struck by the nakedness of Aboriginal Australians, Davidson suggested that if a European 'Samaritan' did distribute clothes they would 'in all probability, appear naked at his door tomorrow, having given away their clothes to some convict, in exchange for a pound of flour or an ounce of tobacco'.[23] Here Davidson's writing follows a well-established tradition of British observers characterising Aboriginal peoples as the most primitive that the Empire had encountered. Colonial observers commonly depicted the indigenous population of New

---

[16] Parliamentary Papers, *Select Committee on Transportation, Report, 1837–38*, 1838 (669).

[17] John Ritchie, 'Towards Ending an Unclean Thing: The Molesworth Committee and the Abolition of Transportation to New South Wales, 1837–40', *Historical Studies*, 17, 67 (1976), 144–64.

[18] Angela Woollacott, *Settler Society in the Australian Colonies: Self-Government and Imperial Culture* (Oxford: Oxford University Press, 2015), 2.

[19] Rebecca Wood, 'Frontier Violence and the Bush Legend: The Sydney Herald's Response to the Myall Creek Massacre Trials and the Creation of Colonial Identity', *History Australia*, 6, 3 (2009), 1–19.

[20] Parliamentary Papers, *Select Committee on Transportation*.

[21] These reforms to land distribution were heavily influenced by the ideas of Edward Gibbon Wakefield. See Woollacott, *Settler Society in the Australian Colonies*, 37–42.

[22] Davidson, *Trade and Travel in the Far East*, 147.

[23] Ibid., 145.

South Wales as a 'stone-age' people, who were lost in time and dismissed as economically unproductive.[24]

As in Singapore, Davidson had immediately accepted and reiterated the colonial trope of the lazy native. Combining ideas about civilisational hierarchy and labour, he remarked that Aboriginal Australians 'are, without exception, the most complete savages I have ever come across. They resist almost every attempt to induce them to labour.'[25] Similarly to colonial views of the Malay population in Southeast Asia, the resistance to capitalist forms of production and contract-based labour relationships was directly equated with civilisational inferiority. Davidson's views of Aboriginal peoples were in line with the dominant frontier narrative in colonial Australia. Existing cultural, social and economic systems, which developed over centuries, meant that Aboriginal peoples were reluctant to enter labour relationships required by colonial employers.[26] As part of the wider critique of Aboriginality, colonial observers interpreted resistance to employment and labour as symbolic of Aboriginal inferiority.

The practical reality was that Aboriginal peoples did form an effective labour force at various points in early colonial Australia. For example, in the 'planned colony' of South Australia, indigenous workers filled gaps left by a shortage of European labour.[27] Similarly, the Australian Agricultural Company's workforce was as high as eight per cent Aboriginal in the 1820s, and demonstrated the suitability of indigenous peoples, and their specialist skills and experiences, for pastoral work.[28] Despite the realities of Aboriginal labour on the frontier, Aboriginal laziness was an essential theme of colonial critiques of the economic structures of Aboriginal society, which stood in contrast to European ideas about land ownership. Prior to colonisation, plentiful resources, hunting techniques and democratic social structures had secured Aboriginal 'affluence'.[29] As Angela Woollacott has emphasised, the brutal frontier violence perpetrated by settlers against Aboriginal peoples was

---

[24] Ann McGrath, '"Modern Stone-Age Slavery": Images of Aboriginal Labour and Sexuality', *Labour History*, 69 (1995), 30–51.

[25] Davidson, *Trade and Travel in the Far East*, 145.

[26] Various texts by Henry Reynolds have illustrated the clash between colonisers and Aboriginal peoples: Henry Reynolds, *The Other Side of the Frontier: Aboriginal Resistance to the European Invasion of Australia* (Ringwood, Vic.: Penguin, 1981), 5. These clashes often revolved around issues of land cultivation and labour during phases of colonial expansion. For an overview of his work see B. Attwood and T. Griffiths, eds, *Frontier, Race, Nation: Henry Reynolds and Australian History* (North Melbourne, Vic.: Australian Scholarly Publishing, 2009). See in particular Reynolds, *The Other Side of the Frontier*; and Henry Reynolds, *Dispossession: Black Australians and White Invaders* (St Leonards, NSW: Allen & Unwin, 1989).

[27] Alan Pope, 'Aboriginal Adaptation to Early Colonial Labour Markets', *Labour History*, 54 (1988), 1–15.

[28] Mark Hannah, 'Aboriginal Workers in the Australian Agricultural Company, 1824–1857', *Labour History*, 82 (2002), 19.

[29] Richard Broome, 'Aboriginal Workers on South-Eastern Frontiers', *Australian Historical Studies* 26, 103 (1994), 205.

'interwoven with the topics of land and labour'.[30] Presenting the indigenous population as lazy was essential to colonial justifications for the taking of land and the logic of the entire project of colonisation. In this context, where laziness justified dispossession, the Australian colonies required alternative sources of labour.

It was apparent to Davidson that the Chinese migrant population of Singapore provided the answer to Australia's labour shortage. From the start of Britain's colonial project in New South Wales there was an awareness that a viable source of imported labour would be required to further the colony's economic development. Long before Davidson's scheme, in 1804, the possibility of Chinese migration to Australia features in official communication between Governor King and the Colonial Secretary, Lord Hobart:

> It would be attended with the most desirable consequences in introducing Chinese into these settlements, which from your knowledge your Lordship has had of the industrious character of that people, and how much the Dutch settlements in India have profited by their residence among them, I presume might be attended with great advantage to this country.[31]

Not only was labour required, but the 'industrious character' of the Chinese made them particularly desirable labourers. But King's scheme was theoretical, and the severity of the shortage had intensified by the 1830s. Few British territories caused more demands and challenges in labour supply than the growing Australian colonies in the 1830s.

Davidson was not alone in recommending imported Asian labour. A rival solution of the 1830s was the proposed importation of Indian coolies. In 1836 John Mackay arrived from Bengal with Bengali servants and sent a memorandum on 'Indian Coolies' to Governor Bourke. A year later J. R. Mayo sent a similar memorandum regarding the success of Indian labour in Mauritius.[32] The supply of labour in Australia, and possible Asian solutions, was a concern of both colonial and imperial governments. Reports, with evidence given from colonists who required labourers, were compiled by 'Governors of the Australian Colonies' and dispatched to the Secretary of State for the Colonies.[33] Thomas Walker, who was a Sydney merchant and cattle owner, revealed that individual proprietors had already made arrangements for the recruitment of Indian and Chinese labour:

---

[30] Woollacott, *Settler Society in the Australian Colonies*, 3.

[31] King to Hobart (1804).

[32] Ohlsson, 'The Origins of a White Australia', 204. See also Cullen, 'Empire, Indentured Labour and the Colony', 84–109.

[33] Parliamentary Papers, *Emigration. Copies of any general report, since the last laid before this House, from the Agent General for Emigration: of any report from the Agent for Emigration in Canada: copies or extracts of any correspondence between the Secretary of State for the Colonies and the governors of the Australian colonies, respecting emigration, since the papers presented to the House on the 14th day of May 1838*, 1839 (536-I) (536-II).

So urgent is the demand for labour, that many settlers have been obliged, in opposition to their own inclination, to send India for Chinese and Coolies, to be hired and introduced at their individual expense. It comes within my own knowledge, that 1,203 such labourers have actually been sent for by 111 settlers, each of whom has paid an advance at the rate of £5 for each labourer, and entered into an engagement to pay the balance of the expense of their introduction on arrival of the parties here.[34]

Given the details discussed here, it appears that Walker was referring, in part, to Davidson's Chinese migration scheme. Crucially, from Walker's perspective, 'Chinese and coolies' were grouped together for the purposes of filling colonial labour shortages.[35]

As early as 1829, texts written by leading colonisation advocates, Robert Gouger and Edward Gibbon Wakefield, recommended Chinese labour as a solution to the Australian problem.[36] The main argument was that voluntary migrants, not slaves or convicts, should be procured for the Australian colonies by the imperial government in London. However, Gouger also looked to China as a possible solution. He noted that: 'the Chinese, especially, who, with a population of 300,000,000, feel the pressure of people upon territory more than any other nation whatsoever, – who are greatly disposed to emigrate, – and are, by far, the most industrious and skilful of Asiatics'.[37] Wakefield expanded upon this, suggesting that it was 'surprising that the Chinese haven't already moved to Australia. And is it not still more surprising that these British settlers, who would gladly purchase slaves at one hundred pounds per head should not have procured labourers from Canton?'[38] As emphasised by Woollacott, though thinkers such as Wakefield advocated specific types of labour migration – namely promoting the emigration of British working-class families – Indian, Chinese and Pacific Islander migrant labour was preferred to coerced or Aboriginal labour.[39] As in Singapore, the use of Chinese labour in Australia was intimately tied to notions of racial hierarchy.

A colonial trailblazer in the employment of Chinese migrants was the Scottish clergyman and politician John Dunmore Lang. After arriving in Sydney

---

[34] Parliamentary Papers, *Emigration*, 44.

[35] As noted in the previous chapter, 'coolie' was generally used in these colonial documents to refer to Indian labourers.

[36] Robert Gouger, ed., *A Letter from Sydney, the Principal Town of Australasia*; together with Edward Gibbon Wakefield, *Outline of a System of Colonization* (London: Joseph Cross, 1829).

[37] Gouger, *A Letter from Sydney*, 202. Additionally Wakefield was also connected to Jardine Matheson through his close friend and patron, John Abel Smith, who represented the firm in London.

[38] Wakefield, *Outline of a System of Colonization*, 219.

[39] Woollacott, *Settler Society in the Australian Colonies*, 40. Wakefield specifically saw female immigration as crucial to ensuring that colonies were 'virtuous and polite'. See Robert Grant, '"The Fit and Unfit": Suitable Settlers for Britain's Mid-Nineteenth-Century Colonial Possessions', *Victorian Literature and Culture*, 33 (2005), 174.

in 1823, Lang employed two Chinese migrants (named Queng and Tchiou) in 1827.[40] Lang, like Wakefield, was an outspoken advocate of assisted migration from Britain to Australia. After a visit to England in 1830, Lang used a Colonial Office loan to assist 140 Scottish tradesmen and their families to emigrate.[41] Yet his advocacy of Chinese immigration into Australia demonstrated the different purposes attributed to different types of migrants. In 1837 Lang mooted the possibility of Australian tea cultivation, which would require a 'numerous' Chinese population.[42] He also demonstrated knowledge of existing systems of Chinese migration and was confident that the success of Chinese migration in Southeast Asia was a model for New South Wales:

> The Chinese … are an emigrating nation; and as they are easily induced, by the prospect of bettering their fortunes to emigrate to Singapore, Batavia, and Calcutta, there is no reason to doubt that a similar prospect would induce them to emigrate to New South Wales.[43]

When there was opposition to large-scale Chinese migration to Australia in the 1850s and 1860s, Lang took the lead in seeking the repeal of anti-immigration legislation.[44] There was demand for Chinese labour in New South Wales. In 1837 Davidson attempted to provide a supply for employers like Lang and establish a regular system of Chinese migration to Australia.

Gordon Forbes Davidson's Chinese Migration Scheme in New South Wales

Gordon Forbes Davidson promoted his migration scheme in June and July 1837. After approaching investors through the 'Sydney Banks', Davidson published nine copies of an advertorial titled 'Chinese Mechanics and Labourers' in the *Colonist, Sydney Gazette, Sydney Herald* and *Hobart Town Courier*. These articles set up further notices from 31 July 1837, which reminded subscribers to pay their deposits. The scheme Davidson laid out in this article was a direct extension of the credit-ticket migration system to Singapore:

[40] D. W. A. Baker, 'Lang, John Dunmore (1799–1878)', *Oxford Dictionary of National Biography*, Oxford University Press, 2004, www.oxforddnb.com/view/article/16005 (accessed 30 September 2018); James Jupp, *The Australian People: An Encyclopaedia of the Nation, Its People and Their Origins* (Cambridge: Cambridge University Press, 2001), 198.

[41] Baker, 'Lang, John Dunmore'.

[42] John Dunmore Lang, *An Historical and Statistical Account of New South Wales, Both as a Penal Settlement and as a British Colony* (London: A. J. Valpy, 1837), 435. This may have been influenced by the ongoing experiment with Chinese labour and tea cultivation in Assam: see Neal, 'Opium and Migration'.

[43] Lang, *An Historical and Statistical Account of New South Wales*, 435.

[44] Neville Meaney, '"In History's Page": Identity and Myth', in Deryck Schreuder and Stuart Ward, eds, *Australia's Empire* (Oxford: Oxford University Press, 2010), 366. Lang's funeral procession was led by 500 Chinese mourners in recognition of his advocacy: see Charles E. Farhadian, ed., *Introducing World Christianity* (Chichester: Wiley-Blackwell, 2012), 208.

My plan is to write to Singapore, in the early part of August, for four or five hundred Chinese, to be hired from the annual supply by the Junks from various ports in China, which arrive there in December and January in large numbers, and may be hired for this or any other country with very little trouble … From a calculation I have made, I feel convinced I can land the men in Sydney at £10 a head, say £11, and add £1 for commission to my Singapore agent, for this the men would serve twelve months after their arrival in the Colony, getting fed of course, and they would serve a second year for £1 per month and rations; after the second year they would expect wages something nearly equal to what free Europeans get here.[45]

The initial advance required from subscribers was £5, with the additional £6 payable on the arrival of the Chinese labourers. The wages of the Chinese employees would be used to pay the subscriber's advances, as they were in Singapore. Davidson mitigated the risk of this large single shipment of 400 labourers by securing numerous investors and had therefore spread potential losses. A list of subscribers and the number of Chinese workers required by each accompanied Davidson's advertisement – Davidson himself had subscribed and paid for five labourers. The list amounted to 335 labourers, a sizeable portion of Davidson's planned total of 400, after just two months of advertising.

In advertising the scheme, Davidson played heavily on his own expertise from Singapore and his first-hand experience of Chinese labour. He emphasised the versatility of Chinese labourers:

From my long experience amongst Chinese, I have no hesitation in recommending strongly to the settlers of New South Wales, the importation of them into this country; as Carpenters, Cabinet-makers, Wheelwrights, Millers, Blacksmiths, Bricklayers and Brick-makers, Gardeners, Cooks, growers of Maize, Sugar, and Tobacco, and general labourers, I can with perfect safety recommend them.[46]

Davidson's knowledge of the Singapore labour market was critical as he confidently stated that the colonists of New South Wales would be able to attract workers: 'If they get £15 a year and rations, it will be double what they earn in and about Singapore, and, in my opinion, will be sufficient to keep up a constant supply of Chinese labour in this market.'[47] Davidson was explicit in his desire to establish a seasonal migration scheme that replicated and drew on excess labour from Singapore.

In Davidson's promotion of Chinese workers he equated them with Europeans and was keen to emphasise his own experience from Singapore: 'for field-work, the China-man is fully equal to the European labourer. I speak

---

[45] *Sydney Herald*, 26 June 1837.
[46] Ibid.
[47] Ibid.

advisedly, having tried them together, side by side, for months at a time.'[48] Yet, Davidson was well aware that the main rival source of labour being proposed for New South Wales was from India. Again, Davidson made use of his first-hand experience that gave him authority on issues of labour and race:

> Many gentlemen have turned their attention to Bengal for a supply of labour. The men procurable from that country, are not equal in physical strength to the Chinamen, nor are they to be had for lower pay. I had six Bengal Coolies in my employ in the Bush, and have no hesitation in saying, that three China-men would have done their work.[49]

In his promotion of Chinese labour as a viable solution to labour shortages in Australia, Davidson continually emphasised his experience in Singapore. Davidson had witnessed the contribution of Chinese colonists in Singapore – occupying an economic, political and social space between European elites and lazy natives – and wished to replicate such an effective system of production in Australia. On the subject of 'ill-treatment' from employers, Davidson cautioned that 'a Chinaman will not put up with it, and will spread such reports about it as will tend to prevent future supplies reaching this part of the world'.[50] This resistance to 'ill-treatment' from Chinese labourers made them the perfect group to replace forced labour. Moreover, labour relations in settler Australia highlighted a contrast between the 'detailed employment of Indian and Chinese labourers on the one hand, and the infantilized employment of Aboriginal workers on the other'.[51] In lieu of white settlers the Chinese would provide a stable, effective and cheap workforce, whilst fulfilling the political imperative for voluntary labour. The success of the scheme in attracting subscribers bolstered Davidson's optimism and belief in the suitability of Chinese labour for an Australian context. In terms of planning and preparation, the project had started with promise.

Whilst the shortage of labour was a widespread concern in 1830s Australia, many Australian colonists opposed Davidson's proposed scheme. The mid-nineteenth century would see the development of white, working-class unionism against Asian migrant labour.[52] As Tony Ohlsson has suggested, the opposition towards Chinese and Indian labour schemes from British settlers in the 1830s can be seen as the genesis of the 'White Australia' policy, created through exclusionary legislation in the late nineteenth century and culminating in the Immigration Restriction Act in 1901.[53] The views of

---

[48] Davidson, *Trade and Travel in the Far East*, 204.
[49] Ibid., 205.
[50] *Sydney Herald*, 26 June 1837.
[51] Woollacott, *Settler Society in the Australian Colonies*, 173.
[52] Ohlsson, 'The Origins of a White Australia', 205.
[53] Ibid., 205.

the Secretary to the Emigration Commission, T. F. Elliot, underline the main points made by opponents to Davidson's scheme:

> There must be a vast superiority in our well-assorted parties of European Families, including a carefully secured equality of females, as compared with any importations that could be made of Chinese, who only come to go away, or of Indian coolies, who are accompanied by a scanty proportion of Women, and who also stipulate to be returned to their own country.[54]

The argument that Asian labour was unreliable, particularly that of the sojourning Chinese, and was morally undesirable, due to the gender imbalance, would be repeatedly made in opposition to non-white immigration in nineteenth-century Australia.[55] That the planned migration to Australia was by private arrangement and consequently was almost entirely undertaken by single men, allowed Chinese migrants, without families to support, to undercut the wages of white Australian settlers. The perceived causes of wage disparity were not limited to family, but included racial tropes, such as the suggestion that Chinese workers could survive solely on rice, unlike white workers who required meat, and therefore could subsist on lower wages.[56] The undercutting of wages would be a major factor in white Australian resistance to Asian migration throughout the nineteenth century, whether based on economic reality or racialised fantasy.[57]

The New South Wales press was critical of Davidson's plan.[58] The *Sydney Monitor* hoped for the failure of Davidson's scheme and warned that, 'to introduce Chinese men by the thousand without women, (they being a gross and sensual people, and addicted to a nameless vice) would be to pollute this land with crimes, which, with all its vices, New South Wales is at present free from'.[59] This suggestion of Chinese criminality and a predilection towards homosexuality notably complemented contemporary criticisms of convict or ex-convict labour. Critics of convict transportation to Van Diemen's Land in the 1840s warned of a plague of 'unnatural' sexual offences.[60] By presenting

---

[54] Elliot to Stephen, 1 December 1837, in Australian Parliament: Joint Library Committee, *Governors' Despatches to and from England, Volume XIX, July 1837–January 1839* (The Library Committee of the Commonwealth Parliament, 1915), 205; Margaret Ray, 'Elliot, Sir Thomas Frederick (1808–1880)', *Oxford Dictionary of National Biography*, Oxford University Press, 2004; online edn, January 2008, www.oxforddnb.com/view/article/41086 (accessed 30 September 2018).

[55] A similar argument about gender surfaced in the United States: Peffer, *If They Don't Bring Their Women Here.* Also note that many Chinese migrants to Australia did settle permanently: Sophie Couchman and Kate Bagnall, eds, *Chinese Australians: Politics, Engagement and Resistance* (Leiden: Brill, 2015).

[56] Lake and Reynolds, *Drawing the Global Colour Line*, 30.

[57] Ibid., 19–50.

[58] Ohlsson, 'The Origins of a White Australia', 205–9.

[59] *Sydney Monitor*, 19 June 1837.

[60] Kirsty Reid, *Gender, Crime and Empire: Convicts, Settlers and the State in Early Colonial Australia*

Chinese male labourers as pre-disposed to sodomy the newspaper was echoing this earlier representation of convicts, repeated by Davidson himself, as undesirable colonists and a moral threat. These discussions of possible labour sources were moving beyond economic necessity and engaging with existential questions about the type of society New South Wales should become. As outlined by Frank Bongiorno, convicts and Chinese immigrants were both 'natural outsiders in a free and self-governing British community'.[61]

The article criticising Davidson's scheme invoked sensational, hyperbolic racism. It described the proposed Chinese immigrants as 'a most outrageous evil' and 'seed of moral pestilence'.[62] This representation of Chinese migrants as a racial threat would be commonly repeated in later anti-immigration discourse. As in Singapore, it was precisely because migrant labourers were overwhelmingly single men, that they were able to provide cheap labour.[63] In colonial imagery the white settler family was emerging as an idealised social unit, in contrast to the threatening single male Chinese sojourner.[64] The *Sydney Monitor*'s stance reflected the editor Edward Smith Hall's avowed aim to represent the interests of the 'poor and labouring classes' through the editorial line of his paper.[65] Hall realised the potential resentment towards competing, cheaper sources of manual labour. Despite Davidson's success in attracting subscribers, the opposition to his scheme revealed the social and economic fissures forming in colonial Australia, which would later become much more overt and politically charged in opposition to Chinese migration to the goldfields from the 1850s. The political disharmony amongst Australian colonists around issues of labour and migration placed additional pressure upon imperial planners to find alternative solutions.

Ultimately, the scheme failed to bring any Chinese labourers to New South Wales. A letter published in both Australian and Singaporean newspapers in May 1839 explained that the advanced money would be returned and the project would be abandoned 'temporarily'. In this letter Davidson explained that:

> Shipping having been so scarce this season, and freight to England so high, has rendered it quite impossible for me to procure a vessel to go to your port with Chinese, and there being still not the latest prospect of my being able to get a

---

(Manchester: Manchester University Press, 2007), 204.

61 Frank Bongiorno, *The Sex Lives of Australians: A History* (Collingwood: Black Inc., 2014), 29.

62 *Sydney Monitor*, 19 June 1837.

63 Peffer, *If They Don't Bring Their Women Here*, 8–9.

64 Tony Ballantyne, *Orientalism and Race: Aryanism in the British Empire* (Basingstoke: Palgrave, 2002), 81.

65 M. J. B. Kenny, 'Hall, Edward Smith (1786–1860)', *Australian Dictionary of Biography*, National Centre of Biography, Australian National University, http://adb.anu.edu.au/biography/hall-edward-smith-2143/text2729 (published first in hardcopy 1966; accessed online 30 September 2018).

vessel, I beg to return, as desired, the first, second, and third of the Treasury Bills for £1,500 sterling.[66]

Despite this setback Davidson did suggest that the project could be successful in the future. He provided details of future prices and contracts 'in case it should be wished to import Chinese from this place next year'.[67] The next year saw the outbreak of Anglo-Chinese hostilities in the First Opium War. As a result, Davidson's scheme never took place. The Opium War disrupted British access to the China coast and Davidson evidently lacked significant connections with the Chinese brokers who were essential for facilitating migration from China to Singapore.[68]

Whilst Davidson's scheme ultimately failed, it had two main implications for Chinese migration to Australia. First, the Singapore to Sydney scheme demonstrated the demand for Chinese labour amongst Australian employers. Attached to this we can see the way that Davidson's praise of Chinese labourers fitted neatly with existing critiques of indigenous Australians. Second, it shows how Australian settler society was primed for racial exclusion before mass migration in the 1850s. This is particularly important as histories of Chinese exclusion in Australia have emphasised the development of negative racial stereotypes in response to mass migration.[69] The issues that Davidson's proposal highlighted would re-emerge, on a much broader scale, after the opening of China to British trade in the Treaty of Nanking in 1842 and the Australian gold rushes of the 1850s.

Singapore and Mass Migration to Australia

Due to Australia's chronic labour shortages, Davidson was not alone in looking to Singapore and Chinese migrant labour as a model for colonisation. This section examines the continued importance of Singapore and Davidson's scheme in Australian discussions around Chinese migration after the cession of Hong Kong to the British and the opening of the Chinese labour market to British merchants in 1842. First, the reports of John Crawfurd to the Colonial Land and Emigration Commission demonstrate that beyond Davidson imperial planners in the metropole saw ways that the lessons of Singapore were applicable to Australia. Second, the case of the *Nimrod* provides an insight into the beginnings of Chinese migration to colonial Australia as well as highlighting the continuities from Davidson's proposed scheme. Third, we

---

[66] *Sydney Gazette*, 4 May 1839.
[67] Ibid.
[68] Kuhn, *Chinese among Others*, 63.
[69] This is also placed in the context of scientific racism and concepts of 'whiteness' that developed in the second half of the nineteenth century. See Atkinson, *The Burden of White Supremacy*.

can trace Singapore as a reference point in Australian discourse on Chinese immigration right through the crucial gold rush period of the 1850s and 1860s, in which the politics of racial exclusion came to the fore.

In Chapter 3 we saw how the Colonial Land and Emigration Commission turned to Chinese labour as a possible alternative to African slave labour. However, one of the Commission's enduring priorities was sourcing cheap, voluntary labour for the Australian colonies. In the early 1840s the Commission again approached John Crawfurd for information about the prospects of a colony at Port Essington to facilitate shipping trade with Asia from the far north of the Australian continent. Various attempts had been made to form a colony at Port Essington since 1824, but success had been limited.[70] One reason for this, which was highlighted by Crawfurd, was the unsuitability of the hot climate for European labourers and the prevalence of disease.[71] After a page discussing the specifics of Port Essington, Crawfurd then spent several pages discussing Singapore as a possible model for the new settlement because the new colony was conceived as an entrepôt that would facilitate trade between Asia and the Australian colonies.[72]

Notably, in suggesting that Singapore might serve as a model for a port in northern Australia, Crawfurd repeated his praise of the Chinese as ideal colonists. On the Chinese population, Crawfurd emphasised their versatility: 'Of the 40,000 [in Singapore], 20,000 are Chinese, and of these certainly not 3,000 are engaged in agricultural pursuits ... The rest are generally merchants, shopkeepers, accountants and porters.'[73] Again, Crawfurd went on to suggest that if the site was 'judiciously selected', Chinese immigrants would be 'sure to pour in' and that 'revenue quickly follows'.[74] As well as his praise of the Chinese as potential colonists, Crawfurd reiterated the free market principles that he had followed in his governance of Singapore and his lobbying against the East India Company monopoly. Here we can detect Crawfurd's confidence that Singapore's economic model taught imperial lessons:

> As Singapore has been looked to as the model of a commercial settlement in these regions ... The only magic to which it has owed its prosperity, but it is a very potent one, has consisted in freedom of commerce, security of life and property, convenience of locality, and the absence of heavy or injudicious taxation.[75]

[70] Jim Allen, *Port Essington: The Historical Archaeology of a North Australian Nineteenth Century Military Outpost* (Sydney: Sydney University Press, 2008)
[71] Appendix No. 6, Notes on Port Essington, in Parliamentary Papers, *General report of the Colonial Land and Emigration Commissioners ... 1843*, 1843 (621) 40.
[72] Ibid., 42.
[73] Ibid., 43.
[74] Ibid., 43.
[75] Ibid., 40.

It is unsurprising that Crawfurd viewed Singapore's Chinese population and free trade economic structure as successful and applicable elsewhere. However, Crawfurd showed little awareness, or acknowledgement, of the concerns of white settlers in the Australian colonies who would view the establishment of a settlement with Chinese colonists in northern Australia with suspicion and fear. Despite Crawfurd's recommendations, the Colonial Office did not populate Port Essington with Chinese colonists and the unfortunate settlement was abandoned in 1849.

Gordon Forbes Davidson's and John Crawfurd's suggestions to use Chinese labour in Australia were hypothetical, but by the late 1840s, with continuing labour shortages in Australia and increased British access to the Chinese labour market, actual experiments with Chinese migration to Australia began to take place. The British firm Tait & Co. chartered the *Nimrod* to take Chinese passengers to Sydney in 1848. The cargo of the *Nimrod* was 120 Chinese labourers under indenture contracts agreed with Captain Thomas Larkins, formerly of the East India Company maritime service. These contracts were for five years' labour in New South Wales at a rate of $2.50 per month for the men and $1.50 for the boys.[76] Larkins had a long career working on the coast of China. He features in the correspondence of the opium traders Jardine Matheson as early as 1825, when Larkins was working as a ship captain for private merchant firms. Larkins arranged the shipment to New South Wales through Tait & Co. from Hong Kong.[77] We can see here the significance of Hong Kong as a British enclave in China and a competing trade entrepôt for Singapore.[78]

The *Nimrod* departed Hong Kong for the treaty port of Amoy to collect labourers in July 1848. Twenty-one of the 120 contract labourers aboard the *Nimrod* were boys below the age of thirteen. Given the age of many of the emigrants and official concerns about the lack of consent, the British Consul T. H. Layton appointed an interpreter to interview passengers before the ship's departure.[79] In a foreshadowing of the Amoy riots of 1852, Hong Kong Governor Bonham, who was nominally responsible for overseeing British subjects at Amoy, informed Palmerston that the 'consul considers it probable that these shipments may give rise to a popular outbreak' in a specific reference to the passage of the *Nimrod*.[80] Poor working conditions and abuses in the

---

[76] Consul T. H. Layton (Amoy) to Governor J. G. Bonham (Hong Kong), 17 July 1848, in Parliamentary Papers, *Emigration. (North American and Australian colonies.) Copies or extracts of any despatches relative to emigration to the North American and Australian colonies; in continuation of the papers presented to this House in August 1848 and February 1849*, 1849 (593). This rate was below average for the Australian colonies at this time.

[77] Various correspondence in MS JM/C2/4, Jardine Matheson Archive (Cambridge University Library).

[78] This is detailed extensively in Chapter 5.

[79] Layton to Bonham, 17 July 1848.

[80] Governor Bonham (Hong Kong) to Viscount Palmerston (London), 10 October 1848, in Parliamentary Papers, *Emigration (North American and Australian colonies)*.

recruitment of Chinese workers continued even during the mass migration of free labourers to Australia in the 1850s.[81] On arrival in Sydney, on 3 October 1848, the Chinese labourers were described in the Australian press as young men who 'appear in sound health' and were suited for work under the supervision of shepherds.[82] Not all of the Chinese labourers had pre-arranged employment. Articles in Australian newspapers between 17 October and 24 November 1848, posted by an 'agent' named Henry Moore, advertised that 'some' of the Chinese immigrants were 'still open for engagement'.[83] These adverts detailed the contracts the labourers had entered into, which were available to be purchased. The contracts covered five years, with provisions for food and clothes, and were estimated to provide one labourer's hire at a total cost of less than £11 per annum for employers.[84]

Much like Davidson's attempted project in 1837, the arrival of the *Nimrod* divided press opinion in Australia. The reaction of the *Goulburn Herald* reflected the criticisms. The newspaper opined, 'we much dislike this copper-colored, anti-Christian emigration'.[85] Whilst the necessity for labour in the colony was recognised – Australian colonies faced many of the same problems with labour shortages in 1848 as they had in 1837 – the critics preferred for the necessary labour to be sourced from the 'virtuous and enlightened' population of 'Christians and born subjects of the British Crown'.[86] In settler society it was one thing for Asian migrants to do jobs that whites would not, but quite another for them to actively compete in the labour market.[87] The origins of the exclusionary, racialised, white working-class resistance to Chinese immigration that became politically mobile in Australia from the mid-1850s onwards can be seen in the criticism of the Chinese labourers who arrived aboard the *Nimrod* in 1848. Angela Woollacott has discussed how newspaper discourse in the 1840s advocated government-funded migration schemes from Britain as opposed to Asian 'coolie' labour, which would lead to a multi-racial colonial population that both the authorities and settlers deemed undesirable.[88] The threat of Asian immigration led to the self-definition

---

[81] Margaret Slocomb, 'Preserving the Contract: The Experience of Indentured Labourers in the Wide Bay and Burnett Districts in the Nineteenth Century', *Labour History*, 113 (2017), 103–31.

[82] *Sydney Morning Herald*, 3 October 1848.

[83] *Sydney Morning Herald*, 17 October 1848.

[84] *Melbourne Argus*, 24 November 1848.

[85] *The Goulburn Herald*, 7 October 1848.

[86] Ibid.

[87] Rachel Bright, 'Asian Migration and the British World, c.1850–1914', in Kent Fedorowich and Andrew Thompson, eds, *Empire, Migration and Identity in the British World* (New York: Manchester University Press, 2013), 130.

[88] Woollacott, *Settler Society in the Australian Colonies*, 89. The exclusionary attitude towards Asian immigrants in Australia was, in many ways, born from the attitudes of racial superiority implicit in the expansion of British colonial control and land ownership, and explicit in campaigns of frontier violence against Aboriginal Australians.

of Australia as a 'white' country.[89] Groups, such as the Irish, who were subject to discrimination in Britain, were incorporated, by virtue of their skin colour, into a vision of colonial labour that excluded non-whites and the Chinese in particular.[90]

Despite settler protests, Australian employers continued to demand Chinese migrant labour. The labour shortages that had created interest in Davidson's 1837 scheme had not abated by the late 1840s. Colonial, pastoral expansion had exacerbated pre-existing shortages. In contrast to the criticisms made in the *Goulburn Herald*, an 1847 letter from the entrepreneurial Australian settler Adam Bogue praised the Chinese and their potential as labourers in New South Wales. Following a visit to Amoy, both Australian and China-coast newspapers published Bogue's letter:

> The great poverty of the majority of the inhabitants, their civility and kind-
> ness to Europeans, their general quiet and inoffensive manners, the tractability
> of their character, and their indomitable industry in agricultural and other
> pursuits, induced me to suppose that it would be of the first advantage to New
> South Wales in her present condition, if she could be supplied with labourers
> from that province.[91]

Note here how Bogue's praise invoked many of the common perceptions of the Chinese character discussed in the 1830s. Again, notions of Chinese 'character' and 'industry' made China a particularly desirable source of labour. The difference between 1847 and 1837 was not the demand for labour in New South Wales, but the easy access Adam Bogue had to China and Chinese labour in contrast to Davidson.

Investors in the *Nimrod* scheme also responded to press criticism. This response came in the form of vociferous praise of the Chinese workers. An advert published on 24 November 1848 included a letter from 'an influential settler and magistrate' who had Chinese labourers in his employ. The mystery settler wrote that the Chinese workers, who had been working as shepherds, 'do the same work as Europeans, with whom they are equally intelligent and hardy'.[92] Aside from the specifics of the author's recruits, praise was extended to other potential forms of employment: 'they are careful … honest, and exceedingly cleanly, and would doubtless answer well for cooks and in-door servants … by their civility and tact they have avoided all quarrelling, and are individually liked by their white fellow servants'.[93] This promotion of Chinese labour is notable for the comparisons and importance placed on the

[89]   Robert A. Huttenback, *Racism and Empire: White Settlers and Coloured Immigrants in the British
       Self-Governing Colonies 1830–1910* (Ithaca, NY: Cornell University Press, 1976), 21.
[90]   Huttenback, *Racism and Empire*, 17–21.
[91]   *Canton Register*, 15 June 1847.
[92]   *Melbourne Argus*, 24 November 1848.
[93]   Ibid.

'European' and 'white' servants, as opposed to comparisons with other Asian groups seen in previous chapters. This letter demonstrates an awareness of the developing context of the Australian clamour for migrants from Britain to preserve the colony's racial homogeneity.

The *Nimrod* shipment was particularly significant as it became a model for importing Chinese labour in Australia in the late 1840s. In May 1849, 'parties who hired the Chinese immigrants per Nimrod, from Amoy, for a further number of those men' placed an advert to try to attract employers who were interested in recruiting Chinese labourers.[94] The continuing expansion of the pastoral industry in the late 1840s and the paucity of labour meant that in spite of criticisms Australian newspapers were aware of the necessity of Chinese labour to fuel the colony's economic development. Articles spoke of how the importation of cheap Chinese labour would lead the river banks 'to be diversified by plantations of sugar-cane, cotton, coffee, rice etc.' and how 'Chinese labourers will be required to colonize the northern and tropical portions of New Holland'.[95] By March 1849 the importation of Chinese labour was referred to as 'not a mere matter of experiment, but a regular and systematic trade' in the colonial press.[96] Before the discovery of gold in 1851 – from which point Chinese migrants tended to be self-funded, free migrants – schemes that involved Chinese contract labour brought an estimated 3,000 migrant workers to Australia.[97]

Australian demand for labour in the late 1840s also combined with increased supply from China. In particular, colonial observers noted that the proximity of Australia to China – as compared with destinations like the West Indies – encouraged immigration, as migrants 'could have frequent communication with their friends in China'.[98] Due to J. T. White's investigation into emigration on behalf of the West India Committee, numbers of Chinese passengers from the China coast between 1848 and 1853 were recorded. Over a four-and-a-half-year period a total of 3,385 Chinese contract labourers departed Amoy and Namoa for Sydney.[99] Of course, given the scrutiny of the system by the British and the continued Qing prohibition on emigration, it is likely that there were unreported shipments. Similarly it is likely that the given mortality figure, with 145 Chinese passengers recorded as having died *en route* to Sydney, is a low estimate. Employers contracted most of these

[94] *Moreton Bay Courier*, 19 May 1849.
[95] *Sydney Morning Herald*, 2 May 1845; *Melbourne Argus*, 5 May 1848.
[96] *The People's Advocate*, 10 March 1849.
[97] Pan, *The Encyclopaedia of the Chinese Overseas*, 274.
[98] *Sydney Morning Herald*, 30 January 1847.
[99] James T. White to S. Walcott, 'Emigration of Contract Labourers to Sydney', 16 April 1853, in CO 885/1/20, *Correspondence Relative to the Emigration of Chinese Coolies* (London: Edward Eyre and William Spottiswoode, 1853).

emigrants for roles in agriculture (including vineyards and olive groves), the wool industry and, from 1851, gold and tin mining.[100]

The discovery of gold, first reported in Hong Kong in August 1851, changed the nature of emigration to Australia as free migrants to the gold-fields soon outnumbered the contracted pastoral labourers.[101] Moreover, the British investigation into the activities of the firms operating at Amoy, due to cases of exploitation such as the *Nimrod*, marked the decline of emigration from that departure point and the ascendance of Hong Kong as the main departure point for Chinese emigrants. An estimated 62,000 Chinese miners travelled from Hong Kong to Australia between 1855 and 1867.[102] The story of Chinese mass migration to the Australia goldfields in the 1850s is well known, but the origins of the Amoy to Sydney passenger route – trailblazed by the *Nimrod* – are less so. The success of the *Nimrod* shipment, and the subsequent shipments of agricultural labourers, stood in contrast to Gordon Forbes Davidson's failed experiment in 1837. The key change here was the firm foothold that the British had established in Hong Kong and the new Chinese treaty ports after 1842.

The discovery of gold in Australia also fundamentally changed the processes of Chinese migration to Australia. In search of a quick fortune on the goldfields, passengers either paid for their own passage or moved under a version of the credit-ticket system, one where they had their passage paid and repaid the debt to their sponsor.[103] Various histories have emphasised the role of Chinese migrants on the Australian goldfields in economic and social terms, as well as resistance to immigration as a significant force in Australian political discourse in the late nineteenth century.[104] For example, John Fitzgerald has discussed how Chinese workers formed the second largest group in mid-nineteenth-century Victoria and how the majority of the population of Darwin was Chinese until the 1920s, in order to outline the significance of the Chinese population.[105] The fact that these migrations followed in the tracks of Gordon Forbes Davidson, John Crawfurd and the *Nimrod* reveals an extended lineage. Nobody illustrates this sense of continuity in an era of rapid change better than John Dunmore Lang who, after first

---

[100] Parliamentary Papers, *Emigration (North American and Australian colonies)*; Carol Matheson Con-nell, *A Business in Risk: Jardine Matheson and the Hong Kong Trading Industry* (London: Praeger, 2004), 29.

[101] *Hong Kong Register*, 12 August 1851.

[102] Margaret Slocomb, *Among Australia's Pioneers: Chinese Indentured Pastoral Workers on the Northern Frontier 1848 to c.1880* (Queensland: Balboa Press, 2014), 92.

[103] Walton, *Indentured Labour*, 45.

[104] Jonathon Hyslop, 'The Imperial Working Class Makes Itself White', *Journal of Historical Sociology*, 12, 4 (1999), 398–421; Barry McGowan, 'The Economics and Organisation of Chinese Mining in Colonial Australia', *Australian Economic History Review*, 45, 2 (2005), 119–39.

[105] John Fitzgerald, *Big White Lie: Chinese Australians in White Australia* (Sydney: UNSW Press, 2007), 43.

employing Chinese migrants in Sydney in 1827, took the lead in arguing for the repeal of New South Wales' proposed anti-Chinese legislation in 1867.[106]

There is a wealth of literature that has discussed Chinese migration to Australia over the nineteenth century in the context of racial exclusion. This existing literature has often been focused specifically on views of Chinese migrants in white settler colonies and the United States – such as *Drawing the Global Colour Line*, *Melancholy Order*, *The Burden of White Supremacy* – and has treated these mass migrations to 'white men's countries' as a separate process from Chinese migrations to Southeast Asia.[107] Scholars like Benjamin Mountford have begun to put the exclusionary responses to Chinese in a broader imperial context, with a particular focus on Anglo-Chinese diplomatic relations, but it is also clear from an examination of debates about Chinese immigration in the Australian colonies that Singapore remained an important part of settler discourse for several reasons.[108] First, as increasing numbers of Chinese migrants settled in Australia, rather than sojourning for a short period before returning to China, comparisons with Singapore's inter-generational Chinese community became more common.[109] Second, the stereotypes applied to Chinese migrants from an exclusionary perspective demonstrated a clear continuity with the tropes repeated by colonial administrators in Singapore. Third, even as Hong Kong emerged as an important departure point for Chinese migrants to Australia, Singapore and the Straits Settlements remained an important centre of onward migration.

As in Singapore itself, characterisations of the Chinese as colonists in the Australian press were not simply positive or negative, even in the context of calls for racial exclusion, but drew on a range of stereotypes that were modified for the specific context of the Australian colonies. Newspaper commentary provides a useful insight into popular discourse because of the rapid proliferation and widespread consumption of newspapers in colonial Australia. Moreover, scholars such as Rebecca Wood and Greg Picker have emphasised the importance of colonial newspapers for the development of a specific Australian settler identity.[110] Crucially, the development of settler identity was often in combination with discriminatory racism. On the one hand this was in opposition to indigenous land rights, with settlers

[106] Schreuder and Ward, *Australia's Empire*, 366.
[107] Lake and Reynolds, *Drawing the Global Colour Line*; McKeown, *Melancholy Order*; Atkinson, *The Burden of White Supremacy*.
[108] Mountford, *Britain, China and Colonial Australia*.
[109] See Mobo Gao, 'Early Chinese Migrants to Australia: A Critique of the Sojourner Narrative on Nineteenth-Century Chinese Migration to British Colonies', *Asian Studies Review*, 41, 3 (2017), 389–404, for a critique of the stereotype that Chinese migrants were exclusively sojourners.
[110] Wood, 'Frontier Violence and the Bush Legend', 1–19; Greg Picker, '"A Nation Is Governed by All That Has Tongue in the Nation": Newspapers and Political Expression in Colonial Sydney, 1825–1850', *Journal of Australian Studies*, 23, 62 (1999), 183–9.

advocating the violent dispossession of indigenous peoples.[111] However, in the Australian context the political articulation of settler identity often included anti-Chinese racism. For example, the famous imagery of the Lambing Flat Riots (1860–61) included a banner that combined the phrase 'no Chinese' with the image of the 'Southern Cross' flag, which rebel miners flew at the Eureka Stockade, an event often credited as the starting point of Australian democracy and political independence.[112] From the very beginning, settler democracy combined with racial exclusion.

In the Australian newspapers in the 1850s and 1860s references to Singapore feature heavily in critiques of racial exclusion. The first, and most obvious, problem with exclusion was that Chinese colonists born in Singapore and Hong Kong were technically British subjects.[113] Advocates of Chinese migration to Australia emphasised the inconsistency of an exclusionary policy: 'If all these [Chinese in Singapore and Hong Kong] are free to emigrate to a British colony by virtue of their being British subjects, how can any objection be raised to the Chinese on the score of their being an alien race?'[114] In addition to discussions around British subjecthood, Australian fears that a large Chinese settler population constituted a political, military and demographic threat could be dispelled with the combined examples of Singapore and Hong Kong. For example, a report of a discussion in which members of the Victorian Chamber of Commerce debated the pros and cons of repealing the infamous poll-tax on Chinese immigrants focused on recent riots at Singapore:

> Mr O'Shanassy asked, if there had not been some strong feeling against Chinese in Singapore, where it was believed they were so numerous as to be powerful enough to seize the place? Mr Marshall said those riots were, in great measure caused by the oppressive behaviour of the Malay police there, and the feeling among the Chinese that they were without redress. When he was in Hong Kong there were only 1,000 Europeans to 4,000 Chinese, and yet no one apprehended riots there.[115]

Within these sources we can see echoes of Singapore's colonial administrators' concerns about the Chinese as an organised political threat. However, the longevity of Singapore as a politically and economically stable

---

111 This phenomenon was not confined to Australia. See Lester's *Imperial Networks* for more on the construction of settler identity in South Africa.

112 S. Thompson, '1860 Lambing Flat Roll Up Banner', Migration Heritage Centre: New South Wales, www.migrationheritage.nsw.gov.au/exhibition/objectsthroughtime/lambing-flatsbanner/index.html (accessed 30 September 2018).

113 Peter Prince, 'The "Chinese" Always Belonged', *History Australia*, 26 August 2018. DOI: 10.1080/14490854.2018.1485463.

114 'Chinese Immigration', *Mount Alexander Mail*, 6 February 1857.

115 'Chinese Immigration', *The Argus*, 6 June 1862.

colony meant that alternative causes, in this case 'oppression', explained Chinese unrest.

In Australia, as in Singapore, even despite earnest defences of Chinese colonists, some negative stereotypes persisted. For example, in an early debate about the possibility of regulating immigration from China, the politician John Lamb, who was a notable opponent of convict transportation, 'opposed the motion' on the grounds that:

> He did not believe in the existence of the vile practices and crimes attributed by the Honourable Member to the Chinese; he had seen great numbers of them in Eastern countries, in Calcutta, Singapore, Penang, and Java, and in none of those places were such habits imputed to them, their prevalent vices being opium eating and gambling.[116]

Here we can detect continuity from the criticisms applied to Gordon Forbes Davidson's proposed shipment in 1837. The charge that Lamb was responding to was that the Chinese were 'a people among whom nameless and shocking vices were habitually indulged in'.[117] Whilst Lamb refuted this often-repeated charge of homosexuality, which had its origins in the criticisms of convict transportation in the 1830s, he did so by invoking the tropes of opium and gambling addiction that were well established in Singapore.

More broadly, the reprinting of sensational stories from Singapore's English-language newspapers continued to reinforce negative stereotypes of the Chinese as a catalyst for social degradation: 'readers of the Singapore papers will find constantly brief details of Chinese vice laid bare by the police, and published by the papers as far as decency will permit'.[118] Additionally, whilst Singapore could be used to provide an example of successful Anglo-Chinese colonialism, in the context of Chinese exclusion the potential of a Chinese majority population as a political threat was a powerful image. Australian newspaper discourse repeated the fears of Singapore's colonial administrators, that Chinese secret societies and factional riots had the potential to develop into fully fledged rebellions against British rule:

> All who have read much of the current history of the British Straits Settlements, for some years past, are aware that the Chinese, although not given to much that could be well objected to, when they are few in number in a European or foreign community, become very vicious, turbulent, and dangerous, when their numbers have increased until they form a relatively large portion of the population. The police records of Singapore and Penang would abundantly bear out this statement; and the Chinese insurrection at Sarawak, with

---

[116] 'Chinese Immigration', *The Maitland Mercury*, 29 November 1851.
[117] Ibid.
[118] 'The Chinese Immigration Bill', *The Maitland Mercury*, 28 September 1861.

its cruel episodes of murder, was only a more complete proof, because there the Chinese chanced to still more exceed in proportionate numbers the Europeans.[119]

This extract from the *Maitland Mercury* perhaps reveals that the ultimate problem with attempts to apply the Singapore model in the Australian colonies was settler concern at the prospect of mass migration leading to a demographic shift that left white settlers outnumbered. Whilst employers and colonial planners looked to the success of Chinese labour in Singapore with specific shortages and small experiments in mind, the rhetoric of exclusion developed a more apocalyptic view of a 'dangerous' and uncontrollable Chinese population.

In Australia, as in Singapore, colonial observers were concerned about the potential social ramifications of the gender imbalance of Chinese migrant populations.[120] Beyond this, tales from Singapore also inform critiques of Chinese gender relations and by extension critiques of the Chinese character. For example, British observers interpreted the practice of foot-binding in China as evidence of domestic despotism on the part of Chinese men, which, if the Chinese held political power, would replicate on a larger scale. Thus, gender relations were a prism through which the Chinese and China could be criticised.[121] A good example of this is an editorial in the *Empire* that suggested 'one of the most decisive tests of the tone of morals, the sense of man's true dignity, is the habitual treatment of woman', before concluding that 'tried by this test the Chinaman does not rise in our estimation'.[122] The article then gives an account of British visitors to the home of a respected and important Chinese merchant in Singapore. The account described the merchant's wife as a 'little thing' that appeared to the guests in a 'bundle' and put 'its hands in the position of a suppliant'.[123] Crucially, the author extrapolated from this specific example to form a general conclusion that 'the [Chinese] husbands who can exact from their wives not reverence but self-abasement in the presence of strangers, are devoid of manly feeling'.[124] Here we can see how insights into Chinese social structures in Singapore were used as supporting evidence for pre-existing Australian prejudices and were

119 'Chinese Immigration', *The Maitland Mercury*, 16 March 1861.
120 For example, some articles in the Australian newspapers referenced the fact that some Chinese women did emigrate to Singapore as a potential solution to the gender imbalance in Australia: 'Chinese Immigration', *The Banner*, 19 September 1854.
121 Note that gender and gender relations were a common factor in the process of racialisation in the British Empire. For example, colonial observers stereotyped Indian men as 'effeminate': Mrinalini Sinha, *Colonial Masculinity: The 'Manly Englishman' and the 'Effeminate Bengali' in the Late Nineteenth Century* (Manchester: Manchester University Press, 1995).
122 'Chinese Immigration', *Empire*, 4 September 1861.
123 Ibid.
124 Ibid.

mobilised in a broader critique of the Chinese character that was essential to exclusionary politics.

Ultimately, Singapore remained an important contact zone, which offered an insight into the positives and negatives of Chinese immigration, even as new systems of migration from the China coast to Australia developed. The 120 Chinese migrants who arrived in Sydney aboard the *Nimrod* in October 1848 were treading a new and unfamiliar path. Around 100,000 more Chinese migrants followed these labourers to Australia by 1901.[125] In 1879 some of these migrants – Lowe Kong Meng, Cheok Hong Cheong and Louis Ah Mouy – wrote a scathing critique of the inconsistencies of Britain's desire to open China economically whilst limiting Chinese migration to Australia.[126] In doing so they also emphasised how Chinese colonists were hardworking and opium consumption was not immoral when compared to British 'drunkenness'.[127] One of the authors of this polemic, Lowe Kong Meng, typified the continuing connection to Singapore. Born in the Straits Settlements, and therefore a British subject, Meng arrived in Melbourne in 1853, ahead of the 10,000 Chinese fortune seekers who arrived in 1854, and set up a business selling tea and other provisions to Chinese gold diggers.[128] A wealth of literature exists on these growing Chinese communities in the second half of the nineteenth century and their significance in the globalisation of border control in the twentieth century.[129] Yet it is the start of these migrations, and in particular the transitional period from the 1830s to the 1860s, that requires further study. Not only does the life story of Lowe Kong Meng bridge this period, but it shows that concepts of Chinese character constructed in the contact zones of the Straits Settlements and China coast were re-configured and re-applied in colonial Victoria.

Conclusion

In the late 1830s Gordon Forbes Davidson's project failed, and the beginning of the Opium War and his return to Britain in 1844 prevented any repeat attempts. However, his attempt to establish such a scheme does show how his experience of Chinese migration in Singapore informed his efforts to procure Chinese labourers for Australia. Davidson was drawing on the stereotypes and ideas about Chinese labourers that circulated in print media, as well as his personal experience of Anglo-Chinese society in Singapore.

---

[125] Fitzgerald, *Big White Lie*, 13.
[126] L. Kong Meng, Cheok Hong Cheong and Louis Ah Mouy, *The Chinese Question in Australia 1878–9* (Melbourne: F. F. Bailliere, 1879), 4. The wider context of this contradiction is effectively outlined in Mountford, *Britain, China and Colonial Australia*.
[127] Meng et al., *The Chinese Question in Australia*, 4.
[128] Lake and Reynolds, *Drawing the Global Colour Line*, 16–17.
[129] McKeown, *Melancholy Order*, 2.

As a result, Singapore fulfilled two functions. It was important both as a representative model of Chinese migration and as a site of onward migration from which Davidson could recruit migrants. However, the long list of subscribers Davidson attracted, and the criticism his scheme faced, show a conflict in Australian society between the need for cheap labour, the economic interests of white workers and the desire for racial homogeneity in the colony. Davidson's scheme was the first attempt to introduce a significant number of Chinese labourers into a colony with a sizeable white settler population. This well-publicised attempt to set up a system of Chinese migration from Singapore does demonstrate the desire for Chinese migrant labour amongst colonial employers and reveals the intersection between concepts of racial hierarchy, land ownership and labour in colonial New South Wales. At the same time, its failure shows the limitation of the idealised narrative of Chinese migrant labour. Whilst employers and colonial authorities desired Chinese labour in both Singapore and New South Wales, there was a growing class of settlers in the Australian colonies who opposed cheap, non-white labour.

Davidson's greatest mistake was that he was a decade too early. In the late 1840s contract labourers began to travel from Hong Kong to Australian colonies and, with the onset of the Australian gold rush in the early 1850s, the number of willing Chinese migrants grew exponentially. The response of white working-class exclusion movements to these migrations echoed the racialised opposition to Davidson's scheme in the 1830s. But, even as the focus of the debate moved away from Davidson's proposed Singapore to Sydney route, to migration direct from China to Australia, the impact of Singapore remained. Both positive and negative stereotypes about Chinese immigrants drew heavily on the example of Singapore. The key difference was the specific colonial context of the Australian colonies and the racialised resistance of Australia's settlers to Chinese labour.

This chapter demonstrates that the economic and social anxieties, as well as the racial prejudice, which underpinned Australian resistance to Chinese immigration in the second half of the nineteenth century were already in place by the 1830s. Hence, John Crawfurd's suggestion that Australian colonies could follow Singapore as a 'model of commercial settlement' was hopelessly naïve. Opponents of Chinese immigration to Australia contorted and adapted Crawfurd's own observations of the Chinese as hardworking but potentially untrustworthy. The Singapore model was problematic in the context of the settler colony, but Chinese migration to Australia from the 1850s demonstrates the significance of British access to the China coast post-1842. Hong Kong and the treaty ports acted as new Anglo-Chinese contact zones and facilitated experiments with the Singapore model in the development of plantation colonies on a global scale.

Chapter 5

HONG KONG VERSUS SINGAPORE: THE DAWN OF MASS MIGRATION

> His Majesty the Emperor of China agrees that British Subjects shall be allowed to reside … at the Cities and Towns of Canton, Amoy, Foochow-fu, Ningpo, and Shanghai … the Island of Hong-Kong [is] to be possessed in perpetuity by her Britannic Majesty.[1]

The Treaty of Nanking was the 'opening' of China that British merchants and commentators had so vehemently lobbied for throughout the 1830s.[2] Historians have identified the treaty as the start of a new age in Anglo-Chinese economic, political and military relations. It is known in Chinese history as the start of China's 'century of humiliation' at the hands of foreign imperialism.[3] In terms of emigration too, the newly opened ports and acquired territory listed in the treaty provided new opportunities for Chinese workers seeking to circumvent the Qing ban on emigration. Historians of Chinese emigration have taken 1842 as the start of a new era and have emphasised changes from, rather than continuities with, the pre-Opium War era.[4] This chapter will situate Chinese emigration in the wake of the Treaty of Nanking as connected to systems and perceptions of Chinese migrants developed in Singapore from 1819. Additionally, with the security of Hong Kong and the Chinese treaty ports, British merchants established new systems of Chinese migration from different departure points and to new, global destinations. British colonies in the Caribbean, which required a replacement for recently abolished African slave labour, were a key destination.

---

[1] Treaty of Nanking (Great Britain – China), in G. E. P. Hertslet and Edward Parkes, *Hertslet's China Treaties. Treaties between Great Britain and China and between China and Foreign Powers, etc.*, 3rd edn (London: Harrison and Sons, for H.M. Stationery, 1908).

[2] For more on the British belief in the necessity to 'liberate' the Chinese from Qing rule see Chapter 2.

[3] See Bickers, *The Scramble for China*, 5–7, for a description of Chinese nationalist historiography.

[4] Note the date range of Adam McKeown, 'Conceptualizing Chinese Diasporas, 1842–1949', *The Journal of Asian Studies*, 58, 2 (1999), 306–37.

First, this chapter examines the role of Hong Kong as an Anglo-Chinese contact zone, as well as a destination and departure point for migrants. Colonial authority in Hong Kong, much like Singapore previously, was simultaneously reliant on Chinese elites and intermediaries, whilst being threatened by the size and organisation of the Chinese labour force. Second, Hong Kong was also important as it provided a base from which British firms could facilitate onward migration to destinations beyond Southeast Asia. The establishment of British judicial hegemony on the China coast, combined with extensive shipping connections that had developed with the growth of Anglo-Chinese trade post-1842, facilitated mass migrations to the goldfields of Australia and California as well as indentured labourers as a cheap alternative to African slave labour in the West Indies.[5] Finally, as these new systems of mass migration developed, which saw the movement of millions of people in the second half of the nineteenth century, Singapore was still important as a model, stopping place and point of onward migration.

Hong Kong versus Singapore

The cession of Hong Kong to Britain in 1842 had implications for systems of Chinese emigration through both the nineteenth and twentieth centuries. Hong Kong became both a point of onward migration to various global locations and a destination for migrants from across southern China. Hong Kong acted as a contact zone in which existing concepts of the Chinese character were further developed by both experienced and new Western observers. For the small indigenous population, seizure of the island and its colonisation by the British would completely change the geographic, economic, social and cultural fabric of Hong Kong.[6] The immigration of thousands of people from across southern China as well as the establishment of a wealthy and powerful foreign merchant elite led to new formations of colonial identity.[7] The mainland Chinese who moved to Hong Kong were criticised by colonial observers, such as the colonial administrator Robert Montgomery Martin who referred to them as the 'scum of Canton'.[8] In addition to Hong Kong's role as a contact zone, it also became an important base for British commercial

---

5   For more on California see Elizabeth Sinn, *Pacific Crossings: California Gold, Chinese Migration, and the Making of Hong Kong* (Hong Kong: Hong Kong University Press, 2013), 143.

6   Solomon Bird, *Traders of Hong Kong: Some Foreign Merchant Houses, 1841–1899* (Hong Kong: Hong Kong Museum of History, 1993), 19. John M. Carroll, *A Concise History of Hong Kong* (Hong Kong: Rowman & Littlefield, 2007), 19, gives an estimated population of 5,000–7,000 prior to British occupation.

7   Namely the developing 'Hong Konger' identity, which is discussed repeatedly in Helen F. Siu and Agnes S. Ku, eds, *Hong Kong Mobile: Making a Global Population* (Hong Kong: Hong Kong University Press, 2008).

8   Wai Kwan Chan, *The Making of Hong Kong Society: Three Studies of Class Formation in Early Hong Kong* (Oxford: Clarendon Press, 1991), 49.

operations on the China coast. As Hong Kong became a busy colony and key site of onward migration globally, the significance of opium-trading firms like Jardine Matheson and Dent & Co. provides a connection to the pre-Opium War context of Anglo-Chinese exchange discussed in Chapter 2.

Frank Welsh's description of Hong Kong as a 'Chinese colony that happened to be run by Britain' is useful as it brings attention to the fact that twentieth-century histories of colonial rule often ignored or oversimplified the role of the island's Chinese inhabitants.[9] Hong Kong was significant both as a migrant destination and a point of onward migration. That a large Chinese population overtly operated outside of the control of the Qing Empire from 1842 both highlighted the ineptitude of existing emigration restrictions and created an environment for establishing new systems of migration. Two historical approaches have resulted in the Chinese being largely written out of the history of Hong Kong. Early Western historiography focused on the Western residents and Hong Kong's success story as a liberal, capitalist, free trade port. In contrast, Chinese scholars had maintained that Hong Kong was a symbol of imperialism, with the Chinese islanders being described either as captives or as collaborators.[10] More recent work by Christopher Munn and John Carroll has focused on the Chinese majority and their relationship with colonial authority and mercantile elites. Munn's *Anglo-China* sets out to redress the balance by dismissing the notion of Chinese inhabitants as passive victims of 'colonial machinery'.[11] Similarly, Carroll has emphasised the close business relationships between Western merchants and their Chinese employees, known as compradors, highlighting cooperation over conflict.[12] These texts build on an increasing body of work that highlights the different social and economic roles played by Chinese migrants – whether labourers, artisans or merchants – in Hong Kong.[13]

Hong Kong's Chinese population was essential to the colony's economic development in the 1840s and 1850s. Initial population counts at the point of Hong Kong's cession to Britain estimated a community of 15,000 at Victoria, of whom more than 12,000 were Chinese.[14] This population increased rapidly over the 1840s, a process that was encouraged by European capital and poor economic conditions in Guangdong province due to the opening of

[9]   Frank Welsh, *A History of Hong Kong* (London: HarperCollins, 1994), 8.

[10]   Carroll, *A Concise History of Hong Kong*, 9.

[11]   Christopher Munn, *Anglo-China: Chinese People and British Rule in Hong Kong, 1841–1880* (Hong Kong: Hong Kong University Press, 2009), 10.

[12]   Carroll, 'The Canton System', 54. For more on the role of Chinese compradors see Chapter 2.

[13]   For example see Elizabeth Sinn, *Power and Charity: A Chinese Merchant Elite in Colonial Hong Kong* (Hong Kong: Hong Kong University Press, 2003); Chan, *The Making of Hong Kong Society*; Jung-fang Tsai, *Hong Kong in Chinese History: Community and Social Unrest in the British Colony, 1842–1913* (New York: Columbia University Press, 1993).

[14]   Welsh, *A History of Hong Kong*, 139; these figures were the estimates of Governor Pottinger's new, under-resourced colonial administration.

the treaty ports.[15] Contemporaries like Arthur Cunynghame described how 'it was almost impossible to prevent the people from the opposite coast from flocking to us'.[16] Early colonial blue books did try to quantify the growing Chinese population in the 1840s.[17] The first such measure in 1845 gave the 'coloured' population as 23,748 (only 4,809 of whom were female).[18] By 1849 'Chinese' had been written in pencil over the term 'coloured', which was already printed in the blue book by the Colonial Office, and the total 'Chinese' population was given as 28,956 (with a similar gender disparity) and was now further split with the sub-category of 'boat people'.[19] The Tanka 'boat people' were placed at the foot of the social stratification by many mainland Chinese contemporaries, but had been extremely useful to the British merchants and colony builders by supplying provisions during the Opium War.[20] As a consequence of British colonisation, many Tanka relocated to Hong Kong in search of economic opportunities. The census information points to the problems local government faced when it came to categorising different Chinese ethnic groups. It was not until 1845, three years into British governance, that a 'Registrar General' was appointed to take responsibility for a Chinese community that constituted ninety-five per cent of the total population.[21] Colonial authorities were aware that the Chinese migrant population was essential to the colony's success.

The Western firms that relocated to Hong Kong during the Opium War were dependent on Chinese employees. As an example, Jardine Matheson employed a large staff of Chinese compradors, interpreters and clerks in their head office and warehouses (buildings which themselves were erected by Chinese labour) at East Point – a prime location in Hong Kong's Victoria Harbour.[22] Other trading operations required Chinese intermediaries, with each opium ship employing at least one comprador and interpreter.[23] Another draw for migrants was the opportunities for entrepreneurship that Hong Kong presented. Early occupational data are as limited as census data, but sporadic

---

15 Elizabeth Sinn, 'Emigration from Hong Kong before 1941: General Trends', in Ronald Skeldon, ed., *Emigration from Hong Kong: Tendencies and Impacts* (Hong Kong: The Chinese University Press, 1995), 21.

16 Captain Arthur Cunynghame, *The Opium War: Being Recollections of Service in China* (first published Philadelphia: G.B. Ziever & Co., 1845, reprint 1972), 40.

17 Chan, *The Making of Hong Kong Society*, 65.

18 Hong Kong Blue Book (1845), CO 133/2 (National Archives).

19 Hong Kong Blue Book (1849), CO 133/6 (National Archives).

20 John Carroll, *Edge of Empires: Chinese Elites and British Colonials in Hong Kong* (London: Harvard University Press, 2005), 23.

21 Tsang, *A Modern History of Hong Kong*, 24.

22 Edward LeFevour, *Western Enterprise in Late Ch'ing China: A Selective Survey of Jardine, Matheson & Company's Operations, 1842–1895* (Cambridge, MA: Harvard University Press, 1968), 22. The word 'comprador' was not in common use until slightly later, but the term serves as a useful description for the important role of Chinese workers.

23 LeFevour, *Western Enterprise in Late Ch'ing China*, 22.

attempts were made to gauge Chinese employment in the 1840s. In March 1842 the *Canton Register* published a table listing the various occupations of Chinese inhabitants. The largest 'shop-based' categories included 566 carpenters, 439 prostitutes, 402 chandlers and 380 masons.[24] In contrast there were also non-'shop-based' employment categories, such as 1,366 labourers, 500 bricklayers and 500 'having no ostensible employment'.[25] The increasingly varied nature of Chinese employment can be seen if we compare this crude list and the *Hong Kong Almanac* of 1846. The 1846 list of 'Chinese traders' covers more than seventy specialist trades, the most popular being forty chandlers, thirty lodging-house keepers, nineteen carpenters and eighteen druggists.[26] Crucially, the growing Chinese population of Hong Kong created new social and economic relationships. The immigrant population brought connections that were essential in turning Hong Kong into a base for later mass migrations to destinations like Australia and California. Hong Kong was a transmission point for money, information and people between southern China and overseas destinations.[27]

As in Singapore in the 1820s and 1830s, there was recognition by colonial authorities and Western merchants in Hong Kong that cooperation with elements of the Chinese community was necessary to ensure the colony's success.[28] Hong Kong also provided a space for new Chinese entrepreneurs to acquire social status and become economically powerful. Examples included figures like Loo Aqui of the Tanka community who was given land in recognition of the provisions he gave to the British during the Opium War and became an extremely wealthy community leader.[29] Whilst the British had referred to the Tanka as 'boat people' in their early census data, colonial Hong Kong provided opportunities for previously marginalised people like Loo Aqui to acquire wealth and power through collaboration. The formation of the Tung Wah Hospital in the late 1860s has been highlighted as an example of the Chinese elite becoming incorporated into the formal political structure of the colony.[30] Indeed Governor John Bowring's failed proposals of 1855, which would have enfranchised propertied Chinese residents and included Chinese representation on the legislative council, did signify an awareness of class distinctions and opportunities for collaboration with elements of the Chinese community.[31]

---

[24] *Canton Register*, 29 March 1842.
[25] Ibid.
[26] A. R. Johnston, *Hong Kong Directory/Almanac* (Hong Kong, 1846).
[27] Michael Williams, 'Hong Kong and the Pearl River Delta Qiaoxiang', *Modern Asian Studies*, 38, 2 (2004), 260.
[28] Carroll, *A Concise History of Hong Kong*, 20.
[29] Ibid., 17.
[30] Chan, *The Making of Hong Kong Society*, 105.
[31] Ibid., 105.

Hong Kong also offered a new colonial contact zone in which British observers could critique Chinese migrants. A common early observation of Western residents and visitors to the colony was the supposedly poor character of the Chinese inhabitants. As in Singapore, Westerners simplified the Chinese population into two groups: a threatening mass of conniving Chinese workers, and complicit Chinese merchants who were crucial to colonial rule. Violent crime blighted the early years of the colony's development. The cause of this, according to colonial observers such as Charles Gutzlaff and Robert Montgomery Martin, was the poor class and character of the Chinese immigrants, which was believed to be exacerbated by the lack of females to act as a pacifying force.[32] 'Disturbances', 'affrays' and 'secret sects' were regularly reported in the pages of the *Hong Kong Register*.[33] Christopher Munn has discussed how allegations of criminality allowed the colonial government to pass law and order legislation that strengthened colonial authority.[34] Hong Kong's vast class of criminal Chinese, whether real or imagined, were particularly maligned as the worst examples of the Chinese character.

Importantly, in Hong Kong in the 1840s the interests and personnel of the colonial state and elite merchant houses overlapped. For example, Alexander Matheson – who became head of Jardine Matheson on the China coast following James Matheson's return to Britain in 1843 – was made an unofficial member of the legislative council.[35] Western elites specifically highlighted distinctions between themselves and the 'criminal' Chinese majority. The early years of the *Hong Kong Register* carried a litany of Chinese crimes, ranging from 'serious disturbances' to illegal gambling establishments.[36] Often these events were distinctly personal. For example, the *Register* gave extensive coverage to the trial of 'Wang Acho', who had committed forgery 'with the intention of defrauding A. Matheson Esq.'.[37] Existing in the midst of a Chinese colonial population, the *Register*'s previous critique of the Chinese authorities was broadened to include Chinese migrants to Hong Kong. The proximity of the powerful Western merchant elite to the colonial authorities meant that legislative action was focused against the 'criminal' Chinese. An article titled 'The Secret Sects of China and Hong Kong Legislation' covered how the first ordinance of 1846 allowed the authorities to 'imprison', 'brand' and 'expel' members of the 'Triad, or other secret

---

[32]   Bird, *Traders of Hong Kong*, 39.
[33]   *Hong Kong Register*, 17 October 1843, 7 May 1844, 17 September 1844. The *Hong Kong Register* was a rebranding of the *Canton Register*, discussed in Chapter 2.
[34]   Munn, *Anglo-China*, 16.
[35]   G. B. Endacott, *A Biographical Sketch-Book of Early Hong Kong* (Hong Kong: Hong Kong University Press, 2005), 160.
[36]   *Hong Kong Register*, 7 May 1844, 23 September 1845.
[37]   *Hong Kong Register*, 8 October 1844.

societies'.[38] For colonial authorities the criminal character of the Chinese population was a particular concern.

The policing of the colony provides a good example of how criminality was intensely racialised by the colonial authorities. The Hong Kong Police Force in 1845 was formed of seventy-one Europeans, fifty-one Chinese and forty-six Indians, with the Chinese component reduced to twenty-three by 1847 and thirteen by 1849 as Chinese officers were believed to be 'untrust-worthy' and were accused of having connections to triad societies.[39] It was the view of colonial authorities that the Chinese of Hong Kong were especially prejudiced against Western residents. This view of an 'ill feeling of people of Hong Kong towards foreigners [Westerners]' also surfaced during the 1847 Select Committee on Commercial Relations with China, and played a role in the Colonial Office's decision to limit representative government in the 1850s.[40]

There are clear comparisons and contrasts between the concerns about Chinese criminality in Hong Kong and the political and social attitudes to Chinese labourers seen in early colonial Singapore. As discussed by Anthony Webster, the extent to which the European community were outnumbered by the Chinese meant the latter were viewed as an 'intimidating presence' by colonial authorities.[41] This intimidation was exacerbated by concerns about secret society membership and increasing rates of opium consumption. The Chinese in Hong Kong were viewed as especially subversive. The contrast between the Straits Settlements and Hong Kong was most vividly illustrated by the shipment of Chinese convicts from Hong Kong to Penang, via Singapore, aboard the *General Wood*.[42] In November 1847 the former opium-trading vessel the *General Wood* was chartered by the Hong Kong government to transport '92 convicted pirates'.[43] Here we can see colonial authorities relocating the 'bad' Chinese from the decadent colony to the 'good' example of the successful Anglo-Chinese colony of Singapore.[44] A passenger uprising whilst

---

[38] *Hong Kong Register*, 20 May 1845.
[39] Norman Miners, 'The Localization of the Hong Kong Police Force, 1842–1947', *The Journal of Imperial and Commonwealth History*, 18, 3 (1990), 299.
[40] Parliamentary Papers, *Report from the Select Committee on Commercial Relations with China*, 552.
[41] Webster, 'The Development of British Commercial and Political Networks in the Straits Settlements', 911.
[42] A. R. Williamson, *Eastern Traders: Some Men and Ships of Jardine, Matheson & Company* (Hong Kong: Jardine, Matheson & Co., 1975), 164–5.
[43] Clare Anderson, 'The Age of Revolution in the Indian Ocean, Bay of Bengal and South China Sea: A Maritime Perspective', *International Review of Social History*, 58 (2013), 239.
[44] Singapore actually received more Indian than Chinese convict labourers. See Anand A. Yang, 'Indian Convict Workers in Southeast Asia in the Late Eighteenth and Early Nineteenth Centuries', *Journal of World History*, 14, 2 (2003), 179–208, for more on this system of convict labour.

the ship was harboured at Singapore served to further underline the perception of Hong Kong's criminal underclass as the 'scum of Canton'.[45]

It is worth noting some of the wider motivations for the emphasis placed on Chinese criminality in Hong Kong. Palmerston famously described the island as a 'barren rock' after Charles Elliot's acquisition of it during the Opium War and many British observers would have preferred the island of Chusan, temporarily held in the 1840s as collateral by British forces, as a colony.[46] Charles Gutzlaff acted as an administrator in Chusan and echoed the common opinion that the Chinese in Hong Kong, in contrast to the Chinese of Chusan, were of the 'lowest moral standard'. Nobody was more critical than Robert Montgomery Martin.[47] Martin was appointed Treasurer of Hong Kong in 1844 and whilst spending time in Chusan recovering from illness wrote a report on the advantages of Chusan over Hong Kong.[48] Martin famously wrote that there was not 'one respectable Chinese inhabitant' in Hong Kong and he lamented how the 'migratory, predatory, gambling and dissolute habits' of the Chinese had made them 'not only useless but highly injurious subjects in the attempt to form a new colony'.[49] Published as the *British Position and Prospects in China*, Martin's work was criticised in the Hong Kong newspaper press. However, Martin's general criticisms of Hong Kong – its limited size, disadvantageous geographical position, lack of natural resources and unfitness for European habitation – gained some currency in London, as evidenced by the stir his resignation in Hong Kong caused in Parliament and the Colonial Office.[50] Though his advocacy of Chusan was in vain, Martin's writing had further promoted the opinion that the Chinese migrants to Hong Kong were of an especially poor character.

As well as being a destination for migrants, Hong Kong developed into a 'clearinghouse' between the *qiaoxiang* region of Guangdong province and various global locations.[51] British firms played a crucial role in both facilitating the movement of people from Hong Kong and supplying support services that allowed for the remittance of goods, money and information. For example, colonial newspapers facilitated mass emigration from Hong Kong through the publication of news from the goldfields that drew thousands

[45] Chan, *The Making of Hong Kong Society*, 49.

[46] Bird, *Traders of Hong Kong*, 39.

[47] Ibid., 39; Christopher Munn, 'The Chusan Episode: Britain's Occupation of a Chinese Island, 1840–46', *The Journal of Imperial and Commonwealth History*, 25, 1 (1997), 82–112.

[48] King, *Survey Our Empire!*, 232.

[49] Endacott, *A Biographical Sketch-Book of Early Hong Kong*, xvi.

[50] The details of Martin's resignation were debated in the metropole and correspondence over the issue was published as a parliamentary paper: Robert Montgomery Martin, *Reports, Minutes and Despatches on the British Position and Prospects in China* (London: Harrison, 1846); Parliamentary Papers, *Mr. Montgomery Martin. Copy of correspondence of Mr. Montgomery Martin with the Secretary of State for the Colonies, relating to his resignation of the office of Treasurer of Hong Kong*, 1847 (743).

[51] Williams, 'Hong Kong and the Pearl River Delta Qiaoxiang', 360.

of migrants each year. The *Hong Kong Register* published numerous original articles and extracts on 'The California Gold Rush', 'Report from the Gold Coast of California', 'The California Trade' and the 'Discovery of Gold in Australia'.[52] Importantly these new pull factors for emigrants drew on the labour pool supplied by the increased Chinese population of Hong Kong over the 1840s. Elizabeth Sinn has discussed three groups that were targeted by emigrant recruiters: those who had settled in Hong Kong and decided to re-migrate; those who had arrived in Hong Kong with the intention to migrate elsewhere; and indigenous villagers from rural Hong Kong.[53] The migration of southern Chinese to Hong Kong in the 1840s was crucial in creating the context for mass emigration from Hong Kong to new destinations in the 1850s.

By the mid-1850s, Hong Kong had developed into a major departure point for Chinese emigrants. For example, the Victoria Harbour Master's list from October 1855 shows the significance of Hong Kong as an emigrant port. Between 1 November 1854 and 30 September 1855 there were 14,991 Chinese passengers recorded departing Hong Kong for overseas destinations.[54] Australian and Californian ports were the destinations for more than ninety per cent of the passenger traffic from Hong Kong due to the ongoing gold rushes. Elizabeth Sinn has detailed the way that these new, large migration systems were extremely profitable for British merchants. The Chinese communities that became resident in various destinations now maintained connections to their homeland through Hong Kong. British merchants, such as the former opium traders Jardine Matheson, were able to profit through their involvement in the growing shipping traffic to the lucrative goldfields, as well as the supplementary postal, goods and financial remittance industries.[55]

The cession of Hong Kong to Britain in 1842 had two main implications for Chinese migration in the British Empire. First, Hong Kong was a new colonial contact zone in which the Chinese character was debated. As before, British colonial authority was contingent on complicit Chinese elites, who were crucial to the colony's commercial success, but Hong Kong also became home to a large Chinese population that observers like Robert Montgomery Martin dismissed as a criminal underclass. Whilst the character of the Hong

---

[52] *Hong Kong Register*, 5 June 1849, 24 July 1849, 4 June 1850, 12 August 1851.

[53] Elizabeth Sinn, 'Hong Kong as an In-between Place in the Chinese Diaspora, 1849–1939', in Gabaccia and Hoerder, *Connecting Seas and Connected Ocean Rims*, 225–51.

[54] 'List of vessels cleared outwards with Chinese passengers from 1 November 1854 to 30 September 1855', Thos. V. Watkins, Harbour Master. Harbour Master's Office, Victoria, Hong Kong, 5 October 1855, in Parliamentary Papers, *Hong Kong. Copies or extracts of correspondence between the Colonial Department and the governor of Hong Kong, and between the Colonial Department and the Foreign Office, on the subject of emigration from Hong Kong and from the Chinese Empire to the British West Indies and to foreign countries and their possessions, since the 1st of January 1853*, 1857–58 (481), 31.

[55] Sinn, *Pacific Crossings*, 143.

Kong Chinese might be criticised, Britain ultimately retained the colony because of the re-centring of Britain's China coast economic and political power in Hong Kong. Second, Hong Kong in the 1840s was an environment in which firms could profit from both Chinese immigration to Hong Kong and Chinese emigration from Hong Kong to new, global destinations. Hong Kong acted as a staging point from which British firms could become involved in new migration systems from the China coast.

The Chinese Passenger Trade from the Treaty Ports

The Chinese 'coolie trade' began life inauspiciously, with a shipment of Chinese labourers from Amoy to Reunion aboard a French ship in 1845.[56] Large-scale emigration from Amoy began in earnest in 1847 through the British firms Tait & Co. and Syme, Muir & Co.[57] The details of these firms' nefarious activities are known largely due to parliamentary interest stimulated by comparisons between Asian indentured labour and the recently abolished system of African slavery by political heavyweights like Lord John Russell.[58] These firms operated in a confusing legal space as, thanks to the extraterritoriality afforded by the Treaty of Nanking, they were bound by British, not Chinese, laws. However, they utilised a network of Chinese brokers (*ketou*) who operated outside of Chinese law.[59] Though neither firm hid their activities from British authorities the records of their migrant shipments are confusing at best. This chapter's discussion of the Chinese passenger trade is based on a cross-referencing of ships discussed in Colonial Office correspondence on Chinese emigration and the various reports on the passenger trade, with shipping lists from the *Hong Kong Register*, the *China Mail* and the *Friend of China*. These shipping records provide limited details on ship cargoes. Ships departing from Amoy were largely recorded as carrying 'ballast' to stabilise the ship, having deposited their imports, but both goods and human passengers could be used as ballast. Correspondence from the British Consulate at Amoy to Hong Kong Governor John Bowring demonstrates the difficulties in tracking the firms' activities: 'Two other British vessels, the "*Inchinnan*" and "*Eleanor Lancaster*" have cleared from Amoy in ballast, with the intention of taking coolies on board at Namoa or some place in its vicinity.'[60]

---

56 Murakami, 'Two Bonded Labour Emigration Patterns in Mid-Nineteenth-Century Southern China', 154. The 'coolie trade' will be referred to as the passenger trade due to the pejorative use of 'coolie'.

57 Irick, 'Chi'ing Policy towards the Coolie Trade', 8.

58 Russell's phrase 'a new system of slavery' was borrowed for the title of Tinker's *A New System of Slavery*: Hugh Tinker, *A New System of Slavery: The Export of Indian Labour Overseas, 1830–1920* (London: Oxford University Press, 1974).

59 Pan, *The Encyclopaedia of the Chinese Overseas*, 61.

60 Consul J. Backhouse (Amoy) to Governor John Bowring (Hong Kong), 24 December 1852,

This section focuses on one of the first passenger shipments, aboard the *Duke of Argyll*, as a key example for several key reasons. First, it demonstrates that new migrant destinations, beyond the British Empire, were available as possible destinations for British shipments of Chinese migrant labour from 1842 onwards – the Singapore model was going global. Second, it set a precedent in terms of contractual arrangements and highlights issues with coercion that continued to blight the Chinese passenger trade over the nineteenth century. Third, of the ships listed in the Colonial Office records the *Duke of Argyll* is amongst the best documented, with various Colonial Office reports, private correspondence and newspaper sources available.

On 7 November 1846 the *Duke of Argyll* arrived in Hong Kong.[61] The ship sat in Victoria Harbour with no listed agent until Jardine Matheson stepped in on 8 December 1846.[62] A letter from the firm to James Tait in January 1847 revealed why the firm had acquired agency of the ship:

> In accordance with the letters which have passed between you and our own Mr Matheson with reference to the charter of a vessel on your account for the Havanna we now beg to enclose a Signed Copy of agreement entered into between us & the commander of the ship 'Duke of Argyle' Capt. Bristow, which we trust will be found in conformity with your wishes on the subject.[63]

This encapsulated the role of the shipping agent. Established China-coast opium firms such as Jardine Matheson acted as a 'middle-man' between ship owners and ship charterers. In 1846 Tait & Co., a fledgling British firm at Amoy, had neither the expertise, connections nor resources to secure a vessel of the necessary specifications for carrying large number of Chinese passengers.[64] We can see here the start of the development of British-operated Chinese migration systems, in contrast to the pre-existing Chinese junk trade that supplied seasonal labour to Singapore. On 13 January 1847 the *Duke of Argyll* proceeded to Amoy from Hong Kong and, after spending time 'seeking coolies', was dispatched to Havana by James Tait with 420 Chinese passengers on 10 March 1847.[65]

The impact of the *Duke of Argyll* as the first of Tait & Co.'s migrant shipments would be felt throughout the initial evolution of the passenger trade.

---

in Parliamentary Papers, *China. Correspondence with the Superintendent of British trade in China, upon the subject of emigration from that country*, 1852–53 (1686).

61 *Friend of China*, 7 November 1846.

62 *Friend of China*, 8 December 1846.

63 Jardine Matheson, & Co. (Hong Kong) to James Tait (Amoy), 2 January 1847, in MS/JM/C13/4, Jardine Matheson Archive (Cambridge University Library).

64 Note that the failure to acquire ships for passage had previously prevented Gordon Forbes Davidson's emigration scheme from taking place.

65 *Hong Kong Register*, 12 January 1847; James Tait (Amoy) to Jardine, Matheson & Co. (Hong Kong), 20 February 1847, in MS JM/B6/6, Jardine Matheson Archive (Cambridge University Library); *Hong Kong Register*, 10 March 1847.

Most significantly the *Duke of Argyll* was identified as a legal precedent. In spite of concerns about coercion, the British Consul at Amoy, T. H. Layton, had been reluctant to prevent the shipment until he had clarification on the extent of his legal authority.[66] James Tait was also insulated from British consular authority as he was the acting consul for Spain, Portugal and the Netherlands at Amoy.[67] That the *Duke of Argyll* was allowed to travel from Amoy to Havana meant that both Tait & Co. and Syme, Muir & Co. could reference it as evidence of the legality of the trade, or more commonly argue that the prevention or regulation of emigration was the responsibility of Chinese officials. In particular, if such emigration to a Spanish 'slave colony' was deemed legal, or was not objectionable to the British Consul, then similar migrant voyages to 'free' British colonies were definitely legal.[68] It also set a standard for passenger conditions. 'The allotment of space was nine superficial feet, or about one ton and a-half to each man; whereas the English rule is two tons, with ten superficial feet', and the allowance of water – which was of 'essential importance' – was 'two pints more than the allowance of vessels carrying English emigrants'.[69] Most significant for future Chinese migrants was news of the poor treatment of the Chinese labourers in Cuba, which had been remitted to Amoy by Spanish doctor Jose Villate from Havana. This reduced the attractiveness of contract emigration in general and contributed to increased coercion of the trade as Chinese recruiters struggled to attract willing labourers.[70]

Within the passenger trade there were two main groups of migrants: contract and free. Contract refers to indentured labourers who would agree to contracts of a set length – examples usually ranged from five to eight years – with emigration brokers who would either have a prior arrangement with specific employers or planned to 'auction' labourers' contracts at their destination. It is clear how this system could be compared to slavery, especially given the visceral image of the 'auction' of labourers. It is also worth noting that in contemporary discourse, free migrants – usually, in the 1850s, using arrangements similar to the credit-ticket system or paying for passage in advance in order to access goldfields in Australia or California – would often be conflated with contract labourers under the pejorative term

66   Consul T. H. Layton (Amoy) to Governor J. G. Bonham (Hong Kong), 17 July 1848, in Parliamentary Papers, *Emigration (North American and Australian Colonies)*, 1849 (593). This was the 'benign neglect' of the British state that allowed British observers to act with autonomy in the treaty ports: see Robert Bickers, 'Shanghailanders: The Formation and Identity of the British Settler Community in Shanghai, 1843–1937', *Past and Present*, 159, 1 (1998), 175.

67   Slocomb, *Among Australia's Pioneers*, 91. Notably the use of an official position on behalf of another European power worked as an insurance policy for British merchants.

68   *Melbourne Argus*, 5 May 1848.

69   'Note by Dr. Winchester', Governor Bowring to Earl of Malmesbury, 25 September 1852, in Parliamentary Papers, *China. Correspondence upon the subject of emigration from China*, 1854–55 (0.7).

70   Murakami, 'Two Bonded Labour Emigration Patterns in Mid-Nineteenth-Century Southern China', 158.

'coolies'.[71] The British Consul at Amoy, T. H. Layton, explained to Hong Kong Governor George Bonham that 'there is a wide distinction between voluntary emigration to Singapore and "buying men" for terms of years'.[72] In particular the concept of 'buying men' was a direct reference to the *Duke of Argyll's* landing in Havana where contracts were auctioned upon arrival.[73] The following contract, entered into at Amoy for five years' labour in British Guiana, demonstrates some of the common terms of these indenture agreements:

> I ___ native of the village of ___ in the province of ___ in China, of the age of ____ years, have agreed to embark in the vessel with the object of proceeding to the colony of British Guiana, obliging myself from and after my arrival, to dedicate myself there to the orders of the honourable the Immigration Agent of that colony, to whatever class of labour I may be destined, whether in plantations or other estates, during the customary hours of work in that colony, or even at other than plantation labour, as may be most convenient to the honourable Immigration Agent, or whoever may become the holder of this engagement, and to perform said work for ____ of monthly salary, maintenance of eight ounces of beef, one and a half pounds of other alimentary food daily medical assistance and medicines, two suits of clothes, one blanket, and one flannel shirt annually ... that I shall find myself in all provisions and other necessities, fulfilling these obligations for five years continuous, which are fixed for the term of this engagement, during which it shall not be permitted me to leave the colony, nor deny my services to the persons to whom this engagement may be transferred; at the end of that period, I shall be at liberty to act as may seem to be best ...[74]

Importantly, from the perspective of those looking to hire contract migrants (in the case of British Guiana to replace slave labour), the contract's vagueness about future employers as well as its limiting of migrants to plantation work ensured a fixed labour market, which, by suppressing entrepreneurial self-employment, benefited employers. After entering into such an agreement, indentured migrants would then undertake passage, arranged by a firm like Tait & Co., and the contract would be auctioned at the destination. As an example, the British Consul General in Cuba, Jos. J. Crawford detailed a scheme by which Villoldo, Wardrop & Co. contracted 8,000 labourers from the Amoy firms and then planned to auction the labourers to employers using the following method: '8,000 colonists of this contract shall be divided into series of eight Chinese each. 800 tickets, numbered from 1 to 800, shall be

---

[71] Arensmeyer, 'The Chinese Coolie Labour Trade and the Philippines', 194; Meagher, *The Coolie Trade*, 104.

[72] Consul T. H. Layton (Amoy) to Governor J. G. Bonham (Hong Kong), 17 July 1848, in Parliamentary Papers, *Emigration*.

[73] Layton to Bonham, 17 July 1848.

[74] Consul Charles A. Winchester (Amoy) to Governor John Bowring (Hong Kong), 26 August 1852, in Parliamentary Papers, *China*, 1854–55.

made and put into an urn, from whence they shall be drawn by the proprietors.'[75] These types of contracts and distribution arrangements were the
speciality of the Amoy firms.

The coercion of migrants blighted the contract passenger trade. Both Tait
& Co. and Syme, Muir & Co. used Chinese brokers who outsourced recruitment to local recruiters ignominiously referred to as 'crimps'. The recruitment
network also encouraged kidnapping as foreign merchant firms hired 'great'
brokers who used subordinate brokers to recruit workers. If brokers could not
fill ship capacities, they had to pay the firm's expenses.[76] The threat of debt to
foreign merchants meant that brokers enforced strict quotas on subordinate
brokers who resorted to kidnap in order to fill them. As well as kidnap, debt
exploitation was a common method of recruitment. Wages offered on indenture contracts, normally around two to four dollars per month or 80 to 120
wen per day, were relatively low and unattractive to skilled labourers. 'First-
class' agricultural labourers in the vicinity of Amoy could expect to earn 160
wen per day.[77] As a result only the most desperate or indebted emigrants took
up these contracts. In particular, opium- or gambling-addicted workers were
most vulnerable to being press-ganged by aggressive crimps.[78]

British authorities knew about the accusations of kidnap. In Consul Layton's
correspondence with Bonham he made reference to a petition for liberty that
had been placed in his hands 'from the father of one of the boys' due to be
shipped aboard the *Duke of Argyll*.[79] Contract migrants were kept in secure
pens prior to embarkation. The utility of these enclosures was ostensibly to
prevent potential migrants collecting advance payments and absconding.
In reality, the British firms were aware of some of the more questionable
recruitment methods of their Chinese brokers and feared those who were
held without their consent breaking free. The inhumane pre-voyage holding
conditions for coerced migrants led to locals in Amoy and the surrounding
area contemptuously referring to the passenger trade as the 'pig trade'.[80]

The Qing Empire's prohibition on emigration technically rendered Tait's
passenger shipment illegal, but the firm's international connections helped to
insulate them from British authority. As Governor Bowring remarked, 'the
principal shipper of coolies is Mr. Tait, a British subject, who has all the
advantages and influence which his being Spanish, Dutch and Portuguese

---

75 Consul Jos. J. Crawford (Cuba) to Lord Stanley (London), 7 August 1852, in Correspondence Relative to the Emigration of Chinese Coolies (1853), CO 885/1/20 (National
Archives).

76 Murakami, 'Two Bonded Labour Emigration Patterns in Mid-Nineteenth-Century Southern
China', 157.

77 Ibid.

78 Pan, *The Encyclopaedia of the Chinese Overseas*, 61.

79 Layton to Bonham, 17 July 1848.

80 Northrup, *Indentured Labour in the Age of Imperialism*, 5.

Consul gives him'.[81] The firms acted in an ill-defined legal space, where their early shipping activities were used to justify their later shipping activities. In correspondence between Syme, Muir & Co. and T. H. Layton, the firm referenced Layton's early allowance of a shipment of Chinese passengers to justify the legality of their proposed shipments to Australian colonies: 'as we need hardly remind you that within a short period back the *Duke of Argyle* left this for Havana with upwards of 400 on board, that she did so with your cognizance, and carried with her your port clearance, stating her cargo and destination'.[82] The British firms operated comfortably within a network of Western mercantile and shipping interests but exploited the poorly defined role of British authority in the treaty ports.

The emigrant destinations most commonly linked to the abuses of the passenger also sat outside of the British Empire. Notably, the *Duke of Argyll's* destination was Havana. The Spanish, and former Spanish, colonies of Cuba, and Peru, became common emigrant destinations in the late 1840s.[83] Between 1853 and 1860, 6,000 Chinese workers travelled to Cuba annually, not necessarily to replace the slave population but to provide additional labour for the expansion of the sugar trade and mill construction.[84] British colonial authorities paid special attention to these passenger shipments to Spanish colonies. For example, the emigration agent James T. White, who was sent to the China coast by the West India Committee to arrange contract labour for the West Indies, catalogued the departure of 4,505 Chinese passengers from Amoy and Namoa to Cuba between 1847 and 1853.[85] It is notable that, despite White's best efforts, mortality figures for most of these voyages are unrecorded. This suggests poor conditions and, potentially, high levels of passenger fatalities.[86] Importantly, the abuses in these new systems of Chinese migration led back to Singapore. As a regular stopping point for passenger shipments from China to the Americas, Singapore was a key site at which colonial observers interacted with and critiqued the Chinese passenger trade. The next section demonstrates how the notions of Chinese character formed in Singapore continued to inform colonial perceptions of Chinese migrant labour and the role of Singapore as a stopping place in the creation of new

---

[81] John Bowring (Hong Kong) to the Earl of Malmesbury, 3 August 1852, in Parliamentary Papers, *China. Correspondence with the Superintendent of British trade in China, upon the subject of emigration from that country*, 1852–53 (1686)

[82] *Melbourne Argus*, 5 May 1848.

[83] Siu and Ku, *Hong Kong Mobile*, 39.

[84] Laird W. Bergad et al., *The Cuban Slave Market, 1790–1800* (Cambridge: Cambridge University Press, 1995).

[85] James T. White to S. Walcott Esq., 'Emigration of Contract Labourers to Cuba', 16 April 1853, from Fohkien province, in CO 885/1/20.

[86] Note that British concerns about abuses in the Chinese passenger trade to Cuba continued into the 1860s. For example, see Register of Correspondence: West India Emigration (1858–61), CO 428/3 (National Archives).

legislation that would signal the beginning of the regulation of the Chinese passenger trade over the nineteenth century.

Chinese Character, Singapore and Regulating Chinese Migration

As new systems of Chinese emigration developed on the China coast under the auspices of private British merchant houses, the Colonial Office made plans for state-managed migration systems to prevent the abuse of labourers and address specific colonial labour shortages.[87] As seen in Chapter 3, there was demand for Chinese labour as replacement for outlawed African slave labour in the British West Indies. Specifically, British sugar plantations required additional labour. In August 1851, the British Guiana Government agreed to pay a bounty of $100 for each Chinese worker landed. The following year the *Lord Elgin* transported Chinese workers from Amoy to Guiana, but forty-eight per cent of the Chinese passengers died on the voyage.[88] In order to ensure sufficient labour was supplied to the West Indies and that such abuses were stopped, the Colonial Office directed the Colonial Land and Emigration Commission to work with the West India Committee in establishing a contract system of Chinese migration to the West Indies, supported by a £50,000 parliament-guaranteed loan, under British Government control.[89] James T. White, who had been the recruiting agent for the British Guiana Government in India, was appointed emigration agent in China and dispatched to Hong Kong in order to manage this new system of migration.[90] White was instructed to secure as large a proportion of female migrants as possible, to find suitable Chinese interpreters and to source labour from the British enclave of Hong Kong to prevent breaking Chinese laws.[91]

White's reports on Chinese migration reveal the continuing influence of Singapore even during the establishment of new migration systems on the Chinese coast. After staying nineteen days in Singapore, White provided Henry Barkly, the Governor of British Guiana, with a comprehensive overview of the role of Chinese migrants in the colony's development. Notably White's views echo those of colonial administrators in Singapore seen in Chapter 1:

> Of the three races who form the principal inhabitants of Singapore the Chinese are the most numerous, and are beyond all comparison the most

---

87 For an overview of the different emigration agents at Hong Kong, see Wang Sing-wu, *The Organization of Chinese Emigration, 1848–1888: With Special Reference to Chinese Emigration to Australia* (San Francisco: Chinese Material Centre, 1978), 355–60.

88 Tinker, *A New System of Slavery*, 94.

89 Campbell, *Chinese Coolie Emigration within the British Empire*, 99.

90 J. W. Murdoch and Frederic Rogers to H. Merivale, 24 July 1852, Letters to the Colonial Office. West Indies, Africa, St. Helena, Mauritius (July 1852–April 1853), CO 386/89 (National Archives).

91 Campbell, *Chinese Coolie Emigration within the British Empire*, 100.

laborious and industrious. They are here the pioneers of civilization, and it is to their indominable energy that Singapore is indebted for clearing the forest and preparing the way for the occupation of men … A few of them are respectable merchants, and are men of wealth … I think it very probable that in time they will, by their superior industry and energy, entirely displace the other races.[92]

Again, we can see here how White's promotion of the Chinese over Singapore's other 'races' followed models of racial hierarchy that had been developed from 1819 and reinforced by the various experiments with Chinese labour. White's description of Singapore also covered the Chinese purchase of Malay women, the disparity of the sexes, details of labour costs and methods of sugar production in the Straits Settlements. White's thirty-four-part overview of Chinese migration in Singapore concluded that 'they possess many prominent vices and defects, but at the same time it is impossible not to admire them for their many virtues'.[93]

As emigration agent in Hong Kong, White continued to report on the character of the Chinese and the suitability of Chinese colonists for the West Indies. He consulted with knowledgeable parties in Hong Kong to procure information 'with regard to their [the Chinese] habits and feelings as English colonists'.[94] One element of White's evaluation was physical. Could the Chinese cope with the hard plantation labour, and often brutal treatment, in the West Indies? In doing so, White repeated John Crawfurd and Gordon Forbes Davidson's earlier favourable comparisons between Chinese and Indian labourers in terms of physical output: 'They are generally a strong muscular race, broad shouldered, and bony, and capable of enduring great and continuous fatigue. They are hardworking and industrious; and in physical ability for labour, and the endurance of toil, I should consider one Chinese equal to two of the inhabitants of Bengal.'[95] Again, we can detect both racial hierarchy and the connected notions of physical masculinity that permeated colonial evaluations of indigenous labour. Additionally, the language of 'character', which was so crucial in representations of the Chinese in the context of Anglo-Chinese tensions over the 1830s, is repeated multiple times in this report. White ascribes to the Chinese a 'quiet and inoffensive character' and a 'mild character', as well as suggesting that the Chinese are inherently 'tractable', 'easily managed' and 'civil'.[96] A careful consideration of the physical and behavioural characteristics of Chinese labour led White to conclude that:

[92] James T. White (Calcutta) to Henry Barkly (British Guiana), 17 November 1851, in Emigration from China to the West Indies, CO 885/1/19 (National Archives).
[93] Ibid.
[94] James T. White Esq. to Henry Barkly Esq., Governor of British Guiana, Macao, 21 June 1851, CO 885/1/19.
[95] Ibid.
[96] Ibid.

> There are two traits in the character of the Chinese which will make them
> valuable labourers in the present state of the West Indies. In the first place, they
> are fond of money, and so devoted to the acquisition of it, that, being never
> satisfied with what they possess, they will continue the pursuit of gain to the
> very last; and in the second place, they are extremely shrewd and intelligent,
> keenly alive to their own interests, and will soon perceive the advantage to be
> derived from cultivating land on their own account, either under lease, or for
> an interest in the produce or need proceeds from the soil. In fact, they have
> sufficient intelligence and ambition to rise in the world, and in a short time
> would become useful and valuable as a middle class in the West Indies.[97]

Notably, though White's instructions were to source Chinese migrant labour as
a replacement for African slave labour on sugar plantations, here he suggests
that the Chinese might fulfil a different economic role, as an entrepreneurial
middle class, based on the experience of the Anglo-Chinese combination in
Singapore and Hong Kong.

Whilst White was impressed by his observations of Chinese migrant
communities in Singapore and Hong Kong, he also identified the same
problems as previous colonial observers. The first difficulty White identified
was the common concern about the 'impossibility of obtaining women and
families'.[98] We see here again the colonial belief in the regulating form of the
family unit, which would negate the social problems and vices associated with
Chinese male labourers.[99] Additionally, White's observations of mixed families at Singapore also connected back to notions of Chinese superiority over
the indigenous population and native laziness: 'the offspring will, from the
pressure of Chinese immigration, become more and more assimilated to the
Chinese race, and I believe that in course of time the Malays will necessarily
succumb to the superior energy of the Chinese, and will ultimately disap-
pear from the soil'.[100] Drawing on concerns and tropes from previous colonial
examples, White concluded that the Chinese would be the 'best labourers'
ever introduced into the West Indies provided females and families could be
procured.[101] Towards the end of his time in Hong Kong, White also invoked
colonial concerns about the Chinese as an organised political threat along the
lines of the *Kongsi* and secret societies in Singapore:

> There is one trait in the character of the Chinese which makes me somewhat
> doubtful as to their conduct in the West Indies. I refer to their habit of *combining*
> together for all purposes, whether good, bad, or indifferent. No Chinaman ever
> acts from individual impulse, but always in concert with others. This principle

---

[97] Ibid.

[98] Ibid.

[99] For more on these assumptions about female migrants see Lisa Lowe, *The Intimacies of Four
     Continents* (Durham, NC: Duke University Press, 2016).

[100] White to Barkly, 21 June 1851.

[101] Ibid. Note that the comparison here is with Indian and African labour.

of their character, if pushed to any extent in such colonies as British Guiana and Trinidad, where the demand for labour is greater than the supply, might be found very inconvenient and injurious.[102]

Note here that White's overview of Chinese migrants as colonists in the 1850s mirrors, almost exactly, the perceptions and tropes formulated in the early years of colonial Singapore and discussed in Chapter 1. Having considered the subject at length, White concluded that Chinese migrants had 'more intelligence, and habits of greater industry, and have attained a higher civilization' than Indian labourers.[103]

White struggled to attract Chinese workers for the West Indies in Hong Kong due to overwhelming competition for ships, which preferred to carry credit-ticket passengers to the goldfields in California, and the high cost of attracting female migrants.[104] He did enjoy some success through the British firm Tait & Co. at Amoy, as indicated by his records which provide the most detailed Chinese emigration figures available.[105] By January 1853 White had secured 1,022 labourers for Trinidad aboard the *Australia* (445 migrants), *Clarendon* (257 migrants) and *Lady Flora Hastings* (320 migrants), with arrangements for a further 800 labourers for Demerara and 700 for Trinidad.[106] However, the Colonial Office had instructed White to source Chinese labour from Hong Kong rather than breaking the Qing Empire's prohibition on emigration in the treaty ports. As a result of the high cost of recruitment at Hong Kong, the Colonial Office recalled White and abandoned the Government-run project. By June 1854 White was already on his way back to London.[107] Despite the reluctance of the British state to get involved in the Chinese passenger trade, the demand for labour in the West Indies persisted. In lieu of the state, private firms and arrangements serviced this demand. Between 1853 and 1884 more than 17,000 Chinese labourers travelled to the West Indies on indenture contracts.[108]

Whilst the Chinese migrations to the West Indies drew on perceptions of Chinese migrants formed in the colonial contact zones of Singapore and Hong Kong, Singapore also played a role as a stopping place on long-distance voyages to the Caribbean. A good example of the role of stopping places in uncovering abuses in the Chinese passenger trade is the case of the *Lady Amherst*. The ship departed Amoy for Havana with 275 officially registered

[102] James T. White (Hong Kong) to Henry Barkly (British Guiana), 19 July 1851, in CO 885/1/19.

[103] Ibid.

[104] Sinn, 'Emigration from Hong Kong before 1941: General Trends', 23.

[105] Skeldon, *Emigration from Hong Kong*, 23.

[106] James T. White to E. A. Blundell (Straits Settlements), 19 January 1853, in CO 885/1/19.

[107] Herman Merivale, 4 July 1854, in Letters to the Colonial Office. West Indies, Mauritius (1854–58), CO 386/91 (National Archives).

[108] Carter and Kwong, *Abacus and Mah Jong*, 33.

emigrants on 3 December 1852 (the real figure was estimated to be closer to 350 by consular authorities).[109] The *Straits Times* recounted how the 'happy demeanour' of the 'coolies' was a cover for an attack on the captain and crew of the ship who fired upon the passengers to regain control of the vessel before stopping at Singapore to 'rid the ship of the worst characters on board'.[110] The Singapore news editorial reflected the increasing concerns over the Amoy contract trade: 'looking at the character of the persons shipped as coolies, and the means resorted to in procuring them, we need not be surprised at the melancholy results which have attended this pernicious trade'.[111] Here both the perceived criminal character of the Chinese emigrants from Amoy and the coercive practices of labour recruiters were combined into a single damning assessment of a trade that was becoming increasingly unpopular in both Britain and China.

Upon stopping again for supplies at Saint Helena, the *Lady Amherst* was inspected by naval officer W. Rowlatt who concluded that the uprisings against the crew could be attributed to 'a small portion [of passengers] who seem generally to have been entrapped into going … the remainder belonging to the dangerous classes'.[112] Rowlatt also noted that of the twenty-seven passengers who had died, 'three or four had been drowned by jumping over-board'.[113] In both Singapore and Saint Helena the indolent character of the passengers was acknowledged but official suspicions were raised over the lack of consent. British observers increasingly echoed John Hurst's comments to emigration agent James T. White that 'the coolies must be misled in some way or they never would prefer going to a slave country to going to a good English free settlement'.[114] Whilst Hurst's observation contained a particular irony – in that the West India Committee White represented had been resistant to abolition – his view was representative of most colonial commenters in that he saw the slavery-tainted destinations of the passenger shipments, arranged by British firms, as their most problematic aspect.

The *Lady Amherst*'s departure point was a Chinese treaty port and its destination was a Spanish colony, but British colonial, shipping and mercantile involvement demonstrates the trans-imperial context of Chinese emigration from the mid-nineteenth century. The example of the *Lady Amherst* indicates the significance of supply ports in tracking the abuses of the contract trade. The stopping of the ship at Singapore and Saint Helena allowed for its story

109 J. Backhouse (Amoy) to Dr. Bowring (Hong Kong), 20 November 1852, in Parliamentary Papers, *China. Correspondence with the Superintendent of British trade in China, upon the subject of emigration from that country*, 1852–53 (1686)

110 *Straits Times*, 21 December 1852.

111 Ibid.

112 'Report of W. Rowlatt' (St Helena, 5 April 1853), Governor Thomas Gore Browne (St Helena) to Duke of Newcastle (London), 22 March 1853, in CO 885/1/20.

113 Ibid.

114 Parliamentary Papers, *Chinese immigration*, 1852–53 (986), 110.

to be catalogued. The Spanish port of Manila was also particularly important in this regard as it was a regular stopping point on trans-Pacific, trans-Atlantic and Australian voyages. Cases of high mortality through overcrowding, such as the *Inglewood*, which involved more than 200 deaths, came to public attention at locations such as Manila and Singapore as opposed to their final destinations.[115] Singapore also continued to supplement the long-distance migrations as a source of compliant Chinese-English interpreters for shipments of passengers from Hong Kong to the West Indies.[116] Singapore also offered a cover to illicit shipments as a pre-existing destination for Chinese migrants, with a large Chinese community. As a result, subsequent legislation, such as the Chinese Passengers Act of 1855, did not apply to these 'short' voyages as 'the passengers are not ignorant Coolies but mechanics, who have either made the passage before, or are acquainted with the circumstances of it from others'.[117]

The passenger trade that emerged from the Chinese treaty ports and Hong Kong after 1842 also came to replace pre-existing migration networks to Southeast Asia serviced by the Chinese junk trade. Records from Singapore show that of a total of 11,484 Chinese immigrants between June 1852 and June 1853, 3,456 Chinese migrants arrived from Amoy aboard European-owned vessels.[118] Over the same period only 330 migrants arrived from Amoy aboard the Chinese junks that had been carrying passengers along this familiar route.[119] The very system of migration that had alerted British colonial observers to the possibility of using Chinese labour came to be directly replicated and controlled by private Western firms. Of the twenty-eight European vessels involved in this new passenger trade route, nineteen were British.[120] In the post-Opium War era, systems of Chinese migration to Singapore were similar to those that had developed over the 1820s; the crucial difference was that the British were no longer reliant on Chinese intermediaries to secure a supply of labour from China itself.

Over the 1850s the increasing number of deaths and uprisings on passenger ships brought the issue to the attention of colonial authorities. Deaths were largely caused by cramped conditions and a shortage of provisions. The death of 170 migrants aboard the *Lady Montagu* in 1850 was attributed to an 'insufficient supply of food and water'.[121] Poor on-board conditions, combined with widespread kidnapping, caused a high frequency of ships being overrun

---

[115] Arensmeyer, 'The Chinese Coolie Labour Trade and the Philippines', 192; *Liverpool Mercury*, 4 February 1853.

[116] Governor W. J. Butterworth, 6 September 1854, in X5: Governor's Diary: General, 1853–54 (National Archives of Singapore).

[117] Parliamentary Papers, *Hong Kong*, 54.

[118] *Hong Kong Register*, 16 August 1853.

[119] Ibid.

[120] Ibid.

[121] *Singapore Free Press and Mercantile Advertiser*, 11 October 1850.

by passengers. An Australian title, the *Inquirer*, blamed poor provisioning for such an incident in 1853: 'Another vessel has been captured by her coolie passengers, and the captain murdered. She was bound for Havannah, with 200 Chinese coolies and a Malay crew. The cause of the riot was a deficiency of water.'[122] Given the combination of factors at play many voyages were interrupted or abandoned, often at stopping places such as Singapore, due to passenger uprisings.

Despite the growing awareness of duplicitous recruitment practices, colonial administrators and English-language newspapers routinely described uprisings on passenger ships as 'piracy'. The accusation of piracy lay within a broader British concern with establishing legal and economic hegemony of the China coast.[123] Piracy was discussed regularly in correspondence with the Colonial Office and was the subject of early colonial ordinances.[124] Throughout the 1850s the Royal Navy would commit vast resources to preventing piracy on the China coast, under the command of celebrated admirals like Thomas Cochrane and Henry Keppel, and the issue was raised repeatedly in parliamentary discussions on the China trade.[125] For example, the seizure of the *Rosa Elias* (a ship chartered by Tait & Co.) on its voyage to Peru was reported as the torrid tale of 'piracy and murder of an English captain and crew' who were killed by '200 Chinese coolies'.[126] The testimony of surviving ship crews confirmed suspicions that the cause of these uprisings was the dishonesty and criminality of the migrants. Colonial observers commonly attributed the frequency of piracy among Chinese passengers to the emigrants being of the 'most vicious classes in Amoy' as opposed to the lack of informed consent in recruitment for labour contracts.[127] There were clear parallels between the accusations of criminality in Hong Kong and amongst Chinese ship passengers as evidence of the innate duplicity of the Chinese racial character.

The event that forced the Colonial Office to seriously investigate coercive recruitment practices was the Amoy riot of November 1852.[128] The flashpoint that led to violence was the attempt by Syme, Muir & Co. to free a

---

[122]   *Inquirer*, 17 August 1853.
[123]   Robert J. Antony, ed., *Elusive Pirates, Pervasive Smugglers: Violence and Clandestine Trade in the Greater China Seas* (Hong Kong: Hong Kong University Press, 2010); Elliot Young, 'Chinese Coolies, Universal Rights and the Limits of Liberalism in an Age of Empire', *Past & Present*, 227, 1 (2015), 121–49.
[124]   'Ordinance on the Prevention of Piracy', in Hong Kong Blue Book (1847), CO 133/4 (National Archives).
[125]   Parliamentary Papers, *Report from the Select Committee on Commercial Relations with China*; Parliamentary Papers, *Piratical Vessels*, 1850 (367).
[126]   *Liverpool Mercury*, 5 July 1853; Adelaide Observer, 23 July 1853.
[127]   *Sydney Morning Herald*, 24 November 1851.
[128]   Murakami, 'Two Bonded Labour Emigration Patterns in Mid-Nineteenth-Century Southern China', 160.

migrant recruiter, who had been accused of kidnap, from jail.[129] The riot was the culmination of building local anger at the kidnap that supplied the contract trade and the poor pre-departure conditions of the 'pig' pens. Additionally, news of fatalities aboard passenger ships and reports of poor working conditions at emigrant destinations had fed back to China itself. Syme, Muir & Co. and Tait & Co. were specifically named by rioters who raised placards explaining that 'if persons among themselves should trade with these hongs their houses would be pulled down, their goods plundered and their lives taken'.[130] The severity of the riot, which threatened not only the merchants concerned but all Western residents in Amoy, led to the republishing of Colonial Office correspondence on emigration as a parliamentary paper. The riot lasted for several days, resulting in the death of several local people, and suppression of the riot even required the assistance of British marines.[131]

The riot marked the decline of the passenger trade from Amoy. It also laid the groundwork for British legislation to regulate the trade in 1855. As a result of the riot the Governor of Hong Kong, John Bowring, instituted a court of inquiry in December 1852. In the short term, F. D. Syme was fined $200 (roughly £40) for his role in creating the conditions for the riot, even though in his evidence to British officials in Amoy he feigned innocence: 'Q – How do you account for the fact of your house and that of Tait and Co. being mentioned in the hostile placard? A – I cannot account for it.'[132] As a consequence of the Amoy riot the passenger trade became spread more evenly across the treaty ports, and Hong Kong, by the late 1850s.[133] The 'opening' of Amoy and Hong Kong to British merchants had led to a new, more overtly politically problematic, framework of Chinese emigration.

By the early 1850s the catalogue of abuses in the Chinese contract trade made state regulation of Chinese migration inevitable. In an article on the case of the *Lady Amherst* in December 1852 the *Straits Times* claimed that it was the 'eleventh vessel' to be the scene of 'cooly violence'.[134] Such a pattern caused concern in the metropole. The high frequency of fatalities and passenger uprisings on British ships, combined with the threat to British trade posed by the Amoy riots, was well known to the Colonial Office. These issues were exacerbated by the perceived poor character of emigrants who were generally young, single, unskilled, male labourers. As before, the character of the Chinese was a ubiquitous topic in correspondence on emigration

---

[129] Parliamentary Papers, *China. Correspondence with the Superintendent of British trade in China, upon the subject of emigration from that country*, 1852–53 (1686), 48.

[130] Ibid.

[131] Slocomb, *Among Australia's Pioneers*, 91.

[132] Parliamentary Papers, *China, Correspondence with the Superintendent of British trade in China, upon the subject of emigration from that country*, 1852–53 (1686), 48.

[133] Irick, 'Chi'ing Policy towards the Coolie Trade', 8.

[134] *Straits Times*, 21 December 1852.

from China, though in references to the treaty port passenger trade it was overwhelmingly negative.

The international context also put pressure on imperial policy makers. The mutiny on the American ship *Robert Browne* on its voyage to San Francisco was arguably the most widely reported incident and applied international pressure on the British state to act, as Syme, Muir & Co. had acted as brokers and agents.[135] The biggest issue facing consular and colonial authorities was the extra-legal space in which the trade operated. The *Lady Amherst* demonstrated this issue as the inspection from Rowlatt had held the ship to the standards of the existing English Passengers Act, but as the ship was transferring Chinese subjects (emigrating illegally under Chinese law) from an extra-territorial treaty port to a Spanish colony it is unclear whether this Act for English passengers was actually applicable.[136] As urged by Governor Bowring, legislation was needed that would simultaneously 'control the cupidity of brokers and captains' in the contract trade and respond to the overcrowding of credit-ticket passengers headed to goldfields in Australia and California.[137]

An Act for the Regulation of Chinese Passenger Ships was passed by Parliament in 1855 to counter the 'abuses [which] have occurred in conveying Emigrants from Ports in the Chinese seas'.[138] In order to cover the different departure points and shipping arrangements, the Act defined a 'Chinese Passenger Ship' as 'every ship carrying from any port in Hong Kong, and every British ship carrying from any port in China or within one hundred miles of the coast thereof, more than twenty passengers, being natives of Asia'.[139] The Act stipulated that Chinese passenger ships required certificates before embarkation.[140] The granting of the certificate required an inspection of the ship by an emigration officer to ascertain the ship's seaworthiness, whether the ship held adequate medical provisions and if the passengers understood the terms of their emigration.[141] The Passengers Act did not stop accusations of abuse and coercion, but it did provide a framework for parliamentary inquiry into abuses as emigration numbers increased throughout the 1850s. The decade saw a vast increase in emigrant numbers motivated by the Taiping Rebellion at home and the increased promise of mineral riches abroad.[142]

[135] *Hong Kong Register*, 25 May 1852; Irick, 'Chi'ing Policy towards the Coolie Trade', 15–36.
[136] 'Report of W. Rowlatt'.
[137] John Bowring (Hong Kong) to Duke of Newcastle (London), 21 April 1854, in Chinese Emigration (1854), CO 129/45 (National Archives); Skeldon, *Emigration from Hong Kong*, 18.
[138] Parliamentary Papers, *Chinese Passenger Ships*.
[139] Ibid., 3.
[140] Ibid., 7.
[141] Ibid., 7.
[142] Parliamentary Papers, *Chinese, &c., emigrants. Copies of recent communications to or from the Foreign Office, Colonial Office, Board of Trade, and other departments of Her Majesty's government, on the subject of mortality on board British ships carrying emigrants from China or India*, 1857–58 (521); Parliamentary Papers, *Hong Kong*.

Ultimately the contract trade from Amoy declined following the riots of November 1852. In 1859 Shanghai saw similar riots in response to kidnapping to fill the quotas of emigration brokers, and in 1867 colonial authorities passed the Hong Kong Emigration Ordinance to further try to protect the health and safety of Chinese ship passengers.[143] In the long term, Hong Kong became the centre of Chinese emigration. By the twentieth century the island acted as a departure point for ninety per cent of Chinese emigrants.[144]

Conclusion

The pre-Opium War context of Anglo-Chinese relations provided the grounding for the mass migrations of the 1850s, which relied on these new systems of Chinese emigration from Hong Kong and Amoy in the 1840s. Hong Kong and Amoy not only acted as new departure points for emigrants, but also as new locations for changing interpretations of the Chinese character. Hong Kong was a new contact zone in which representations of the majority of Chinese emigrants as criminal and untrustworthy were again constructed in an environment in which colonial authority was contingent on a complicit Chinese merchant elite. The vessels on which migrants travelled, and the stopping points on voyages, even became locations in which colonial observers formed assessments of the Chinese character, as a result of passenger uprisings and piracy.

On a practical level these systems of emigration also drew on previous experiences. The credit-ticket arrangements entered into by some migrants heading to the Australian and Californian goldfields mirrored those that had been used to reach various locations in Southeast Asia, aboard both European vessels and Chinese junks. Migrant journeys from southern China to Southeast Asia itself were also increasingly undertaken aboard Western vessels. The new shipping networks that emerged in the treaty ports were essential to this. Additionally the indenture contracts signed in Amoy were extremely similar to those used to supply Indian labour for Mauritius and mirrored the contracts from the Assam experiment in terms of duration and conditions, if not pay. Ironically, systems of Chinese migration that emerged from a colonial need for free labour in the wake of abolition were criticised for their similarities to slavery. Debates about desirable forms of labour and racial

---

[143] Murakami, 'Two Bonded Labour Emigration Patterns in Mid-Nineteenth-Century Southern China', 161; Irick, 'Chi'ing Policy towards the Coolie Trade', 3; Young, 'Chinese Coolies, Universal Rights and the Limits of Liberalism in an Age of Empire', 148–9.

[144] Carroll, *A Concise History of Hong Kong*, 3. Note that the stipulations of the relevant Passengers Acts and the colonial interest in monitoring and regulating the Chinese passenger trade provided more detailed emigration statistics for the second half of the nineteenth century, which have underpinned the work of scholars examining Chinese migration in the British Empire in the era of racial exclusion.

hierarchy in the British Empire persisted, and continued to affect perceptions of Chinese migrants, post-1842.

In the second half of the nineteenth century the mass migration of Chinese labourers across the British Empire was facilitated by the opening of the Chinese treaty ports and the cession of Hong Kong. The demand for this migrant labour came from the rapid economic transformation of various British colonies. Through this era of rapid change, the colonial model of Singapore, and its significance as an Anglo-Chinese contact zone, remained crucial to perceptions of Chinese migrant labour in the British Empire.

CONCLUSION

In 1874 the English entomologist William Lucas Distant published a short article giving an overview of 'Eastern Coolie Labour', which was based on his observations of plantations in Singapore and Johor.[1] In this article Distant compares Chinese workers favourably against their indigenous counterparts: 'The Chinese ... seem to prosper better under the employment of their own countrymen, cultivate their plots of ground, breed their fowls and pigs, and seem contented with their position and lot. The Chinaman seems also to prosper in contact with the European, he bargains with him.'[2] Whilst he repeatedly praised the role of Chinese workers and middle management in the development of the plantation economy, he also confirmed long-standing stereotypes as essential to the character of Chinese workers: 'Of course they gamble – all Chinamen do – and the head Chinaman makes a considerable profit from the opium with which he supplies them.'[3] Distant's analysis could pass for that of a colonial observer in Singapore in the 1820s and demonstrates the longevity of these tropes from the early colonial period.

In 1879 several prominent Chinese migrants in Australia – Lowe Kong Meng, Cheok Hong Cheong and Louis Ah Mouy – wrote a defence of Chinese immigration in a pamphlet that responded to the anti-Chinese political rhetoric sweeping the Australian colonies. In doing so they placed Chinese migration in the broader context of Anglo-Chinese conflict and highlighted the nexus between free trade and the free movement of people that was key to the success of early colonial Singapore:

> The freedom to come and go, to trade and settle, which you [the British] insisted upon claiming for yourselves, you also accorded to the subjects of his Imperial Majesty. He has fulfilled the first part of the compact, and the trade of Great Britain with China has trebled during the last fourteen years, to say nothing of the indirect commerce transacted with that country via Singapore and Hong Kong. Well, our countrymen begin to emigrate to these colonies, and to seek employment on board Australian vessels, in the fullest confidence that the second portion of the compact will be carried out, and they are astounded

1 W. L. Distant, 'Eastern Coolie Labour', *The Journal of the Anthropological Institute of Great Britain and Ireland*, 3 (1874), 139–45.
2 Ibid., 143.
3 Ibid., 142.

to find that its fulfilment is resisted by the subjects of Her Majesty Queen Victoria in Australia.[4]

Here they explicitly connected the development of the Anglo-Chinese contact zones of Singapore and Hong Kong to the broader global flows of Chinese migration. A wealth of literature exists on these growing Chinese communities in the second half of the nineteenth century and their significance in the globalisation of border control in the twentieth century.[5] Yet it is the start of these migrations, and in particular the importance of Anglo-Chinese contact zones, that requires further study. Concepts of Chinese character constructed in the contact zones of the Straits Settlements and China coast were re-configured and re-applied in colonial Victoria.

This book provides a comprehensive overview of the way that British observers identified Singapore as a colonial model: as a dynamic combination of British leadership working in tandem with a Chinese merchant elite to control a large, productive Chinese labour force. As an Anglo-Chinese contact zone, Singapore conceptually underpinned global migration systems in the later period. As different experiments with Chinese labour sought to replicate the success of Singapore, the mid-nineteenth century was also a vitally important period for the ranking of Chinese migrants in colonial racial hierarchies. There were two main drivers of the British obsession with defining who the Chinese were and what they were like: concern over British commercial access to China and concerns over the shortage of labour in British colonies. Many of the stereotypes about the Chinese character, which would become widespread across the West over the nineteenth and twentieth centuries, were formed in this period. Many of these stereotypes were riven with contradictions. For example, James Matheson simultaneously criticised Chinese deceitfulness and praised Chinese entrepreneurship. Both of these views were manifest in the anti-immigration discourse of the late nineteenth century. Chinese workers were simultaneously a pernicious moral force but also so industrious that white workers needed protection from economic competition. Characterisations of Chinese workers were not fundamentally positive or negative. More accurately, Chinese immigrants in the British Empire were viewed as a useful economic force and a tool of colonial governance.

Importantly, Singapore did not just act as a template, but continued to be a popular destination for Chinese migrant labour. Southeast Asia had attracted Chinese migrants prior to the British imperial presence and continued to attract Chinese migrants after decolonisation. As of the 2010 census, Singapore was home to 2.8 million residents who were Chinese nationals or identified as

---

4   Meng et al., *The Chinese Question in Australia*, 29.
5   McKeown, *Melancholy Order*, 2.

Chinese (seventy-four per cent of the resident population).[6] Today, Singapore is a country where the legacy of colonial-era racial hierarchies is all too clear. State-issued identity cards and official documents still follow a race categorisation model that assigns residents an ethnic identity: Chinese, Malaysian, Indian or Other. Despite the obvious unsuitability of this system for people of mixed heritage, particularly in the context of Singapore as a global hub in the hypermobile twenty-first century, Government ministers have stressed that it is unlikely to change any time soon.[7] Evidently, the legacy of the racial categories that were deemed so important in the 1820s is long-lasting.

Beyond Singapore itself, the systems, arrangements and economic value of Chinese labour in Singapore had a significant impact on colonial observers and imperial planners. The development of Singapore over the 1820s and 1830s combined with the removal of the East India Company monopoly in 1833 changed the economic, political and social dynamics of the British Empire in Asia. Discussions of Chinese character in the debate around the Charter Act demonstrate why historians of Chinese migration into the British Empire must ground their work in the broader context of Anglo-Chinese relations and British economic and imperial expansion in Asia. As seen in Chapter 2, the broad narrative of English-language publications on China and the Chinese was that of a fundamental division. This division was between an enterprising, industrious, liberty-deserving, southern Chinese population and a despotic, insular, tyrannical, northern Manchu state. Not only did this division justify British opium smuggling on the China coast but it also acted as an implicit, and sometimes explicit, advocacy of Chinese emigration. Criticism of the Qing was persistent and intensified over the nineteenth century. The Second Opium War, and consequent legalisation of Chinese emigration, again demonstrates the connection between freedom of movement and the defiance of Qing authority.

The 1830s and 1840s was also a crucial period for establishing new systems of migration to service developing plantation colonies. The procurement of Chinese labour for Assam drew heavily on the Singapore model and economic necessity. In Assam, the experiment had a vast economic, ecological and social impact. The success of tea planting in Assam changed the region, trade in the British Empire and the commodification of tea globally.[8] Demand for Chinese workers also reveals the far-reaching impact of contemporary debates over labour and colonisation in the British Empire. Experiments

6 Department of Statistics Singapore, Singapore Government, 2010, www.singstat.gov.sg/publications/cop2010/census10_stat_release3 (accessed 30 September 2018).
7 Faris Mokhtar, 'Singapore "Far from Ready" to Do Away with Race Categorisation: Ong Ye Kung', *Channel News Asia*, 11 September 2016, www.channelnewsasia.com/news/singapore/singapore-far-from-ready-to-do-away-with-race-categorisation-ong-7810834 (accessed 30 September 2018).
8 Markman Ellis, Richard Coulton and Matthew Mauger, *Empire of Tea: The Asian Leaf that Conquered the World* (London: Reaktion Books, 2014), 202–21.

with Chinese migrant labour took place in a patchwork of colonial contexts, which were afflicted by labour shortages. The phasing out of coercive forms of employment – slave labour, convict labour and the suspension of Indian indentured labour – left questions about how free, or voluntary, labour could fill colonial labour shortages. In this context, Governor James Alexander Stewart-Mackenzie twice attempted to introduce Chinese migrants to Ceylon. He was interested in both 'Chinese with capital', like the prominent Chinese merchant class in Singapore, and tea cultivators so that he could develop new tea plantations. At the same time a new layer of imperial bureaucracy, the Colonial Land and Emigration Commission, began to address problems with labour, colonisation and land distribution across the Empire. This was a key period for testing systems of indentured labour that would continue to service plantation colonies over the nineteenth century. From the 1850s onwards an estimated 18,000 Chinese labourers migrated to the West Indies on indenture contracts.[9]

At the same time as these experiments with Chinese labour in developing plantation colonies, Gordon Forbes Davidson's migration scheme to New South Wales gave an early indication that the white settlers of Australia would politically mobilise in resistance to cheap Chinese labour. A commonality of these experiments was that indigenous populations were seen as candidates for replacement by industrious Chinese workers. The pattern of replacement of indigenous peoples was replicated across the British Empire and beyond. In particular, Aboriginal Australian communities were subject to such marginalisation repeatedly over the nineteenth and twentieth centuries.[10] This destruction of Aboriginal Australian society was driven by the same notions of economic progress and racial hierarchy that had created a demand for Chinese labour. Beyond Davidson's failed experiment, thousands of Chinese migrants did move to Australia in the nineteenth century. Here we can trace the continuing influence of Singapore in the different ways that Chinese immigrants were represented during the gold rush era. Whilst most histories of exclusionary politics in Australia emphasise ideological connections between white settler colonies, it is clear that stereotypes applied to Chinese immigrants also drew heavily on the colonial experience in Singapore.

This was also a period in which the most significant shift in Anglo-Chinese relations took place with the opening of China after the First Opium War. The cession of Hong Kong, the opening of the treaty ports, the

9   Marjory Harper, 'Exile into Bondage? Non-White Migrants and Settlers', in Marjory Harper and Stephen Constantine, *Migration and Empire* (Oxford: Oxford University Press, 2010), 152.

10 For more on this process of destruction see Stuart Macintyre and Anna Clark, *The History Wars* (Carlton, Vic.: Melbourne University Press, 2004); Henry Reynolds, *This Whispering in Our Hearts* (St Leonards, NSW: Allen & Unwin, 1998); Tom Lawson, *The Last Man: A British Genocide in Tasmania* (London: I.B. Tauris, 2014).

granting of legal extraterritoriality for foreigners in China – these changes all had an impact on Chinese migration into the British Empire. Colonial authorities in Hong Kong, much like Singapore previously, simultaneously praised Chinese elites and were wary and critical of the Chinese majority. Most importantly, Hong Kong acted as a point of onward migration to destinations around the globe and a strategic base for Western firms looking to extract labour from China. The Chinese treaty ports also allowed British firms to establish 'new systems of slavery'.[11] The indenture system and mass migration to the goldfields in the 1850s have been discussed as the two main systems in the vast body of literature on Chinese migration in the nineteenth century. The Chinese passenger trade established by British firms has been treated as a new and distinct phenomenon post-1842, yet Singapore remained an important point of connection as both a stopping place and a model migrant destination.

All of the case studies examined in this book demonstrate the mobility of ideas about race, economics and colonisation between Singapore and other colonial contexts. In terms of race, this was the idea that the Chinese had an unchanging racial character. Even in different colonial racial hierarchies the Chinese were deemed to be superior to indigenous populations. Ideas about economics informed these racial hierarchies. The Chinese were seen as superior because they were industrious and commercially minded. At the same time they were seen as particularly well suited to the free trade model of Singapore and the economic liberalism that emerged as a defining feature of British colonialism from the 1830s onwards. In turn, this combination of ideas about race and economics informed the idea that British colonial governance combined with Chinese colonists was a desirable model of colonisation.

In terms of source material, this study of Chinese migration in the British Empire has largely dealt with the colonial lives of powerful individuals and organisations. A focus on such powerful individuals in histories of empire is increasingly unpopular as scholars seek to tell the story of voiceless groups that have been omitted from the historical record. A study of these sources does not directly tell us the story of the Chinese migrant experience. However it does tell us about how migrants were perceived, and the ideas that shaped the colonial contexts in which migrants lived. Importantly, these figures had agency. They were not just reacting to change, but actively changing the British Empire in Asia. Crucially, the examination of Chinese migration through these individuals has allowed for a subversion of some of the methodological binaries that often exist in studies of migration that focus on specific national examples. Historians who dismiss colonial officials, wealthy merchants and

---

11 This phrase, used by Lord John Russell before his ascension to Prime Minister, is discussed in Chapter 5.

powerful organisations as over-examined or disconnected from the realities of migration are failing to utilise a rich resource.

Colonial observers are particularly important as perceptions of Chinese migrants formed in colonial contact zones have significant implications for histories of immigration restriction and white, working-class anti-Asian movements in the late nineteenth century. The narrative of these movements is often straightforward. After large amounts of Chinese, as well as Indian and Japanese, immigration into settler colonies – namely Australia, New Zealand, South Africa and Canada – and the United States from the 1850s onwards, white working-class movements emerged that agitated for the exclusion of cheap Asian labour.[12] This political pressure meant that a legislative framework for exclusion was in put in place across these nations, forming the basis of modern-day systems of border control.[13] These political processes, and associated prejudices, have been interpreted as a reaction to Asian immigration. However, they were actually informed by perceptions of the Chinese that had been formed much earlier in Asian contact zones. Intensely racialised, sensationalist anti-Chinese rhetoric appeared in late nineteenth-century Australia and Chinese migrants were criticised as strike-breaking criminals. As shown in this book, notions of the Chinese as a cheap labour force – who were also flawed opium addicts, gamblers and thieves – were constructed in colonial Singapore in the 1820s and 1830s. These traits re-emerged in the late nineteenth century as criticisms of Chinese immigrant labour. Anti-immigrant discourse clearly drew on the narratives of a much longer tradition of Anglo-Chinese exchange in colonial contact zones.

There is broad scope for a comparative analysis of perceptions of Chinese migrant labour in new, multi-ethnic contexts. For example, Donna Gabaccia has previously discussed how Italian immigrants in North America were labelled the 'Chinese of Europe'.[14] Notions of Italian and Chinese labour sat uneasily between the dichotomy of 'free white' and 'unfree black' labour.[15] Further comparison with different groups that migrated from Europe is possible. This book demonstrates how white settlers simultaneously viewed Chinese labour as uniquely effective and as part of a broad category of harmful Asian labour. Such perceptions were contingent on specific local circumstances and similar distinctions were applied to other migrant groups. For example, Irish immigrants often faced discrimination in Britain and the

12 Victoria in 1854 is often cited as the start of such movements in the British Empire: Hollinsworth, *Race and Racism in Australia*, 101; Hyslop, 'The Imperial Working Class Makes Itself White', 398–421.

13 McKeown, *Melancholy Order*, 2; Lucy E. Salyer, *Laws as Harsh as Tigers: Chinese Immigrants and the Shaping of Modern Immigration Law* (Chapel Hill: University of North Carolina Press, 1995).

14 Donna Gabaccia, 'The "Yellow Peril" and the "Chinese of Europe": Global Perspectives on Race and Labour, 1815–1930', in Jan Lucassen, ed., *Migration, Migration History, History: Old Paradigms and New Perspectives* (Bern: Peter Lang, 1999), 177–97.

15 Gabaccia, 'The "Yellow Peril" and the "Chinese of Europe"', 196.

United States but, in the exclusionary rhetoric of 'white' Australia, were preferred to non-white immigrants. Migrants from Europe, Asia and elsewhere were all part of and subject to confused notions of racial hierarchy as settler colonies developed. Future work needs to place Chinese migration in this comparative model.

More broadly, Chinese migration and the development of the British Empire must be situated in the wider context of Anglo-Chinese relations. The British desire for China to open its borders meant the movement of labour and capital out of China as much as it meant the movement of missionaries, Western imports and foreign merchants into China. This connection between free trade and the free movement of people has clear parallels with the present. This book was researched and written as the United Kingdom voted to leave the European Union and began to negotiate Brexit. These modern debates have struggled to reconcile the desire to limit immigration with the desire to maintain a free and unrestricted trading relationship. Put simply, nineteenth-century British colonial observers similarly grappled with the connection between the free movement of people and the free movement of goods. There is an irony then that people who invoke visions of empire as a potential roadmap for Britain post-Brexit fail to recognise this historical parallel.[16]

Modern debates about Britain's relationship with the wider world need to be situated in this historical context of Britain and the British Empire as a facilitator of mass migration. Perhaps even more pernicious is the echo of the colonial discussions from Singapore that evaluated migrants according to their economic contribution. In the broader debate around Brexit there has been an emphasis on distinguishing between migrants who make a positive contribution to Britain's economy and those who extract capital to send abroad. Often it is people making the case for immigration who make these distinctions as they highlight the valuable contribution of dedicated public-sector workers or hardworking entrepreneurs. However, as early colonial Singapore demonstrates, even positive stereotypes about valuable or useful migrants feed into narratives that justify exploitation and exclusion. Moreover, the distinction between 'good' and 'bad' immigrants is overly simplistic and almost always impossible to delineate.

On 1 April 1867 the Straits Settlements became a Crown Colony. By this point colonial observers had established common tropes about Singapore's Chinese colonists in line with broader ideas about race, economics and colonisation. Singapore's early colonial period (1819–67) did not just lay the groundwork for the development of the colony itself, it was also crucial in shaping the view of China as a source of high-quality, low-cost labour

16 For a discussion of this distorted historical view, see Stan Neal, 'The Commonwealth and Britain: The Trouble with "Empire 2.0"', *The Conversation*, 6 March 2017, https://theconversation.com/the-commonwealth-and-britain-the-trouble-with-empire-2-0-73707 (accessed 30 September 2018).

for imperial shortages. The foundations of the Chinese mass migrations and racialised responses to them, that would lead to the development of global systems of border control in the early twentieth century, were established in this period. The Singapore model re-shaped the British Empire and the resulting systems of Chinese migration re-shaped the world we live in today.

BIBLIOGRAPHY

Primary Sources

Unpublished Archival Sources

Jardine Matheson Archive (Cambridge University Library)

MS JM/B1: Private letters: non-local, 1813–1913.
MS JM/B6: Business letters: non-local, 1844–81.
MS JM/C2: Letters from Yrissari & Co., 1822–30.
MS JM/C5: Private letters from James Matheson, 1831–41.
MS JM/C10: Letters to India, 1800–83.
MS JM/C13: Letters to the China coast, 1839–83.
MS JM/F11: Employment contracts, 1834–1940.

London Metropolitan Archives

MS 9924/1: Assam Company Records.

National Archives of Scotland

GD46/9/6: Mackenzie Papers.

Official Documents

UK National Archives (Colonial Office Records)

CO 129: Hong Kong, Original Correspondence.
CO 133: Hong Kong, Miscellanea.
CO 172: Mauritius, Miscellanea.
CO 273: Straits Settlements Original Correspondence.
CO 277: Prince Edward Island Entry Books.
CO 386: Land and Emigration Commission.
CO 428: Emigration Register of Correspondence.
CO 57: Ceylon, Sessional Papers.
CO 58: Ceylon, Government Gazettes.
CO 885: Subjects Affecting Colonies Generally.

British Library (India Office Records)

IOR/V/17/450: Singapore Shipping and Commerce, 1823–44.
IOR/F/4/1271: Board's Collection, 1820s–1830s.
IOR/F/4/1846/77642: Board's Collection, 1810s–1840s.
IOR/Z/E/4/19/C671, Index to India and Bengal Despatches, 1846–48.

National Archives of Singapore (Straits Settlements Records)

A18: Penang Consultations.
L15: Raffles: Letters from Singapore.
M2: Singapore: Letters from Bengal to the Resident.
M4: Singapore: Letters from Bengal to the Resident.
U39: Governor: Letters to Resident Councillors.
X5: Governor's Diary: General, 1853–54.
Z15 Singapore: Letters from the Governor.

National Library of Australia

Australian Parliament: Joint Library Committee, *Historical Records of Australia: Series I, Volume V* (The Library Committee of the Commonwealth Parliament, 1915).
Colonial Land and Emigration Commissioners, *Colonization Circular* (30 October 1843).

United Kingdom Parliamentary Papers

Parliamentary Papers, *Capabilities of the Chinese to become good emigrants to the colony of New South Wales*, 1838 (389).
Parliamentary Papers, *China. Correspondence upon the subject of emigration from China*, 1854–55 (0.7).
Parliamentary Papers, *China. Correspondence with the Superintendent of British trade in China, upon the subject of emigration from that country*, 1852–53 (1686).
Parliamentary Papers, *Chinese Passenger Ships. A bill intituled an act for the regulation of Chinese passenger ships*, 1854–55 (293).
Parliamentary Papers, *Colonial Land and Emigration Commission. Ninth general report of the Colonial Land and Emigration Commissioners*, 1849 (1082).
Parliamentary Papers, *Colonial Land and Emigration. General Report of the Colonial Land and Emigration Commissioners*, 1842 (567).
Parliamentary Papers, *Emigration. (North American and Australian colonies.) Copies or extracts of any despatches relative to emigration to the North American and Australian colonies; in continuation of the papers presented to this House in August 1848 and February 1849*, 1849 (593).
Parliamentary Papers, *Emigration. Copies of any general report, since the last laid before this House, from the Agent General for Emigration: of any report from the Agent for Emigration in Canada: copies or extracts of any correspondence between the Secretary of State for the Colonies and the governors of the Australian colonies, respecting emigration, since the papers presented to the House on the 14th day of May 1838*, 1839 (536-I) (536-II).
Parliamentary Papers, *Emigration. West Indies and Mauritius. Correspondence relative to emigration of labourers to the West Indies and the Mauritius, from the west coast of Africa, the East Indies, and China, since the papers already laid before the House*, 1844 (530).
Parliamentary Papers, *Fifth general report of the Colonial Land and Emigration Commissioners*, 1845 (617).
Parliamentary Papers, *General report of the Colonial Land and Emigration Commissioners*, 1843 (621).

Parliamentary Papers, *Hong Kong. Copies or extracts of correspondence between the Colonial Department and the governor of Hong Kong, and between the Colonial Department and the Foreign Office, on the subject of emigration from Hong Kong and from the Chinese Empire to the British West Indies and to foreign countries and their possessions, since the 1st of January 1853*, 1857–58 (481).

Parliamentary Papers, *Mauritius. Copies of correspondence addressed to the Secretary of State for the Colonial Department, relative to the introduction of Indian labourers into the Mauritius; and of the report of the Commissioners of Inquiry into the present condition of those already located in that colony*, 1840 (331).

Parliamentary Papers, *Mr. Montgomery Martin. Copy of correspondence of Mr. Montgomery Martin with the Secretary of State for the Colonies, relating to his resignation of the office of Treasurer of Hong Kong*, 1847 (743).

Parliamentary Papers, *Piratical Vessels*, 1850 (367).

Parliamentary Papers, *Report from the committee appointed to consider the practicability and expediency of supplying our West India colonies with free labourers from the East*, 1810–11 (225).

Parliamentary Papers, *Report from the Select Committee of the House of Lords appointed to inquire into the present state of the affairs of the East India Company, and into the trade between Great Britain, the East Indies and China; with the minutes of evidence taken before the committee*, 1830 (646).

Parliamentary Papers, *Report from the Select Committee on Commercial Relations with China; together with the minutes of evidence, appendix, and index*, 1847 (654).

Parliamentary Papers, *Report from the Select Committee on West India Colonies*, 1842 (479).

Parliamentary Papers, *Select Committee on Transportation, Report, 1837–38*, 1838 (669).

Parliamentary Papers, *Slave trade (East India) – Slavery in Ceylon. Return to an order of the Honourable the House of Commons, dated 1 March 1838*, 1837–38 (697).

Parliamentary Papers, *Tea Cultivation (India). Return to an order of the Honourable the House of Commons, dated 15 February 1839;—for, copy of papers received from India relating to the measures adopted for introducing the cultivation of the tea plant within the British possessions in India*, 1839 (63).

Parliamentary Papers, *West Indies. Copies or extracts of correspondence relative to the labouring population in the West Indies*, 1845 (642).

Sessional Papers of the House of Lords, Vol. IX (House of Lords, 1844).

Published Books, Pamphlets and Articles

Anonymous, *Assam: a sketch of its history, soil, and productions* (London: Smith, Elder and Co., 1839).

Bowring, John, *Autobiographical Recollections of Sir John Bowring* (London: Henry S. King, 1877).

Brown, Sampson, 'Life in the Jungle, or letters from a planter to his cousin in London', *Ceylon Magazine*, 11, 17 (1842), 234–343.

Chitty, Simon Casie, *The Ceylon Gazetteer* (Ceylon: Gotta Church Mission Press, 1834).

Crawfurd, John, *Chinese Monopoly Examined* (London: James Ridgeway, 1830).

Crawfurd, John, *Grammar and Dictionary of the Malay Language* (London: Smith, Elder, 1852).

Crawfurd, John, *History of the Indian Archipelago, Vol. I* (Edinburgh: Archibald, Constable & Co., 1820).

Crawfurd, John, *History of the Indian Archipelago, Vol. II* (Edinburgh: Archibald, Constable & Co., 1820).

Crawfurd, John, *History of the Indian Archipelago, Vol. III* (Edinburgh: Archibald, Constable & Co., 1820).

Crawfurd, John, *Journal of an Embassy from the Governor-General of India to the Courts of Siam and Cochin China, Vol. II* (London: Henry Colburn and Richard Bentley, 1830).

Crawfurd, John, *View of the Present State and Future Prospects of the Free Trade and Colonisation of India* (London: James Ridgway, 1829).

Cunynghame, Arthur, *The Opium War: Being Recollections of Service in China* (first published Philadelphia: G.B. Ziever & Co., 1845, reprint 1972).

Davidson, G. F., *Trade and Travel in the Far East; or recollections of twenty-one years passed in Java, Singapore, Australia, and China* (London: Madden and Malcolm, 1846).

Davis, John Francis, *The Chinese: a general description of the empire of China and its inhabitants* (New York: Harper & Brothers, 1836).

de Butts, *Rambles in Ceylon* (London: W. H. Allen & Co., 1841).

Distant, W. L., 'Eastern Coolie Labour', *The Journal of the Anthropological Institute of Great Britain and Ireland*, 3 (1874), 139–45.

Downing, C. Toogood, *The Stranger in China* (Philadelphia: Lea & Blanchard, 1838).

Gouger, Robert, ed., *A Letter from Sydney, the Principal Town of Australasia*; together with Edward Gibbon Wakefield, *Outline of a System of Colonization* (London: Joseph Cross, 1829).

Gow, Wilson, and Gow, Stanton, eds, *Tea Producing companies of India and Ceylon: showing the History and Results of those Capitalised in Sterling* (London: A. Southey & Co., 1897).

Gutzlaff, Charles, *China Opened, Vol. I* (London: Smith, Elder and Co., 1838).

Gutzlaff, Charles, *Journal of a Residence in Siam: and of a Voyage Along the Coast of China to Mantchou Tartary* (Canton: Chinese Repository, 1832).

Gutzlaff, Charles, *A Sketch of Chinese History, Ancient and Modern, Vol. I* (London: Smith, Elder and Co., 1834).

Johnston, A. R., *Hong Kong Directory / Almanac* (Hong Kong, 1846).

Knox, Robert, *An Historical Relation of the Island of Ceylon in the East Indies* (London: Royal Society, 1681).

Lang, John Dunmore, *An Historical and Statistical Account of New South Wales, Both as a Penal Settlement and as a British Colony* (London: A. J. Valpy, 1837).

Lay, George Tradescant, *The Chinese as They Are: Their Moral, Social and Literary Character* (London: William Ball & Co., 1841).

Lindsay, Hugh Hamilton, *The Rupture with China and Its Causes; Including the Opium Question, and Other Important Details: In a Letter to Lord Viscount Palmerston, Secretary for Foreign Affairs* (London: Sherwood, Gilbert, and Piper, 1840).

Martin, Robert Montgomery, *British Relations with the Chinese Empire in 1832* (London: Parbury, Allen & Co., 1832).

Martin, Robert Montgomery, *A History of British Possessions in the Indian and Atlantic Oceans* (London: Whittaker & Co., 1837).

Martin, Robert Montgomery, *Reports, Minutes and Despatches on the British Position and Prospects in China* (London: Harrison, 1846).

Martin, Robert Montgomery, *Statistics of the Colonies of the British Empire: From the Official Records of the Colonial Office* (London: W. H. Allen and Co., 1839).

Matheson, James, *The Present Position and Prospects of the British Trade with China* (London: Smith, Elder and Co., 1836).

Medhurst, Walter Henry, *China: its State and Prospects* (Boston: Crocker & Brewster, 1838).

Meng, L. Kong, Cheong, Cheok Hong, and Mouy, Louis Ah, *The Chinese Question in Australia 1878–9* (Melbourne: F. F. Bailliere, 1879).

Milne, William, 'Account of a Secret Association in China, Entitled the Triad Society', *Transactions of the Royal Asiatic Society of Great Britain and Ireland*, 1, 2 (1826), 240–50.

Mudie, Robert, *China and its Resources, A Notice of Assam* (London: Grattan and Gilbert, 1840).

Murray, Hugh, and Crawfurd, John, et al., *An Historical and Descriptive Account of China, Vol. I* (Edinburgh: Oliver & Boyd, 1836).

Murray, Hugh, and Crawfurd, John, et al., *An Historical and Descriptive Account of China, Vol. II* (Edinburgh: Oliver & Boyd, 1836).

Robbins, Helen H., *Our first ambassador to China: an account of the life of George, Earl of Macartney, with extracts from his letters, and the narrative of his experiences in China, as told by himself, 1737–1806, from hitherto unpublished correspondence and documents* (London: John Murray, 1908).

Scarth, John, *British Policy in China: is our war with the Tartars or the Chinese* (London: Smith, Elder and Co., 1860).

Smith, Adam, *An Inquiry into the Nature and Causes of the Wealth of Nations* (London: W. Strahan, 1776).

Smith, Arthur Henderson, *Chinese Characteristics* (New York: Fleming H. Revell Company, 1894).

Staunton, Sir George, *An authentic account of an Embassy from the King of Great Britain* (London: G. Nicol, 1797).

Tennent, J. Emerson, *Ceylon: an account of the island physical* (London: Longman, 1859).

Thompson, George, *Report of a Public Meeting and Lecture at Darlington … on China and the Opium Question* (Durham: J. H. Veitch, 1840).

Treaty of Nanking (Great Britain – China), in G. E. P. Hertslet and Edward Parkes, *Hertslet's China Treaties. Treaties between Great Britain and China and between China and Foreign Powers, etc.*, 3rd edn (London: Harrison and Sons, for H.M. Stationery, 1908).

U'Chin, Siah, 'The Chinese in Singapore', *Journal of the Indian Archipelago*, Vol. II (1848), 283–90.

Newspapers and Periodicals

Australia

Adelaide Observer
The Argus
The Banner
Empire
The Goulburn Herald
Inquirer
The Maitland Mercury
Melbourne Argus
Moreton Bay Courier
Mount Alexander Mail
The People's Advocate
Straits Times
Sydney Gazette
Sydney Herald
Sydney Monitor
Sydney Morning Herald

China

Canton Press
Canton Register
Chinese Courier
Chinese Repository
Friend of China
Hong Kong Register

Singapore

Singapore Chronicle
Singapore Free Press
Singapore Free Press and Mercantile Advertiser
Straits Times

United Kingdom

Asiatic Journal
The Era
Essex Standard
Hull Packet
Leeds Times
Liverpool Mercury
London Morning Post
Yorkshire Gazette

Secondary Sources

Books, Book Chapters and Journal Articles

Alatas, Syed, *The Myth of the Lazy Native: A Study of the Image of the Malays, Filipinos and Javanese from the 16th to the 20th Century and Its Function in the Ideology of Colonial Capitalism* (London: Cass and Co., 1977).

Allen, Jim, *Port Essington: The Historical Archaeology of a North Australian Nineteenth Century Military Outpost* (Sydney: Sydney University Press, 2008).

Allen, Richard B., 'Satisfying the "Want for Labouring People": European Slave Trading in the Indian Ocean, 1500–1800', *Journal of World History*, 21, 1 (2010), 45–73.

Allen, Richard B., 'Slaves, Convicts, Abolitionism and the Global Origins of the Post-Emancipation Indentured Labour System', *Slavery & Abolition*, 35, 2 (2014), 328–48.

Anderson, Benedict, *Imagined Communities: Reflections on the Origin and Spread of Nationalism* (London: Verso, 1983).

Anderson, Clare, 'The Age of Revolution in the Indian Ocean, Bay of Bengal and South China Sea: A Maritime Perspective', *International Review of Social History*, 58 (2013), 229–51.

Anderson, Kay, *Race and the Crisis of Humanism* (New York: UCL Press, 2006).

Anthony, Robert J., ed., *Elusive Pirates, Pervasive Smugglers: Violence and Clandestine Trade in the Greater China Seas* (Hong Kong: Hong Kong University Press, 2010).

Antrobus, H. A., *The History of the Assam Company, 1839–1953* (Edinburgh: T. and A. Constable Ltd, 1957).

Arensmeyer, Elliot C., 'The Chinese Coolie Labour Trade and the Philippines: An Inquiry', *Philippine Studies*, 28 (1980), 187–98.

Atkinson, David C., *The Burden of White Supremacy: Containing Asian Migration in the British Empire and the United States* (Chapel Hill: University of North Carolina Press, 2017).

Attwood, B., and Griffiths, T., eds, *Frontier, Race, Nation: Henry Reynolds and Australian History* (Melbourne: Australian Scholarly Publishing, 2009).

Baker, Jim, *Crossroads: A Popular History of Malaysia and Singapore* (Singapore: Marshall Cavendish, 2008).

Ballantyne, Tony, *Orientalism and Race: Aryanism in the British Empire* (Basingstoke: Palgrave, 2002).

Ballaster, Rosalind, *Fabulous Orients: Fictions of the East in England, 1662–1785* (Oxford: Oxford University Press, 2005).

Bard, Solomon, *Traders of Hong Kong: Some Foreign Merchant Houses, 1841–1899* (Hong Kong: Hong Kong Museum of History, 1993).

Barron, T. J., 'Science and the Nineteenth-Century Ceylon Coffee Planters', *The Journal of Imperial and Commonwealth History*, 16 (1987), 9–17.

Bayly, C. A., *Empire and Information: Intelligence Gathering and Social Communication in India, 1780–1870* (Cambridge: Cambridge University Press, 1996).

Beals, Melodee, 'The Role of the Sydney Gazette in the Creation of Australia in the Scottish Public Sphere', in Catherine Feely and John Hinks, eds, *Historical Networks in the Book Trade* (Abingdon: Routledge, 2017), 148–70.

Belich, James, *Replenishing the Earth: The Settler Revolution and the Rise of the Anglo-World, 1783–1939* (Oxford: Oxford University Press, 2009).

Berg, Maxine, 'Britain, Industry and Perceptions of China: Matthew Boulton, "Useful Knowledge" and the Macartney Embassy to China', *Journal of Global History*, 1, 2 (2006), 269–88.

Bergad, Laird W., et al., *The Cuban Slave Market, 1790–1800* (Cambridge: Cambridge University Press, 1995).

Bickers, Robert, 'The Challenger: Hugh Hamilton Lindsay and the Rise of British Asia, 1832–1865', *Transactions of the Royal Historical Society*, 6th series, 22 (2012), 141–69.

Bickers, Robert, *The Scramble for China: Foreign Devils in the Qing Empire, 1832–1914* (London: Allen Lane, 2011).

Bickers, Robert, 'Shanghailanders: The Formation and Identity of the British Settler Community in Shanghai, 1843–1937', *Past & Present*, 159, 1 (1998), 161–211.

Bongiorno, Frank, *The Sex Lives of Australians: A History* (Collingwood: Black Inc., 2014).

Bosma, Ulbe, and Webster, Anthony, eds, *Commodities, Ports and Asian Maritime Trade since 1750* (Basingstoke: Palgrave Macmillan, 2015).

Braddell, Roland, et al., *One Hundred Years of Singapore, 1819–1919, Vol. I* (London: John Murray, 1921).

Braddell, Roland, et al., *One Hundred Years of Singapore, 1819–1919, Vol. II* (London: John Murray, 1921).

Bright, Rachel, 'Asian Migration and the British World, c.1850–1914', in Kent Fedorowich and Andrew Thompson, eds, *Empire, Migration and Identity in the British World* (New York: Manchester University Press, 2013).

Broeze, Frank, ed., *Gateways of Asia: Port Cities of Asia in the 13th–20th Centuries* (London: Routledge, 2010).

Broome, Richard, 'Aboriginal Workers on South-Eastern Frontiers', *Australian Historical Studies*, 26, 103 (1994), 202–20.

Burke, Peter, and Hsia, R. Po-Chia, *Cultural Translation in Early Modern Europe* (Cambridge: Cambridge University Press, 2007).

Cain, P. J., and Hopkins, A. G., *British Imperialism: Innovation and Expansion, 1688–2000* (London: Longman, 2013).

Caliendo, Stephen M., and McIlwain, Charlton D., eds, *The Routledge Companion to Race and Ethnicity* (London: Routledge, 2011).

Campbell, Gwyn, and Stanziani, Alessandro, eds, *Bonded Labour and Debt in the Indian Ocean World* (London: Pickering & Chatto, 2013).

Campbell, Persia Crawfurd, *Chinese Coolie Emigration within the British Empire* (London: P.S. King & Son, 1923).

Cangi, Ellen C., 'Civilising the People of Southeast Asia: Sir Stamford Raffles' Town Plan for Singapore, 1819–1823', *Planning Perspectives*, 8, 2 (1993), 166–87.

Carroll, John M., 'The Canton System: Conflict and Accommodation in the Contact Zone', *Journal of the Royal Asiatic Society Hong Kong Branch*, 50 (2010), 51–66.

Carroll, John M., *A Concise History of Hong Kong* (Hong Kong: Rowman & Littlefield, 2007).

Carroll, John, *Edge of Empires: Chinese Elites and British Colonials in Hong Kong* (London: Harvard University Press, 2005).

Carter, Marina, and Kwong, James Ng Foong, *Abacus and Mah Jong: Sino-Mauritian Settlement and Economic Consolidation* (Boston: Brill, 2009).

Carter, Marina, and Kwong, James Ng Foong, *Forging the Rainbow: Labour Immigrants in British Mauritius* (Port Louis: S. N., 1997).

Cassels, Nancy Gardner, *Social Legislation of the East India Company: Public Justice versus Public Instruction* (New Delhi: Sage, 2011).

Chan, Wai Kwan, *The Making of Hong Kong Society: Three Studies of Class Formation in Early Hong Kong* (Oxford: Clarendon Press, 1991).

Chang, Chen-tung, 'Chinese Coolie Trade in the Straits Settlements in the Late Nineteenth Century', *Bulletin of the Institute of Ethnology Academia Sinica*, 65 (1988), 1–29.

Chen, Jeng-Guo, 'The British View of Chinese Civilization and Emergence of Class Consciousness', *The Eighteenth Century*, 45 (2004), 193–205.

Chen, Songchuan, 'An Information War Waged by Merchants and Missionaries at Canton: The Society for the Diffusion of Useful Knowledge in China, 1834–1839', *Modern Asian Studies*, 46, 6 (2012), 1705–35.

Cheong, W. E., *Mandarins and Merchants: Jardine Matheson & Co., a China Agency of the Early Nineteenth Century* (London: Curzon Press, 1979).

Chung-Huang, Yen, *Community and Politics: The Chinese in Colonial Singapore and Malaysia* (Singapore: Times Academic, 1995).

Chung-Huang, Yen, 'Early Chinese Clan Organizations in Singapore and Malaya, 1819–1911', *Journal of Southeast Asian Studies*, 12, 1 (1981), 62–86.

Cohen, Robin, *Global Diasporas: An Introduction* (London: Routledge, 2008).

Connell, Carol Matheson, *A Business in Risk: Jardine Matheson and the Hong Kong Trading Industry* (London: Praeger, 2004).

Corfield, Justin, *Historical Dictionary of Singapore* (Toronto: Scarecrow Press, 2011).

Couchman, Sophie, and Bagnall, Kate, eds, *Chinese Australians: Politics, Engagement and Resistance* (Leiden: Brill, 2015).

Cullen, Rose, 'Empire, Indentured Labour and the Colony: The Debate Over "Coolie" Labour in New South Wales, 1836–1838', *History Australia*, 9, 1 (2012), 84–109.

Derks, Hans, *The History of the Opium Problem: The Assault on the East, ca.1600–1950* (Boston: Brill, 2012).

Dillon, Nara, and Oi, Jean C., eds, *At the Crossroads of Empires: Middlemen, Social Networks, and State-Building in Republican Shanghai* (Stanford, CA: Stanford University Press, 2008).

Dirks, Nicholas, *The Scandal of Empire: India and the Creation of Imperial Britain* (London: Harvard University Press, 2008).

Ebrey, Patricia Buckley, *The Cambridge Illustrated History of China* (Cambridge: Cambridge University Press, 2010).

Elbourne, Elizabeth, 'Freedom at Issue: Vagrancy Legislation and the Meaning of Freedom in Britain and the Cape Colony, 1799 to 1842', *Slavery & Abolition: A Journal of Slave and Post-Slave Studies*, 15, 2 (1994), 114–50.

Ellis, Markman, Coulton, Richard and Mauger, Matthew, eds., *Empire of Tea: The Asian Leaf that Conquered the World* (London: Reaktion Books, 2015).

Endacott, G. B., *A Biographical Sketch-Book of Early Hong Kong* (Hong Kong: Hong Kong University Press, 2005).

Fairbank, John King, *The Great Chinese Revolution, 1800–1985* (New York: Harper & Row, 1986).

Farhadian, Charles E., ed., *Introducing World Christianity* (Chichester: Wiley-Blackwell, 2012).

Fee, Lian Kwen, 'The Construction of Malay Identity across Nations: Malaysia, Singapore, and Indonesia', *Journal of the Humanities and Social Sciences of Southeast Asia*, 157, 4 (2001), 861–79.

Fitzgerald, John, *Big White Lie: Chinese Australians in White Australia* (Sydney: UNSW Press, 2007).

Frost, Mark Ravinder, 'Emporium in Imperio: Nanyang Networks and the Straits Chinese in Singapore, 1819–1914', *Journal of Southeast Asian Studies*, 36, 1 (2005), 29–66.

Frost, Mark, *Singapore: A Biography* (London: Thames & Hudson, 2009).

Fryer, Donald W., and Jackson, James C., *Indonesia* (London: Ernest Benn, 1977).

Gabaccia, Donna, 'The "Yellow Peril" and the "Chinese of Europe": Global Perspectives on Race and Labour, 1815–1930', in Jan Lucassen, ed., *Migration, Migration History, History: Old Paradigms and New Perspectives* (Bern: Peter Lang, 1999), 177–97.

Gallagher, John, and Robinson, Ronald, 'The Imperialism of Free Trade', *The Economic History Review*, 6, 1 (1953), 1–15.

Gao, Hao, 'The Amherst Embassy and British Discoveries in China', *History*, 99, 337 (2014), 568–87.

Gao, Hao, 'Prelude to the Opium War? British Reactions to the "Napier Fizzle" and Attitudes towards China in the Mid Eighteen-Thirties', *Historical Research*, 87, 237 (2014), 491–509.

Gao, Mobo, 'Early Chinese Migrants to Australia: A Critique of the Sojourner Narrative on Nineteenth-Century Chinese Migration to British Colonies', *Asian Studies Review*, 41, 3 (2017), 389–404.

Glendinning, Victoria, *Raffles and the Golden Opportunity, 1781–1826* (London: Profile, 2012).

Grace, Richard J., *Opium and Empire: The Lives and Careers of William Jardine and James Matheson* (Montreal & Kingston: McGill-Queen's University Press, 2014).

Grant, Robert, '"The Fit and Unfit": Suitable Settlers for Britain's Mid-Nineteenth-Century Colonial Possessions', *Victorian Literature and Culture*, 33 (2005), 169–86.

Gregory, John S., *The West and China since 1500* (New York: Palgrave Macmillan, 2003).

Hack, Karl, and Margolin, Jean-Louis, eds, *Singapore from Temasek to the 21st Century: Reinventing the Global City* (Singapore: National University of Singapore, 2010).

Hall, Catherine, *Civilising Subjects: Metropole and Colony in the English Imagination 1830–1867* (Chicago: University of Chicago Press, 2002).

Hannah, Mark, 'Aboriginal Workers in the Australian Agricultural Company, 1824–1857', *Labour History*, 82 (2002), 17–33.

Harper, Marjory, 'Exile into Bondage? Non-White Migrants and Settlers', in Marjory Harper and Stephen Constantine, eds, *Migration and Empire* (Oxford: Oxford University Press, 2010).

Harrison, Henrietta, *China: Inventing the Nation* (London: Bloomsbury Academic, 2011).

Harrison, Peter, '"Fill the Earth and Subdue It": Biblical Warrants for Colonization in Seventeenth Century England', *Journal of Religious History*, 29, 1 (2005), 3–24.

Hevia, James, *The Imperial Security State: British Colonial Knowledge and Empire-Building in Asia* (New York: Cambridge University Press, 2012).

Hilton, Boyd, *A Mad, Bad and Dangerous People? England 1783–1846* (Oxford: Oxford University Press, 2006).

Hitchins, Fred H., *The Colonial Land and Emigration Commission, 1840–78* (Philadelphia: Philadelphia University Press, 1931).

Hillemann, Ulrike, *Asian Empire and British Knowledge: China and the Networks of British Imperial Expansion* (New York: Palgrave Macmillan, 2009)

Hollinsworth, David, *Race and Racism in Australia* (Katoomba: Social Science Press, 1998).

Horsman, Reginald, 'Origins of Racial Anglo-Saxonism in Great Britain before 1850', *Journal of the History of Ideas*, 37, 3 (1976), 387–410.

Huguette, Ly-Tio-Fane Pineo, *Chinese Diaspora in Western Indian Ocean* (Mauritius: MSM, 1985).

Hussin, Nordin, *Trade and Society in the Straits of Melaka: Dutch Melaka and English Penang, 1780–1830* (Singapore: NUS Press, 2007).

Huttenback, Robert A., *Racism and Empire: White Settlers and Coloured Immigrants in the British Self-Governing Colonies 1830–1910* (Ithaca, NY: Cornell University Press, 1976).

Hyslop, Jonathan, 'The Imperial Working Class Makes Itself White', *Journal of Historical Sociology*, 12, 4 (1999), 398–421.

Jupp, James, *The Australian People: An Encyclopaedia of the Nation, Its People and Their Origins* (Cambridge: Cambridge University Press, 2001).

Kawamura, Tomotaka, 'The British Empire and Asia in the Long Eighteenth Century', *Global History and Maritime Asia*, 17 (2010).

Kawamura, Tomotaka, 'Maritime Asian Trade and Colonization of Penang, c.1786–1830', in Taukasa Mizushima, George Bryan Souza and Dennis O. Flynn, eds, *Hinterlands and Commodities: Place, Space, Time and Political Economic Development of Asia over the Long Eighteenth Century* (Leiden: Brill, 2015), 145–65.

Keith, Jeffrey A., 'Civilization, Race, and the Japan Expedition's Cultural Diplomacy, 1853–1854', *Diplomatic History*, 35, 2 (2011), 179–202.

King, Frank H. H., *A Research Guide to China-Coast Newspapers, 1822–1911* (Harvard: Harvard University Press, 1965).

King, Frank H. H., *Survey Our Empire! Robert Montgomery Martin (1801–1868): A Bio-Bibliography* (Hong Kong: University of Hong Kong, 1979).

King, Michelle T., 'Replicating the Colonial Expert: The Problem of Translation in the Late Nineteenth-Century Straits Settlements', *Social History*, 34, 4 (2009), 428–46.

Kitson, Peter J., *Forging Romantic China: Sino-British Cultural Exchange, 1760–1840* (Cambridge: Cambridge University Press, 2013).

Knapman, Gareth, *Race and British Colonialism in Southeast Asia, 1770–1870: John Crawfurd and the Politics of Equality* (New York: Routledge, 2017).

Knight, Roger, *Sugar, Steam and Steel: The Industrial Project in Colonial Java, 1830–1885* (Adelaide: University of Adelaide Press, 2014).

Kobayashi, Atsushi, 'The Role of Singapore in the Growth of Intra-Southeast Asian Trade, c.1820s–1852', *Southeast Asian Studies*, 2, 3 (2013), 443–74.

Kuhn, Philip A., *Chinese among Others: Emigration in Modern Times* (Lanham, MD: Rowman & Littlefield, 2008).

Kumagai, Yukihisa, *Breaking into the Monopoly: Provincial Merchants and Manufacturers' Campaigns or Access to the Asian Market, 1790–1833* (Boston: Brill, 2013).

Kumagai, Yukihisa, 'Kirkman Finlay and John Crawfurd: Two Scots in the Campaign of the Glasgow East India Association for the Opening of the China Trade, 1829–1833', *Journal of Scottish Historical Studies*, 30, 2 (2010), 175–99.

Laidlaw, Zoë, *Colonial Connections, 1815–1845: Patronage, the Information Revolution and Colonial Government* (Manchester: Manchester University Press, 2005).

Laidlaw, Zoë, 'Investigating Empire: Humanitarians, Reform and the Commission of Eastern Inquiry', *The Journal of Imperial and Commonwealth History*, 40, 5 (2012), 749–68.

Lake, Marilyn, and Reynolds, Henry, *Drawing the Global Colour Line: White Men's Countries and the International Challenge of Racial Equality* (Cambridge: Cambridge University Press, 2008).

Lambert, David, and Lester, Alan, eds, *Colonial Lives across the British Empire: Imperial Careering in the Long Nineteenth Century* (Cambridge: Cambridge University Press, 2006).

Lawson, Philip, *The East India Company: A History* (London: Longman, 1993).

Lawson, Tom, *The Last Man: A British Genocide in Tasmania* (London: I.B. Tauris, 2014).

Le Pinchon, Alain, ed., *China Trade and Empire: Jardine, Matheson & Co. and the Origins of British Rule in Hong Kong, 1827–1843* (Oxford: Oxford University Press, 2006).

Lee, Edwin, *The British as Rulers: Governing Multiracial Singapore, 1867–1914* (Singapore: Singapore University Press, 1991).

Lees, Lynn Hollen, *Planting Empire, Cultivating Subjects: British Malaya, 1786–1941* (Cambridge: Cambridge University Press, 2017).

LeFevour, Edward, *Western Enterprise in Late Ch'ing China: A Selective Survey of Jardine, Matheson & Company's Operations, 1842–1895* (Cambridge, MA: Harvard University Press, 1968).

Lester, Alan, *Imperial Networks: Creating Identities in Nineteenth Century South Africa and Britain* (London: Routledge, 2001).

Liew, Clement, 'Ordo ab Chao at the Far End of India: Chinese Settlers and Their Colonial Masters', *Journal of Asian History*, 50, 1 (2016), 141–65.

Liu, Gretchen, *Singapore: A Pictorial History, 1819–2000* (Singapore: Archipelago Press, 1999).

Lockard, Craig A., 'Chinese Migration and Settlement in Southeast Asia Before 1850: Making Fields from the Sea', *History Compass*, 11, 9 (2013), 765–781

Lockard, Craig A., *Southeast Asia in World History* (Oxford: Oxford University Press, 2009).

Lorimer, Douglas A., *Science, Race Relations and Resistance: Britain, 1870–1914* (Manchester: Manchester University Press, 2013).

Lovell, Julia, *The Great Wall: China Against the World* (London: Atlantic Books, 2006).

Lovell, Julia, *The Opium War: Drugs, Dreams and the Making of China* (London: Picador, 2011).

Low, Kelvin E. Y., 'Chinese Migration and Entangled Histories: Broadening the Contours of Migratory History', *Journal of Historical Sociology*, 27, 1 (2014), 75–102.

Lowe, Lisa, *The Intimacies of Four Continents* (Durham, NC: Duke University Press, 2016).

Lutz, Jessie Gregory, *Opening China: Karl F. A. Gutzlaff and Sino-Western Relations, 1827–1852* (Cambridge: William B. Eerdmans, 2008).

Macintyre, Stuart, and Clark, Anna, *The History Wars* (Carlton, Vic.: Melbourne University Press, 2004).

Mackenzie, John M., *Propaganda and Empire: The Manipulation of British Public Opinion, 1880–1960* (Manchester: Manchester University Press, 1984).

Mackerras, Colin, *Sinophiles and Sinophobes: Western Views of China* (New York: Oxford University Press, 2000).

Mandler, Peter, *The English National Character: The History of an Idea from Edmund Burke to Tony Blair* (London: Yale University Press, 2006).

Mandler, Peter, '"Race" and "Nation" in Mid-Victorian Thought', in Stefan Collini, Richard Whatmore and Brian Young, eds, *History, Religion, and Culture: British Intellectual History, 1750–1950* (Cambridge: Cambridge University Press, 2000), 224–45.

Manickam, Sandra Khor, 'Common Ground: Race and the Colonial Universe in British Malaya', *Journal of Southeast Asian Studies*, 40, 3 (2009), 593–612.

Mann, Harold H., *The Early History of the Tea Industry in North-East India* (Bengal Economic Journal, 1918).

Markovits, Claude, 'The Political Economy of Opium Smuggling in Early Nineteenth Century India: Leakage or Resistance?', *Modern Asian Studies*, 43, 1 (2009), 89–111.

Marshall, P. J., 'British-Indian Connections c.1780 to c.1830: The Empire of the Officials', in Michael J. Franklin, ed., *Romantic Representations of British India* (London: Routledge, 2006), 45–64.

McGowan, Barry, 'The Economics and Organisation of Chinese Mining in Colonial Australia', *Australian Economic History Review*, 45, 2 (2005), 119–39.

McGrath, Ann, '"Modern Stone-Age Slavery": Images of Aboriginal Labour and Sexuality', *Labour History*, 69 (1995), 30–51.

McKeown, Adam, 'Conceptualizing Chinese Diasporas, 1842–1949', *The Journal of Asian Studies*, 58, 2 (1999), 306–37.

McKeown, Adam, *Melancholy Order: Asian Migration and the Globalization of Borders* (New York: Columbia University Press, 2008).

Meagher, Arnold J., *The Coolie Trade: The Traffic in Chinese Laborers to Latin America, 1847–1874* (Philadelphia: Xlibris, 2008).

Meaney, Neville, '"In History's Page": Identity and Myth', in Deryck Schreuder and Stuart Ward, eds, *Australia's Empire* (Oxford: Oxford University Press, 2010).

Melancon, Glenn, *Britain's China Policy and the Opium Crisis: Balancing Drugs, Violence and National Honour, 1833–1840* (London: Ashgate, 2003).

Melancon, Glenn, 'Peaceful Intentions: The First British Trade Commission in China, 1833–5', *Historical Research*, 73 (2000), 33–47.

Mendis, G. C., *Ceylon under the British* (New Delhi: Asian Educational Services, 2005; first published 1952).

Meyering, Isobelle Barrett, 'Abolitionism, Settler Violence and the Case against Flogging: A Reassessment of Sir William Molesworth's Contribution to the Transportation Debate', *History Australia*, 7, 1 (2010), 1–18.

Miksic, John, and Low Mei Gek, Cheryl-Ann, eds, *Early Singapore, 1300s–1819: Evidence in Maps, Text and Artefacts* (Singapore: Singapore History Museum, 2004).

Mills, Lennox A., *Ceylon under British Rule, 1795–1932* (London: Oxford University Press, 1933).

Miners, Norman, 'The Localization of the Hong Kong Police Force, 1842–1947', *The Journal of Imperial and Commonwealth History*, 18, 3 (1990), 298–315.

Morrell, W. P., *British Colonial Policy in the Age of Peel and Russell* (London: Frank Cass & Co., 1966).

Mountford, Benjamin, *Britain, China and Colonial Australia* (Oxford: Oxford University Press, 2016).

Munn, Christopher, *Anglo-China: Chinese People and British Rule in Hong Kong, 1841–1880* (Hong Kong: Hong Kong University Press, 2009).

Munn, Christopher, 'The Chusan Episode: Britain's Occupation of a Chinese Island, 1840–46', *The Journal of Imperial and Commonwealth History*, 25, 1 (1997), 82–112.

Murakami, Eli, 'Two Bonded Labour Emigration Patterns in Mid-Nineteenth-Century Southern China: The Coolie Trade and Emigration to Southeast Asia', in Gwyn Campbell and Alessandro Stanziani, eds, *Bonded Labour and Debt in the Indian Ocean World* (London: Pickering & Chatto, 2013), 153–65.

Murphey, Rhoads, 'Colombo and the Remaking of Ceylon: A Prototype of Colonial Asian Port Cities', in Frank Broeze, ed., *Gateways of Asia: Port Cities of Asia in the 13th–20th Centuries* (London: Routledge, 2010), 191–211.

Nasir, Kamaludeen Mohamed, 'Protected Sites: Reconceptualising Secret Societies in Colonial and Postcolonial Singapore', *Journal of Historical Sociology*, 29, 2 (2016), 232–49.

Neal, Stan, 'Imperial Connections and Colonial Improvement: Scotland, Ceylon and the China Coast, 1837–1841', *Journal of World History*, 29, 2 (2018), 213–38.

Neal, Stan, 'Opium and Migration: Jardine Matheson's Imperial Connections and the Recruitment of Chinese Labour for Assam, 1834–1839', *Modern Asian Studies*, 51, 5 (2017), 1626–55.

Northrup, David, *Indentured Labour in the Age of Imperialism, 1834–1922* (Cambridge: Cambridge University Press, 1995).

Ohlsson, Tony, 'The Origins of a White Australia: The Coolie Question, 1837–43', *Journal of the Royal Australian Historical Society*, 97, 2 (2011), 203–17.

Ortmann, Stephan, and Thompson, Mark R., 'China and the "Singapore Model"', *Journal of Democracy*, 27, 1 (2016), 39–48.

Pan, Lynn, ed., *The Encyclopaedia of the Chinese Overseas* (Richmond: Curzon, 1998).

Peffer, George, *If They Don't Bring Their Women Here: Chinese Female Immigration before Exclusion* (Urbana: University of Illinois Press, 1999).

Perry, John Curtis, *Singapore: Unlikely Power* (New York: Oxford University Press, 2017).

Picker, Greg, '"A Nation Is Governed by All That Has Tongue in the Nation": Newspapers and Political Expression in Colonial Sydney, 1825–1850', *Journal of Australian Studies*, 23, 62 (1999), 183–9.

Pitts, Jennifer, *A Turn to Empire: The Rise of Imperial Liberalism in Britain and France* (Princeton: Princeton University Press, 2005).

Pope, Alan, 'Aboriginal Adaptation to Early Colonial Labour Markets', *Labour History*, 54 (1988), 1–15.

Potter, Simon, ed., *Imperial Communication: Australia, Britain and the British Empire, 1830–1850* (London: University of London, 2005).

Potter, Simon, *News and the British World: The Emergence of an Imperial Press System, 1876–1922* (Oxford: Oxford University Press, 2003).

Pratt, Mary Louise, *Imperial Eyes: Travel Writing and Transculturation* (London: Routledge, 1992).

Read, W. H., *Play and Politics: Recollections of Malaya by an Old Resident* (London: Wells Gardner, Darton & Co., 1901).

Reid, Kirsty, *Gender, Crime and Empire: Convicts, Settlers and the State in Early Colonial Australia* (Manchester: Manchester University Press, 2007).

Reynolds, Henry, *Dispossession: Black Australians and White Invaders* (St Leonards, NSW: Allen & Unwin, 1989).

Reynolds, Henry, *The Other Side of the Frontier: Aboriginal Resistance to the European Invasion of Australia* (Ringwood, Vic.: Penguin, 1981).

Reynolds, Henry, *This Whispering in Our Hearts* (St Leonards, NSW: Allen & Unwin, 1998)

Ritchie, John, 'Towards Ending an Unclean Thing: The Molesworth Committee and the Abolition of Transportation to New South Wales, 1837–40', *Historical Studies*, 17, 67 (1976), 144–64.

Roberts, David Andrew, 'Beyond "the Stain": Rethinking the Nature and Impact of the Anti-Transportation Movement', *Journal of Australian Colonial History*, 14 (2012), 205–79.

Roberts, J. A. G., *China through Western Eyes: The Nineteenth Century* (Bath: Alan Sutton, 1991).

Roberts, Michael, 'Problems of Social Stratification and the Demarcation of National and Local Elites in British Ceylon', *The Journal of Asian Studies*, 33, 4 (1974), 549–77.

Rogers, John D., 'Early British Rule and Social Classification in Lanka', *Modern Asian Studies*, 38, 3 (2004), 625–47.

Salyer, Lucy E., *Laws as Harsh as Tigers: Chinese Immigrants and the Shaping of Modern Immigration Law* (Chapel Hill: University of North Carolina Press, 1995).

Samaraweera, Vijaya, 'The Ceylon Charter of Justice of 1833: A Benthamite Blueprint for Judicial Reform', *The Journal of Imperial and Commonwealth History*, 2 (1974), 263–77.

Samaraweera, Vijaya, 'Governor Sir Wilmot-Horton and the Reforms of 1833 in Ceylon', *The Historical Journal*, 15, 2 (1972), 209–28.

Schrikker, Alicia, *Dutch and British Colonial Intervention in Sri Lanka, 1780–1815: Expansion and Reform* (Leiden: Brill, 2007).

Scott, James C., *The Art of Not Being Governed: An Anarchist History of Upland Southeast Asia* (New Haven: Yale University Press, 2009).

Sharma, Jayeeta, *Empire's Garden: Assam and the Making of India* (London: Duke University Press, 2011).

Sharma, Jayeeta, 'Lazy Natives, Coolie Labour, and the Assam Tea Industry', *Modern Asian Studies*, 43, 6 (2009), 1287–324.

Sharma, S. K., and Sharma, Usha, eds, *North-East India: Volume 5 Assam – Economy, Society and Culture* (New Delhi: Mittal, 2005).

Sinha, Mrinalini, *Colonial Masculinity: The 'Manly Englishman' and the 'Effeminate Bengali' in the Late Nineteenth Century* (Manchester: Manchester University Press, 1995).

Sinn, Elizabeth, 'Emigration from Hong Kong before 1941: General Trends', in Ronald Skeldon, ed., *Emigration from Hong Kong: Tendencies and Impacts* (Hong Kong: The Chinese University Press, 1995), 35–50.

Sinn, Elizabeth, 'Hong Kong as an In-between Place in the Chinese Diaspora, 1849–1939', in Donna Gabaccia and Dirk Hoerder, eds, *Connecting Seas and Connected Ocean Rims: Indian, Atlantic, and Pacific Oceans and China Seas Migrations from the 1830s to the 1930s* (Leiden: Brill, 2011), 225–51.

Sinn, Elizabeth, *Pacific Crossings: California Gold, Chinese Migration, and the Making of Hong Kong* (Hong Kong: Hong Kong University Press, 2013).

Sinn, Elizabeth, *Power and Charity: A Chinese Merchant Elite in Colonial Hong Kong* (Hong Kong: Hong Kong University Press, 2003).

Siu, Helen F., and Ku, Agnes S., eds, *Hong Kong Mobile: Making a Global Population* (Hong Kong: Hong Kong University Press, 2008).

Sivasundaram, Sujit, *Islanded: Britain, Sri Lanka, and the Bounds of an Indian Ocean Colony* (London: University of Chicago Press, 2013).

Slocomb, Margaret, *Among Australia's Pioneers: Chinese Indentured Pastoral Workers on the Northern Frontier 1848 to c.1880* (Queensland: Balboa Press, 2014).

Slocomb, Margaret, 'Preserving the Contract: The Experience of Indentured Labourers in the Wide Bay and Burnett Districts in the Nineteenth Century', *Labour History*, 113 (2017), 103–31.

Song, Ong Siang, *One Hundred Years' History of the Chinese in Singapore* (London: John Murray, 1923).

Soothill, William Edward, *China and the West: A Short History of Their Contact from Ancient Times to the Fall of the Manchu Dynasty* (London: Oxford University Press, 1925).

Stanley, Brian, '"Commerce and Christianity": Providence Theory, the Missionary Movement, and the Imperialism of Free Trade, 1842–1860', *The Historical Journal*, 26, 1 (1983), 71–94.

Stanziani, Alessandro, *Labor on the Fringes of Empire: Voice, Exit and the Law* (Cham: Palgrave Macmillan, 2018).

Stockwell, Sarah, ed., *The British Empire: Themes and Perspectives* (Oxford: Blackwell Publishing, 2008).

Suzuki, Hideaki, ed., *Abolitions as a Global Experience* (Singapore: NUS Press, 2016).

Swee-Hock, Saw, 'Population Trends in Singapore, 1819–1967', *Journal of Southeast Asian History*, 10, 1 (1969), 36–49.

Tai Peng, Wang, *The Origins of Chinese Kongsi* (Selangor: Pelanduk Publications, 1994).

Talbot, John M., 'On the Abandonment of Coffee Plantations in Jamaica after Emancipation', *Journal of Imperial Commonwealth History*, 43, 1 (2015), 33–57.

Taylor, Miles, 'Joseph Hume and the Reformation of India, 1819–1833', in Glenn Burgess and Matthew Festenstein, eds, *English Radicalism, 1550–1850* (Cambridge: Cambridge University Press, 2007), 285–309.

Thuno, Mette, *Beyond Chinatown: New Chinese Migration and the Global Expansion of China* (Copenhagen: NIAS Press, 2006).

Tinker, Hugh, *A New System of Slavery: The Export of Indian Labour Overseas, 1830–1920* (London: Oxford University Press, 1974).

Trocki, C., 'Opium and the Beginnings of Chinese Capitalism in Southeast Asia', *Journal of Southeast Asian Studies*, 33, 2 (2002), 297–314.

Trocki, Carl A., *Opium and Empire: Chinese Society in Colonial Singapore, 1800–1910* (London: Cornell University Press, 1990).

Trocki, Carl A., *Singapore: Wealth, Power and the Culture of Control* (London: Routledge, 2006).

Trocki, Carl A., 'Singapore as a Nineteenth Century Migration Node', in Donna Gabaccia and Dirk Hoerder, eds, *Connecting Seas and Connected Ocean Rims: Indian, Atlantic, and Pacific Oceans and China Seas Migrations from the 1830s to the 1930s* (Leiden: Brill, 2011), 198–225.

Tsai, Jung-fang, *Hong Kong in Chinese History: Community and Social Unrest in the British Colony, 1842–1913* (New York: Columbia University Press, 1993).

Tsang, Steve, *A Modern History of Hong Kong* (London: I.B. Tauris, 2007).

Turnbull, C. M., 'The European Mercantile Community in Singapore, 1819–1867', *Journal of Southeast Asian History*, 10 (1969), 12–35.

Turnbull, C. M., *A History of Singapore, 1819–1988* (Singapore: Oxford University Press, 1989).

Uragoda, C. G., 'History of Opium in Sri Lanka', *Medical History*, 27 (1983), 69–76.

Van Dyke, Paul, *Life and Enterprise on the China Coast, 1700–1845* (Hong Kong: Hong Kong University Press, 2005).

Van Kley, Edwin J., 'Europe's "Discovery" of China and the Writing of World History', *American Historical Review*, 76 (1971), 358–85.

Walton, L. L., *Indentured Labour, Caribbean sugar: Chinese and Indian migrants in the British West Indies, 1838–1918* (Baltimore, Maryland: The Johns Hopkins Press, 1993).

Wang, Sing-wu, *The Organization of Chinese Emigration, 1848–1888: With Special Reference to Chinese Emigration to Australia* (San Francisco: Chinese Material Centre, 1978).

Warren, James Francis, *Rickshaw Coolie: A People's History of Singapore, 1880–1940* (Singapore: Singapore University Press, 2003).

Webster, Anthony, 'British Expansion in South East Asia and the Role of Robert Farquhar, Lieutenant-Governor of Penang 1804–5', *The Journal of Imperial and Commonwealth History*, 23, 1 (1995), 1–25.

Webster, Anthony, 'The Development of British Commercial and Political Networks in the Straits Settlements 1800 to 1868: The Rise of a Colonial and Regional Economic Identity?', *Modern Asian Studies*, 45, 4 (2011), 899–929.

Webster, Anthony, *The Twilight of the East India Company: The Evolution of Anglo-Asian Commerce and Politics, 1790–1860* (Woodbridge: Boydell Press, 2009).

Welsh, Frank, *A History of Hong Kong* (London: HarperCollins, 1994).

Williams, Laurence, 'Anglo-Chinese Caresses: Civility, Friendship and Trade in English Representations of China, 1760–1800', *Journal for Eighteenth Century Studies*, 38, 2 (2015), 277–96.

Williams, Michael, 'Hong Kong and the Pearl River Delta Qiaoxiang', *Modern Asian Studies*, 38, 2 (2004), 257–82.

Williamson, A. R., *Eastern Traders: Some Men and Ships of Jardine, Matheson & Company* (Hong Kong: Jardine, Matheson & Co., 1975).

Wood, Rebecca, 'Frontier Violence and the Bush Legend: The Sydney Herald's Response to the Myall Creek Massacre Trials and the Creation of Colonial Identity', *History Australia*, 6, 3 (2009), 1–19.

Woollacott, Angela, *Settler Society in the Australian Colonies: Self-Government and Imperial Culture* (Oxford: Oxford University Press, 2015).

Wright, Jonathan Jeffrey, '"The Belfast Chameleon": Ulster, Ceylon and the Imperial Life of Sir James Emerson Tennent', *Britain and the World*, 6, 2 (2013), 192–219.

Yang, Anand A., 'Indian Convict Workers in Southeast Asia in the Late Eighteenth and Early Nineteenth Centuries', *Journal of World History*, 14, 2 (2003), 179–208.

Yarwood, A. T., *Asian Migration to Australia: The Background to Exclusion 1896–1923* (Melbourne: Melbourne University Press, 1964).

Yen, Ching-Hwang, *The Chinese in Southeast Asia and Beyond: Socioeconomic and Political Dimensions* (London: World Scientific Publishing, 2008).

Yew, Lee Kuan, *From Third World to First: The Singapore Story, 1965–2000* (Singapore: Singapore Press Holdings, 2000).

Young, Elliot, 'Chinese Coolies, Universal Rights and the Limits of Liberalism in an Age of Empire', *Past & Present*, 227, 1 (2015), 121–49.

Unpublished Papers and Theses

Abe, Kaori, 'The City of Intermediaries: Compradors in Hong Kong, 1830s to 1880s' (Ph.D. thesis, University of Bristol, 2014).

Daily, Christopher Allen, 'From Gosport to Canton: A New Approach to Robert Morrison and the Beginnings of Protestant Missions in China' (Ph.D. thesis, SOAS, 2009).

Gao, Hao, 'Sino-British Encounters: Perceptions and Attitudes from Macartney's Mission to the Opium War, 1792–1840' (Ph.D. thesis, Edinburgh, 2014).

He, Sibing, 'Russell and Company in Shanghai, 1843–1891: U.S. Trade and Diplomacy in Treaty Port China', Paper presented to 'A Tale of Ten Cities: Sino-American Exchange in the Treaty Port Era, 1840–1950', Hong Kong University (23–24 May 2011).

Irick, Robert Lee, 'Chi'ing Policy towards the Coolie Trade, 1847–1878' (Ph.D. thesis, Harvard University, 1971).

Kumagai, Yukihisa, 'The Lobbying Activities of Provincial Mercantile and Manufacturing Interests against the Renewal of the East India Company's Charter, 1812–1813 and 1829–1833' (Ph.D. thesis, University of Glasgow, 2008).

Meagher, Arnold Joseph, 'The Introduction of Chinese Laborers to Latin America: The "Coolie Trade", 1847–1874' (Ph.D. thesis, University of California, Davis, 1975)

Tsao, Ting Man, 'Representing China to the British Public in the Age of Free Trade, c. 1833–1844' (Ph.D. thesis, State University of New York at Stony Brook, 2000).

Wright, Nadia Helen, 'Image Is All: Lt-Colonel William Farquhar, Sir Stamford Raffles, and the Founding and Early Development of Colonial Singapore' (Ph.D thesis, University of Melbourne, 2012).

Websites and Digital Sources

'1819 Singapore Treaty', Singapore Government: National Library Board, http://eresources.nlb.gov.sg/infopedia/articles/SIP_2014-05-16_133354.html (accessed 30 September 2018).

'An Overview of the History of Indenture', Aapravasi Ghat World Heritage Site, www.aapravasighat.org/English/Resources%20Research/Documents/History%20of%20Indenture.pdf. (accessed 30 September 2018).

'Sling the Singapore Model out of the Brexit Debate', *Financial Times*, 31 July 2017, www.ft.com/content/08726b32-75f2-11e7-a3e8-60495fe6ca71 (accessed 30 September 2018).

Baker, D. W. A., 'Lang, John Dunmore (1799–1878)', *Oxford Dictionary of National Biography*, Oxford University Press, 2004, www.oxforddnb.com/view/article/16005 (accessed 30 September 2018).

Chew, Ernest C. T., 'Dr. John Crawfurd (1783–1868): The Scotsman Who Made Singapore British', *The Literature, Culture and Society of Singapore*, www.postcolonialweb.org/singapore/history/chew/chew10.html (accessed 30 September 2018).

Department of Statistics Singapore, Singapore Government, 2010, www.singstat.gov.sg/publications/cop2010/census10_stat_release3 (accessed 30 September 2018).

Douglas, R. K., 'Morrison, Robert (1782–1834)', rev. Robert Bickers, *Oxford Dictionary of National Biography*, Oxford University Press, 2004; online edn, May 2007, www.oxforddnb.com/view/article/19330 (accessed 30 September 2018).

Harris, C. A., 'Colebrooke, Sir William Macbean George (1787–1870)', rev. Lynn Milne, *Oxford Dictionary of National Biography*, Oxford University Press, 2004 www.oxforddnb.com/view/article/5867 (accessed 30 September 2018).

Kenny, M. J. B., 'Hall, Edward Smith (1786–1860)', *Australian Dictionary of Biography*, National Centre of Biography, Australian National University, http://adb.anu.edu.au/biography/hall-edward-smith-2143/text2729 (published first in hardcopy 1966, accessed online 30 September 2018).

Mokhtar, Faris, 'Singapore "Far from Ready" to Do Away with Race Categorisation: Ong Ye Kung', *Channel News Asia*, 11 September 2016, www.channelnewsasia.com/news/singapore/singapore-far-from-ready-to-do-away-with-race-categorisation-ong-7810834 (accessed 30 September 2018).

Moore, Peter, 'Torrens, Robert (1780?–1864)', *Oxford Dictionary of National Biography*, Oxford University Press, 2004, www.oxforddnb.com/view/article/27565 (accessed 30 September 2018).

Moss, David J., 'Wakefield, Edward Gibbon (1796–1862)', *Oxford Dictionary of National Biography*, Oxford University Press, 2004; online edn, May 2007, www.oxforddnb.com/view/article/28415 (accessed 30 September 2018).

Neal, Stan, 'The Commonwealth and Britain: The Trouble with "Empire 2.0"', *The Conversation*, 6 March 2017, https://theconversation.com/the-commonwealth-and-britain-the-trouble-with-empire-2-0-73707 (accessed 30 September 2018).

Peers, Douglas M., 'Bentinck, Lord William Henry Cavendish- (1774–1839)', *Oxford Dictionary of National Biography*, Oxford University Press, 2004; online edn, October 2009, www.oxforddnb.com/view/article/2161 (accessed 30 September 2018).

Prince, Peter, 'The "Chinese" Always Belonged', *History Australia* (26 August 2018). DOI: 10.1080/14490854.2018.1485463.

Ray, Margaret, 'Elliot, Sir Thomas Frederick (1808–1880)', *Oxford Dictionary of National Biography*, Oxford University Press, 2004; online edn, January 2008, www.oxforddnb.com/view/article/41086 (accessed 30 September 2018).

Seah, Brandon, 'Seah Eu Chin', http://seaheuchin.info/ (accessed 30 September 2018).

Smith, G. B., 'Farquhar, Sir Robert Townsend, first baronet (1776–1830)', rev. Lynn Milne, *Oxford Dictionary of National Biography*, Oxford University Press, 2004, www.oxforddnb.com/view/article/9180 (accessed 30 September 2018).

Thompson, S., '1860 Lambing Flat Roll Up Banner', Migration Heritage Centre: New South Wales, www.migrationheritage.nsw.gov.au/exhibition/objectsthroughtime/lambingflatsbanner/index.html (accessed 30 September 2018).

Tsao, Ting Man, 'Representing "Great England" to Qing China in the Age of Free Trade Imperialism: The Circulation of a Tract by Charles Marjoribanks on the China Coast', *Victorians Institute Journal*, 6, www.nines.org/exhibits/Representing_Great_England?page=2 (accessed 30 September 2018).

Turnbull, C. M., 'Crawfurd, John (1783–1868)', *Oxford Dictionary of National Biography*, Oxford University Press, 2004, www.oxforddnb.com/view/article/6651 (accessed 30 September 2018).

INDEX

WORLDS OF THE EAST INDIA COMPANY